Overview

Contents

Acknowledgments

Written by: Starr Andersen, Troy Batterberry, Bill Birney, Nancy Buchanan, Brian Crites, Brooks Cutter, Mark Galioto, Douglas Goodwin, John Green, Scott Harrison, Lori Kane, Laura Landstad, Amir Majidimehr, John Michalak, David M. Nelson, John Paddleford, Andrea Pruneda, Richard Saunders, Howard Stateman, and Tom Woolums.

Project managed by: John Michalak

Edited by: Lori Kane and Karen Strudwick

Illustrations by: Greg Lovitt

Produced and formatted by: C. Keith Gabbert and Robert L. Porter

Technical content reviewed by: David Bristol, David del Val, Tim Elhajj, Josh Helm, Steve Hug, Anders Klemets, Ming-Chieh Lee, Jeff McKune, Peter Turcan, Zach Robinson, and Mark VanAntwerp.

Other assistance provided by: Anthony Bay, Donna Corey, Mike Flanagan, April Gabbert, Dan Karwoski, Tom Melberg, and Glenn Schroeder.

JumpStart CD provided by: John Green, David Workman, and Angela Nelson.

Foreword

The possibilities of computer technology continue to expand at an incredible pace. Personal computers provide far more than a platform for entertainment, education, and business applications; they are becoming rich digital media tools. The explosion of new form factors and devices is allowing us to take our audio and video with us wherever we go. A digital media phenomenon is emerging on the Web, and Windows Media is poised to change the way entertainment, news and information, corporate communications, and distance learning are delivered. Technological innovations and greater bandwidth are helping streaming multimedia mature from jerky, grainy, postage-stamp-sized images into a new mass medium. This is the Web—Phase 2.

World wide, more than 100 million digital media players have been downloaded onto personal computers. Fifteen million consumers tune into 300,000 hours of programming on the Web each week. Revenues from digital media on the Web have already reached over $200 million a year. Yet, for the most part, it remains an untapped market loaded with opportunities for artists, record labels, content providers, broadcasters, Web-hosting companies, media portals, solution providers, authoring tool developers, and others.

Compelling content is the driving force behind the digital media revolution taking place on the Web. Rich streaming media content on an otherwise static Web page attracts new visitors and improves the overall user experience. Major new music releases, radio stations, live pay-per-view events, and movie trailers are becoming commonplace on the Web. Streaming and downloading audio and video content afford amateurs and progressive artists the pervasive reach of the Web to distribute their content. Businesses large and small are using digital media to enhance communications and information sharing.

The open architecture of Windows Media Technologies provides the infrastructure for integrating digital media into all types of applications. It supplies all of the components essential for a complete end-to-end digital media solution. From creating compelling content in the highly efficient Windows Media format, to reliably delivering the best user experience at any bandwidth with Windows Media Services, to providing the highest quality playback with Windows Media Player, and helping artists and distributors make their content more secure with Windows Media Rights Manager, Windows Media Technologies offers the highest-quality streaming media platform for an excellent price: free.

Inside Windows Media, written by the developers who created this technology, aims to unravel some of the mysteries of digital media as well as illustrate some of the opportunities Windows Media Technologies offers. I hope you enjoy using Windows Media as much as we have enjoyed creating it.

Anthony Bay

General Manager, Streaming Media Division

Microsoft Corporation

Introduction

Inside Windows Media is a guide to Internet broadcasting and streaming digital media. This book describes the opportunities and challenges presented by this exciting new technology and explains how you can use Microsoft® Windows Media™ Technologies to build a comprehensive solution to create and distribute digital media in a variety of ways on the Internet or on your intranet. *Inside Windows Media* was designed to help you understand and use the components of Windows Media Technologies: Microsoft® Windows Media™ Tools, Microsoft® Windows Media™ Services, and Microsoft® Windows Media™ Player.

Who should read this book

Inside Windows Media is really for anyone interested in learning how to use Windows Media Technologies to stream digital media content across a local area network (LAN) or over the Internet. You can read *Inside Windows Media* to learn how to create and distribute applications ranging from news and entertainment to presentations, corporate communications, and distance learning.

Although we hope that anyone can use *Inside Windows Media* to learn about our technology, this book was written with three audience segments in mind:

- Content creators, who need to know how to create content that can work as either an Internet broadcast or an intranet streaming event across a corporate LAN. Content creators may already be familiar with either audio or video production concepts; however, they may need to learn how to leverage their expertise to create content that can work in a Windows Media Technologies environment.

- Content distributors, who need to know how to install, configure, and administer a Windows Media Technologies system. Content distributors may already be familiar with corporate LAN technology; however, they may need to learn how to leverage their expertise to deliver digital media content over their LAN or the Internet.

- Web developers, who need to understand core digital media concepts and why they should deploy this technology on their Web sites. Web developers may want a front-to-back solution, including all of the information and software they need to encode a stream and host it on a Web site.

Organization of the book

Inside Windows Media is a quick way for you to familiarize yourself with this technology. The book is divided into four sections. You can either read the book from cover to cover or skip right to the section that interests you the most.

Section I—Getting Started. This section presents an overview of Windows Media Technologies, a description of how these technologies work together, a summary of the terms and ideas you need to understand how streaming works, practical examples of how this technology can be used, and tips on how to create quality content for streaming. Chapters include:

> **Chapter 1:** Understanding Windows Media Technologies
> **Chapter 2:** Creating and Improving Multimedia Content

Section II—Using Windows Media Technologies Components. This section describes Windows Media Tools and how to use them to create digital media content, explains how to set up and administer Windows Media Services, discusses how to use and customize Windows Media Player, and shows how to use these components together using real-world examples. Chapters include:

> **Chapter 3:** Using Windows Media Tools
> **Chapter 4:** Using Windows Media Services
> **Chapter 5:** Using Windows Media Player
> **Chapter 6:** Putting It All Together

Section III—Advanced Uses of Windows Media Technologies. This section explains how to encrypt content using Microsoft® Windows Media™ Rights Manager, how to stream Microsoft® PowerPoint® Presentations, and how to customize Windows Media Technologies using scripts and applications. Several code examples are provided in Chapter 9 to give you a head start; the code listings are on the JumpStart CD included with this book so that you can copy and paste them into your own applications. Chapters include:

> **Chapter 7:** Packaging Media Files Using Windows Media Rights
>   Manager
> **Chapter 8:** Streaming PowerPoint Presentations
> **Chapter 9:** Designing and Developing with Windows Media
>   Technologies

Section IV—Underlying Concepts. This section contains detailed information about digital compression, the codecs included with Windows Media Technologies, Advanced Streaming Format, networking concepts and protocols, network capacity, and firewall considerations. Chapters include:

> **Chapter 10:** Principles of Digital Compression and Encoding
> **Chapter 11:** Principles of Networking

Appendix A, "Audio and Video Capture Cards," lists the video capture cards that have been tested with Windows Media™ Encoder and are known to be reliable for encoding Windows Media content. Appendix B, "Getting Help," provides information about where and who to go to if you need help. Appendix C, "Using Content Legally," provides information about creating and compiling content legally.

The Microsoft® Windows Media™ Technologies 4.0 JumpStart CD demonstrates the key features of version 4.0. Free downloads of the components and supporting Help documentation are available on the CD as well as from the Windows Media Web site (http://www.microsoft.com/windows/windowsmedia/).

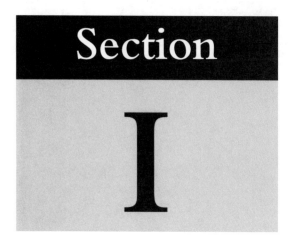

Section

I

Getting Started

This section presents an overview of Microsoft Windows Media Technologies, a description of how these technologies work together, a summary of the terms and ideas you need to know to understand how streaming works, practical examples of how to use this technology, and ideas about how to create high-quality content for streaming. Chapters in this section include:

Chapter 1—Understanding Windows Media Technologies. This chapter introduces the components, features, and formats of Windows Media Technologies and gives examples of how to communicate with streaming media.

Chapter 2—Creating and Improving Multimedia Content. This chapter describes many of the issues to be aware of when you create or edit multimedia content for streaming. Tips about creating, improving, and archiving your audio and video are also provided.

Chapter

1

Understanding Windows Media Technologies

You can use the components of Microsoft® Windows Media™ Technologies to create, deliver, and play digital media content. This chapter introduces the components, features, and formats of Windows Media Technologies and gives examples of how to communicate with streaming media. After reading this chapter, you'll be able to answer the following questions:

- What are the components that make up Windows Media Technologies?

- What are the key features of each Windows Media Technologies component?

- How do you use these components to create, distribute, and render content?

- What are some of the core technologies that support streaming digital media?

■ How can Windows Media Technologies be used in a corporate setting?

■ How can Windows Media Technologies be used to deliver content to an Internet audience?

■ How can Windows Media Technologies be used to create interactive distance learning courses?

Introducing streaming media

The emergence of streaming media can be compared to that of television. Both began as technological novelties: Interesting gadgets that made the covers of technical magazines and amused folks at tradeshows. In the first years of television, the picture and sound quality was bad, and the set required a lot of fussing by end users. A viewer had to adjust rabbit-ear antennas and continuously turn knobs to keep the image from flipping, rolling, and turning to snow. At some point in the history of television, though, the technological improvements hit a point where everything suddenly snapped into place. From that point on, growth in the industry took off. Television was no longer a novelty. It became a part of our lives. It became TV. Control passed from the technical wizards with slide rules and pocket protectors to the creative people who designed and produced entertainment and information programming. At some point in the early 1950s, TV evolved from amusing novelty to communications medium, then to mass medium, business enterprise, industry, and then to institution.

If we use the evolution of television as a model, streaming media is somewhere at the crossover point between novelty and communications medium. The technology is emerging and the creative community is taking notice. To reach the point where control finally passes from the technical wizards to the communicators and on to the business people requires a convergence of several elements. Today most of the elements are in place: The number of end users with players is well into the tens of millions, thousands of creative business people are discovering innovative ways to stream their messages, and massive improvements have been made in networking, compression, and streaming technologies. The emergence of high-speed Internet access from cable modems and DSL (digital subscriber lines) could be the key factor that brings streaming media to the masses in the next few years. It could even herald the convergence of the personal computer and the television.

Windows Media Technologies is an innovative digital media platform that provides end users with unmatched audio and video quality. Windows Media Technologies also provides the emerging streaming media industry with the tools to develop powerful applications, to create high-quality multimedia content, and to reliably distribute their content.

Version 4.0 of Windows Media Technologies contains a rich suite of products and features that you can use to create, deliver, and play streaming media for applications ranging from news and entertainment to e-commerce, corporate communications, and distance

learning. In this chapter, we explore Windows Media Technologies and the emerging
world of streaming media.

Windows Media Technologies components

Windows Media Technologies consists of a number of software components. With these
components, you can create complete streaming media solutions. Unlike a word processor
or a database program, a complete streaming media solution involves a number of
programs and spans several different technologies. For example, Windows Media™
Encoder is just one of the Microsoft® Windows Media™ Tools features. You could say,
Windows Media Encoder is to Windows Media™ Technologies, as a word processor is to
a book publishing system.

The components include Windows Media Tools, Microsoft® Windows Media™ Services,
and Microsoft® Windows Media™ Player. Within each component is a suite of related
programs, plug-ins, tools, and utilities. Together, these components provide an end-to-end
solution for streaming multimedia, from content authoring, to delivery and playback.

- **Windows Media Tools.** The tools component includes programs, plug-ins, and
  utilities for creating content. With several of the tools you can convert other file
  formats, such as the Windows multimedia formats WAV and AVI, the Apple
  QuickTime format, and the Internet music format MP3, to the Windows Media
  format, which is called the Advanced Streaming Format (ASF). In addition to
  creating files, the Windows Media Encoder tool can be used to create a live stream,
  with which you can broadcast audio and video over a network. You can use
  Windows Media™ Author to create illustrated presentations by embedding graphics
  and scripting elements (script commands). Windows Media™ ASF Indexer can be
  used to edit content after it has been encoded to the Windows Media format.
  Windows Media™ On-Demand Producer can be used to edit, process, and encode
  source content and to add markers and script commands. Chapter 2, "Creating and
  Improving Multimedia Content," discusses factors to consider as you create and edit
  multimedia content for streaming. Chapter 3, "Using Windows Media Tools,"
  describes how to use the tools.

- **Windows Media Services.** The Windows Media server components are a set of
  services running on Microsoft® Windows NT® Server. These services distribute
  audio, video, and other media to players on end-user computers. Media can be in the
  form of a file or it can be a live stream. To broadcast a live stream, Windows Media
  Encoder encodes audio and video in real-time and then distributes the encoded
  stream to the Windows Media server for delivery to end users over a network. The
  Windows Media server components are described in detail in Chapter 4, "Using
  Windows Media Services."

- **Windows Media Player.** End users play ASF streams and other multimedia content with Windows Media Player. Intranet and Internet surfers can use Windows Media Player to play audio, illustrated audio (synchronized sound and still images), and full-motion video files, as well as many other multimedia data types. Many of the Windows Media Player components seen by the end user are described in Chapter 5, "Using Windows Media Player."

Information about the Windows Media Technologies components is presented in the first five chapters of this book. This information is brought together and put to use in Chapter 6, "Putting It All Together." Chapter 6 provides information to help you make an important primary decision—whether to produce a live event or create stored content. Then the chapter takes you through, from start to finish, the steps you must take to add audio clips to your Web site, put your radio station signal on the Web, convert your VHS tapes to ASF, and put your television signal on the Web.

Key features of Windows Media Technologies

Windows Media Technologies includes powerful features for creating, delivering, and viewing content. Other features enhance the authoring and presentation of media. Key features include:

- **Highest quality audio.** The Windows Media™ Audio codec provides FM-radio quality sound to all modem users and CD quality at half the bit rate of MP3.

- **Fast video encoding.** Windows Media Encoder encodes lengthy, on-demand content at the fastest rate in the industry.

- **Scalable to full screen.** The video playback window in Windows Media Player can be enlarged to full screen.

- **Integration with other Microsoft products.** You can leverage your investment in other Microsoft products, such as Windows NT Server, Microsoft® Site Server, and the rest of the Microsoft® BackOffice® family of products.

- **Digital rights management.** Microsoft® Windows Media™ Rights Manager enables content owners to make their intellectual property more secure. Chapter 7, "Packaging Media Files Using Windows Media Rights Manager," describes how you can use Windows Media Rights Manager to help control the distribution and preserve the rights of digital media you put on the Internet.

- **PowerPoint 2000 Presentation Broadcasting.** This feature is a complete system for synchronizing the live presentation of Microsoft® PowerPoint® slides with audio and video over a network. Chapter 8, "Streaming PowerPoint Presentations," describes how to use this feature.

Other Windows Media Technologies features relate to the reliability and scalability of the stream delivered to an end user. Reliability means that end users can connect, stay connected, and receive an uninterrupted presentation. Scalability means that components can handle variations in bandwidth and the number of client connections to a server (server load). (The *client* is the computer that is rendering or playing back a stream.) The following features help ensure a quality end-user experience:

- **Wide bandwidth range.** Windows Media Technologies offers one of the industry's widest range of bandwidths for high-quality streaming, from mono-quality audio at 2.4 kilobits per second (Kbps) to broadcast-quality video at greater than 6 megabits per second (Mbps). Windows Media Technologies provides high quality at every bit rate.

- **Intelligent streaming.** The Windows Media server monitors and automatically adjusts the bit rate of each client stream according to current bandwidth. This ensures that the highest-quality stream is delivered to end users, regardless of network conditions.

- **Multiple bit rate encoding.** You can create a live stream or file containing multiple streams, each of which is encoded for a different bit rate. Multiple bit rate encoding is part of intelligent streaming.

- **High scalability.** Windows Media Technologies supports more than 2,000 unicast clients connecting at 28.8 Kbps on a single-processor Pentium II server.

- **Built-in multicast service.** Windows Media Technologies conserves network bandwidth by delivering a single multicast stream to support unlimited end users.

- **Seamless stream switching.** Windows Media Technologies provides a smooth viewing experience by reducing the delay that occurs when switching between content in a playlist. For more information about playlists, see Chapter 9, "Designing and Developing Using Windows Media Technologies."

Streaming media concepts

Before using Windows Media components, you should know the basics of streaming media: about the types of streaming and delivery methods and about the streaming media production process. Chapters 10 and 11, "Principles of Digital Compression and Encoding" and "Principles of Networking" discuss these underlying concepts in more detail.

Streaming and downloading

There are two ways to deliver multimedia content to a client on a network: by streaming the content and by downloading it. Windows Media Technologies components create and deliver files that are streamed. Other types of multimedia files can only be downloaded. Each method has its advantages. The choice of which to use depends on the nature of the content, how you would like it presented to an end user, and the type of network that is used to deliver the content.

To implement the downloading method, you simply place the multimedia content on a Web server. An end user clicks a link on a Web page, downloads the media file to a local hard drive, and then renders it with an appropriate player. The main advantage of downloading is that the file can be of any type. The main disadvantages are that downloading takes time and the file takes up space on the end-user's hard drive. A 30-second video file can take twenty minutes to download on a slow network like the Internet. Downloading the same file on a fast network can take only few seconds and may be a good solution in some cases. Hard drive space and download time are also issues if the running time of the media is long, an hour or two for example, or if your content is live.

To implement the streaming method, you place content that has been encoded in the ASF format on a Windows Media server. An end user clicks a link, but instead of downloading a file, the content remains on the server and plays back to the client as a stream. Windows Media Player on the client computer renders the stream as soon as it is received. There is no 20-minute wait and no downloaded file to take up space on the end-user's hard drive. The main advantage is that media of any length, even live media of an unlimited length, can be played by a client almost immediately.

The main disadvantage of streaming media is that real-time playback of the media is highly dependent on the bandwidth and quality of the network over which the stream is being delivered. The focus of Windows Media Technologies is to provide a system for creating and delivering streaming content that takes into account all of the limitations inherent in networks, so that the end user experiences a seamless, quality presentation.

Delivering streaming media over a network

A stream originates on a Windows Media server that is connected to the Internet or an intranet and is rendered by Windows Media Player on an end user's computer. To get from here to there, the data must be in a form that can be read by routers, modems, browsers, and all of the other components that make up the network. A Windows Media server does this by streaming the data in packets. When Windows Media Player receives the stream, it disassembles the packets and renders the data as images and sound.

The rules that govern how the packets are to be assembled and disassembled are contained within various *Internet Protocols*. The Transmission Control Protocol (TCP) is used for transporting most types of data, such as Web pages, images, documents, and other downloaded data. The User Datagram Protocol (UDP) is preferred for transporting streaming media because it allows Windows Media components greater control over how and when packets are sent. For more details on network protocols, see Chapter 11, "Principles of Networking."

To render a stream properly, a player must receive all of the data in time to recreate the audio waveform and video frames. The speed with which data must be transferred for the player to render the media properly is called the bit rate of the stream. The one greatest limitation to streaming on the Internet is bandwidth. *Bandwidth* is the maximum bit rate that a connection can handle, and unfortunately, the bit rate of high quality audio and video is far higher than the bandwidth of most Internet connections. Because of the popularity of streaming media, however, there have been many technological advances in networking, compression, and media delivery.

The quality of a stream, therefore, is highly dependent on the quality and speed of the connection between server and player. The Windows Media server and Windows Media Player must work as a unit to regulate the flow of the stream, so that the data is received by the player in time to render the media in a continuous fashion. Windows Media Technologies offers two methods of delivering a stream: unicast and multicast.

Unicast and multicast streaming

Unicast and multicast are the two network transport methods that are used to deliver streaming content to end users. Unicast and multicast describe how client computers receive data packets.

Unicast

Unicast has a one-to-one client/server connection during which the client receives a distinct stream from the server. No other client has access to the stream. Each client has its own connection to the server and a separate content stream must be generated for each client requesting content from the server.

The main advantage of a one-to-one connection is that data flows both ways between client and server. As the media is streamed to the client, control and feedback information is sent back to the server. Control information allows the end user to start, stop, pause, and seek to different positions within a stream. Feedback information is used by the server to implement intelligent streaming and error correction. Figure 1.1 shows a unicast data flow.

Figure 1.1.

Unicast data flow.

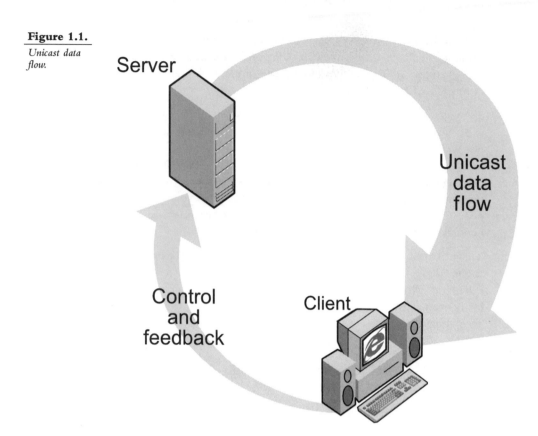

Multicast

Multicast, as implemented by Windows Media Technologies, is a connectionless data transmission method in which a server provides one stream from which many clients can receive data. Connectionless means that clients receive the stream but do not connect to the server. Because there is no connection, control or feedback information cannot be sent to the server.

For each event that is multicast, only a single stream is generated. This saves network bandwidth and reduces the load placed on the server. To distribute a multicast transmission, the network must have multicast-capable routers that have been enabled to forward multicast packets. Most of the Internet is not yet multicast-capable, but multicast can be used on many intranets. Figure 1.2 shows a multicast data flow.

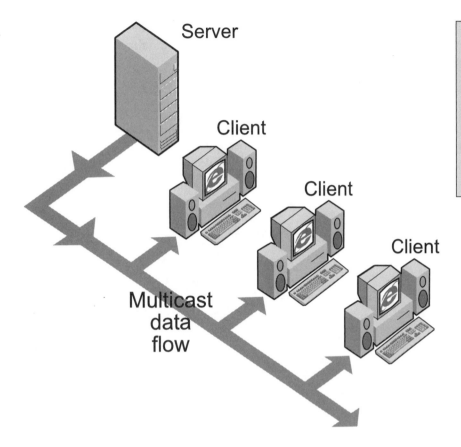

Figure 1.2.
Multicast data flow.

Server

Client

Client

Client

Multicast data flow

On-demand and broadcast content

With Windows Media Technologies, there are two types of streaming media, each of which is defined by the point at which playback is controlled. Playback of an on-demand stream is controlled by the end user. Playback of a broadcast stream is controlled at the point where the stream originates, the server.

Broadcast streams provide a passive end-user experience during which the only choice the end user can make is whether to continue receiving the stream. The end-user experience with a broadcast stream is very similar to the viewer or listener experience with a television or radio broadcast. If the content is a specific live event (such as a press conference), the end user must initiate the connection to the broadcast stream when the event is scheduled to take place.

On-demand streams are initiated at the request of the client. While the stream is playing, the end user can send commands through the client to the server to control playback of the stream. The end-user experience with an on-demand stream is similar to the end-user experience of pre-recorded audio or video. The source of an on-demand stream is always a Windows Media file. The source of a broadcast stream can originate directly from Windows Media Encoder as a live event or from a Windows Media file.

Table 1.1 shows the relationship between the delivery methods, unicast and multicast, and the streaming media types, on-demand and broadcast.

Table 1.1. Streaming media types and delivery methods.

	On-demand content viewing experience	*Broadcast content viewing experience*
Unicast	On-demand unicast provides individual playback control.	Broadcast unicast provides a shared viewing experience, and it is currently available for deployment across the Internet.
Multicast	N/A	• Broadcast multicast is often more efficient than unicast. Broadcast multicast enables low bandwidth usage. • Broadcast multicast can only be deployed across an intranet; most of the Internet is not yet multicast-capable. • Broadcast multicast requires the deployment of multicast-capable routers across the network.

Streaming media production

The three Windows Media Technologies components, Windows Media Tools, Windows Media Services, and Windows Media Player, map directly to the three phases of a streaming media production: content creation, content distribution, and content rendering.

Figure 1.3 shows the elements of the streaming media production process from beginning to end.

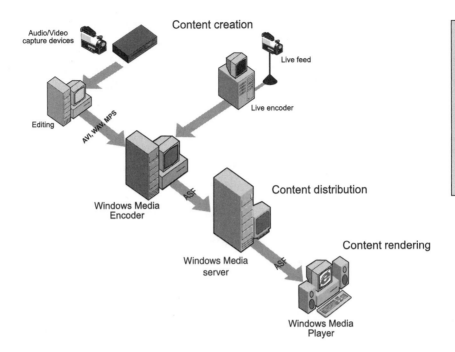

Figure 1.3.

The streaming media process.

Content creation phase

During the content creation phase, audio and/or video content is created and edited. When creating audio and video content for streaming, care should be taken to ensure the highest quality possible, because flaws will be amplified during the compression process. For more information about optimizing your content for streaming media, see Chapter 2 "Creating and Improving Multimedia Content."

To prepare content for streaming, it must be encoded using the Windows Media Tools component that is most appropriate for the particular job. Windows Media Encoder is the basic encoding tool. For more information, see Chapter 3, "Using Windows Media Tools." For more information about file formats and compression, see Chapter 10, "Principles of Digital Compression and Encoding."

In addition to streaming audio and video, you can use Windows Media Technologies to create multimedia presentations that include text, images, commands, Web pages, and HTML. Text synchronized with audio and video can be used to provide closed-captioned text or supplemental information for the media clip. Web page URLs can be synchronized with clips to enrich the clip and provide interactivity, and images can be added to create a slide show. For more information, see Section 3 of this book, "Advanced Uses of Windows Media Technologies." Figure 1.4 shows how these elements are combined during the content production process.

Figure 1.4.

*Content
production
process.*

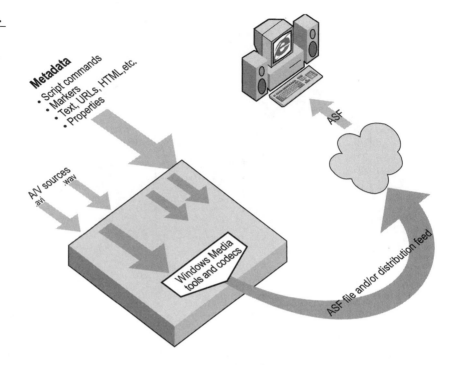

You can use Windows Media Technologies to stream, or make available for download, the
following media types:

- **Prerecorded or live audio.** Audio multimedia files or the live input from a
  computer sound card can be used to create files or broadcast live in the ASF format.

- **Prerecorded or live video.** Video multimedia files or the live input from a
  computer video capture card can be used to create files or broadcast live in the ASF
  format.

- **Still images.** Image files in formats such as JPEG and GIF, can be synchronized
  with an audio file and encoded into an .asf file.

- **Captions.** You can use a script command or Synchronized Accessible Media
  Interchange (SAMI) file to add text to the Windows Media Player closed-captioned
  text display panel.

- **Script commands.** If a script command is added to an .asf file, Windows Media
  Player will be able to perform the command at a specified time during the rendering
  of a stream. Some of the script command types you may choose to add to an .asf file
  include:

  - **URL**, to launch a browser and view a specified Web page.

  - **Filename**, to open a specified file.

  - **Text**, to display specified text in the closed-captioned text display panel.

Content delivery phase

During the content delivery phase, a Windows Media server is used to deliver the .asf file or live stream over a network to a client computer. Before you start streaming content, determine the capacity of your servers and configure them to set limits on the number of concurrent connections. On-demand content is copied into folders that are associated with unicast publishing points. Live streams are delivered to clients from multicast stations and broadcast publishing points. For more information about configuring and administering your server, see Chapter 4, "Using Windows Media Services."

Streaming server versus Web server

A Windows Media server is designed specifically for streaming Windows Media content; however, a standard Web server can also be used to host .asf files. If you decide to use a Web server, you should be aware of the differences in the way the content is delivered that can affect the quality of the playback. For example, many Web sites cannot justify the cost of adding servers. In some cases, Web server delivery may be the best or only method that makes sense. If your site uses streaming media prominently, you should consider the advantages of using a Windows Media server.

When an end user accesses streaming content from a Web server, the content is either downloaded or it is streamed, depending on how the content is referenced and on the configuration of an end-user's browser. If the content is referenced directly, the browser may attempt to download the content first. This could be a problem if the content is copyrighted. However, if the content is referenced through an ASF Stream Redirector (.asx) file, Windows Media Player opens the file and streams it. For more information about .asx files, see Chapter 9, "Designing and Developing Using Windows Media Technologies."

As the file streams from a Web server, the quality of the delivery is not monitored, and no adjustment to the bit rate is made because a Web server is simply not equipped for handling streaming media. Intelligent streaming or other error correction methods are not employed. In addition, the preferred delivery protocol, UDP, cannot be used, so delivery of media is more likely to be interrupted by periods of silence while Windows Media Player buffers data. (Windows Media Player stores data in advance of playing it in a memory buffer.) Live streaming and multicasting are also not possible with a Web server.

Most importantly, the method of actually sending the data is different. A Web server is designed to send as much data as it can, as quickly as possible. Where this is the preferred method for sending packets containing static images, text, and Web page script, it is not the best method for sending packets containing streaming media. Streaming media content should be delivered in real-time, not in large bursts. The client should receive packets just ahead of rendering them. The Windows Media server properly meters the delivery of packets, according to feedback information it receives while sending a stream to a client. When Windows Media Player receives packets in this way, the presentation is much more likely to be smooth. Also, because bandwidth use is controlled, more end users can connect concurrently to your site and receive streams that are free of interruptions.

Content rendering phase

Rendering is the process of converting digital information from the stream into sound and pictures. During the content rendering phase, the data is received by the client computer and rendered by Windows Media Player. Windows Media Player can play content in the stand-alone configuration, or you can embed Windows Media Player in a Web page using the Microsoft® ActiveX® control and plug-in. For more information, see Chapter 5, "Using Windows Media Player." More advanced presentations can synchronize text, images, and audio and video with other items on the Web page. For more information, see Chapter 9, "Designing and Developing Using Windows Media Technologies."

Using Windows Media Technologies

This section describes three ways that Windows Media Technologies is commonly used:

- **Entertainment and information.** If a performance can be captured as audio or video, it can be streamed over the Internet.

- **Corporate communications.** An internal network or intranet is used to exchange information across the enterprise.

- **Distance learning.** This audience uses the Internet as the framework for a global classroom.

Entertainment and information

News, information, music, and many other types of content (from comedy to traffic cams) are available as streaming media on the Internet. You can browse sites, such as WindowsMedia.com (http://www.windowsmedia.com/), to find an entry point to some of the available content. In addition, you can personalize the Microsoft® Internet Explorer default home page and add media clips from various content providers.

The following list gives examples of end-user experiences that can be created using Windows Media Technologies components:

- **On-demand library or archive.** This is the most common end-user experience. The end user visits a Web site and is presented with links to .asf files. She clicks a link, and Windows Media Player starts, locates the file on the Windows Media or

Web server, and plays it. The end user has complete control over playback. She can stop, start, pause, and move backward or forward through the media. The on-demand site can offer any number of files. Large sites may have hundreds of files and provide a search system to help end users locate media. An on-demand site often provides end users with a choice of bandwidths and formats. For example, end users with standard dial-up modems can play clips made for a 28.8-Kbps bandwidth; end users with ISDN modems can play 56-Kbps clips.

■ **Radio and television broadcasts.** This is another very popular use of streaming media. Hundreds of broadcasters are extending their coverage area to the Internet by streaming their on-air signal. End users visit a radio station's site and click a link to open Windows Media Player and play the live stream. Radio stations have traditionally written off listeners during mid-day working hours, but now thousands of end users tune in using their office computers. Because of global accessibility, end users can listen to a radio station from another continent as easily as a local station. To make streaming easy for broadcasters and end users, there are Internet service providers (ISPs) that specialize in streaming media. These ISPs are often referred to as aggregators. One of them, broadcast.com (http://www.broadcast.com/), offers end users a choice of hundreds of radio stations throughout the world.

■ **Pay-per-view sites.** Windows Media Technologies provides a way for developers to create pay-per-view Web sites. The software developer creates plug-ins to the Windows Media server that authenticate and authorize end users to view protected on-demand or broadcast content. The system can be expanded to include e-commerce and bookkeeping functions. The result is a site that offers streaming content for a fee. An end user can come to a pay-per-view site and preview content to decide what to purchase. Then he can pay with a credit card and view the content for a set duration. Windows Media Technologies provides the way to protect streaming content. For more information about creating pay-per-view plug-ins, see the Windows Media Technologies Software Development Kit (SDK), which can be installed from the Welcome page of the JumpStart CD included with this book. For additional information about pay-per-view, see the Windows Media Web site (http://www.microsoft.com/windows/windowsmedia/).

■ **Personalized playlists.** An ASP page contains server-side scripting that can be used to create Web pages on the fly that are personalized to individual end users. By using Windows Media Technologies and ASP pages, a Web site can be built that enables end users to create their own playlists. A playlist is a list of .asf files that are played one after the other and delivered to Windows Media Player in an .asx file. In a playlist's simplest form, you can give an end user a choice of media to view, such as a list of news stories. After the end user chooses from the list, an ASP page is used to build an .asx file that is then sent back to the end user. In a more complex example of personalization, an end user provides a Web server database with personal information, such as news story preferences. The Web server and other server components then build a playlist based on those preferences. An .asx file containing a playlist can also be written manually with a basic text editor and ASX scripting. For information about writing a playlist manually, see Chapter 9, "Designing and Developing Using Windows Media Technologies."

- **Synchronized multimedia.** An ASF stream contains digital media that is played by Windows Media Player. With the addition of script commands, the stream can control events outside the player. For example, an end user can view video in an embedded player, in one frame of a Web page, and images and text in other frames that are synchronized with the stream. For more information on synchronized multimedia, see Chapter 9, "Designing and Developing Using Windows Media Technologies."

- **Encrypted music.** Windows Media Rights Manager provides owners of audio or video content a way to deter unauthorized use of their content. An end user can download the packaged content but cannot play it without a license. After an end user either enters information that you'd like to know about them (like an e-mail address) or pays for the right to play the content, the end user receives the license and can play it according to the terms of the license. For more information, see Chapter 7, "Packaging Media Files Using Windows Media Rights Manager."

Entertainment and information fictional scenarios

The following fictional scenarios provide detailed descriptions of how Windows Media Technologies can be used to enhance the end-user experience:

- **News and information site.** This fictitious site is as dynamic as its cable news television counterpart because of the many creative implementations of Windows Media Technologies.

- **Internet radio automation site.** This site demonstrates how a radio station can extend its reach to the Internet.

- **Encrypted music site.** With Windows Media Technologies, Internet music is no longer a novelty.

News and information site

A large cable television news company, News Network (NN), expanded its communication base to include the Internet. NN is a very successful news Web site with complete coverage of daily news and a vast archive of more than 20,000 stories. As part of their package, they offer end users video of the stories, clips, and newscasts as streaming media using Windows Media Technologies.

As an end user browses the news stories, he discovers three uses of streaming media by NN: on-demand stories, special live broadcasts, and a personalized newscast.

On almost every recent-story page, an end user can click one or more on-demand clips. NN simply encodes edited stories that are broadcast into .asf files and places links to them on story pages. For example, a story on peace efforts has three clips: a story on one country's reaction, a story on activity in the other country's government, and a story on the reaction from a family living near the conflict. For each story, three .asf files are encoded at different bandwidths: 28.8 Kbps, 56 Kbps, and 100 Kbps. The end user can select the one that is most suitable for the current connection speed.

NN performed a poll of end users and discovered a large hearing-impaired audience. Because the broadcast was already available with closed-captioned text, NN engineers invented a simple method of retrieving the text that had already been encoded into the television signal. The text is automatically inserted into a Synchronized Accessible Media Interchange (SAMI) file as the story is being encoded into an .asf file. As a hearing-impaired end user plays the story, Windows Media Player displays the text in synch-ronization with the media in a special closed-captioned text display area on the player.

In the course of delivering the news, News Network often produces special stories that require continuous live coverage for a period of one day to several months. A special live feed is made available to end users on the Web site. The special live feed often does not include cut-ins from the news anchors or commercials. An end user can tune in and watch events as they happen, 24 hours a day, seven days a week. For example, during coverage of a two-week strike by workers at a factory, the special feed comes from one camera at the factory locked-down on a telephoto shot of picketers at the main factory entrance. An end user can tune in at 5:00 a.m. and see what is happening at that moment from the locked-down camera.

The most innovative use of Windows Media Technologies, however, is the personalized newscast. An end user is presented with a list of the day's top stories. The end user browses the list and selects the check box beside the stories she is interested in, then clicks **Create Newscast**. Using the list, the NN Web server creates a playlist of the stories. Then, to make the newscast complete, the server also inserts a show open, a show close, and bumpers (short transitional pieces). The Web server also inserts commercials, the selection of which is determined by a personalization server that makes the choices based on the types of stories that the end user chooses. The result is an .asx file containing a playlist. When played back, this file appears as a complete newscast containing only the stories that the end user wants to see.

The complete stories are edited into individual .avi files, then encoded as .asf files. The show open, show close, bumpers, teases, and commercials are also encoded into separate .asf files. It's very important that video and audio levels match from clip to clip as they are being captured. Keywords concerning the character of the stories are entered into the personalization database. For example, NN is most concerned with targeting commercials by gender and age. A code is created that a producer assigns to a story, labeling it as most likely to be viewed by a certain demographic type. For example, a producer may label a story about a rap singer as most likely to be viewed by young people of a certain gender. When the story is chosen by an end user, a commercial for some youth-targeted soft drink is added to the playlist.

Internet radio automation site

The popularity of Internet radio is growing. Thousands of radio stations throughout the world are streaming globally. One fictional radio station in Tucson, Arizona, however, had a problem when they decided to stream their signal. ABCD radio runs a 24-hour talk radio format. Roughly two-thirds of its programming is produced locally and the rest is from syndicated sources. ABCD radio looked into streaming their on-air signal live over the Internet. A radio station aggregator offered to carry the stream for no fee and even to provide the station with a computer for encoding the signal. The only problem with the plan arose when ABCD radio went to the program syndicators. Two of them would not give permission for ABCD radio to rebroadcast their programming on the Internet. This meant that six hours of programming every day would have to be deleted from the Internet stream: 9:00 a.m. to noon and 8:00 p.m. to 11:00 p.m.

ABCD radio saw the value in using the Internet and decided to invest some time and effort in finding a solution. The operations staff did some research and purchased equipment and software. They built a simple automation system using Windows-based software. The system now runs mostly unattended and switches between the live, on-air signal and automation at the appropriate times. ABCD radio simply reruns programming to fill the holes in the schedule. The show that runs from 11:00 p.m. to 2:00 a.m. is recorded and rebroadcast on the Internet the next day from 9:00 a.m. to noon. The morning talk show is replayed that night from 8:00 p.m. to 11:00 p.m.

On Sunday night from 7:00 p.m. to 6:00 a.m., the system is programmed to automate the play of individual music cuts and to intersperse the cuts with generic announcer one-liners, station identifications, commercials, promotional spots, and live news at the top of each hour. To keep the automated feed fresh, so the end user does not hear the same music every week, the automation is programmed to randomize the playback of music cuts and one-liners. In addition, new material and promos are added periodically.

An end user in New York can tune in to this Tucson-based radio station. ABCD radio effectively extends its reach globally, the syndicated material is copyright protected, and the entire system runs mostly unattended.

Encrypted music site

The Internet has become a major distribution point for recorded music. End users can stream on-demand music clips or download full-fidelity clips and then use them to create custom CDs. A fictional Northwest music group, called The Trumpets, has successfully distributed some of their recordings free on the Internet. Now the novelty has worn off. The group was excited in the beginning to see that 2,000 copies of their first single had been downloaded. However, in looking toward the future, the group envisions a time when their parents will ask them to leave the house and support themselves. Therefore, they must either find a way to make money with their music or get jobs.

They record enough material to release a CD and decide to offer a few clips free on the Internet using Windows Media Rights Manager to gather end-user information. They can use the list of people who downloaded the clips to create a mailing list for sending e-mail promotional material about the CD.

The music clips are captured from the master digital audiotape (DAT) using a Windows-based audio-editing program such as Sonic Foundry's Sound Forge. Sound Forge also enables the person editing the audio to encode the finished file in the ASF format.

After the files are encoded, Windows Media Rights Manager is used to digitally protect, sign, and apply licensing terms to the content. Files that have been through this process are said to be *packaged*. Packaged content requires the acquisition of a license by the end user before it can be played. The owners of the content, The Trumpets, can issue a license based on any criteria they choose. In this case, the group simply wants an e-mail address in exchange for the license. However, issuance can be based on payment; Windows Media Rights Manager can be fully integrated with an e-commerce solution for billing and payment collection. After a license has been acquired for a particular clip, the clip can be played back only on the computer for which the license was issued. If the clip is copied to another person's computer, the second person will also have to perform the license acquisition procedure when she tries to play the clip.

The end-user experience can begin in many different ways. One way an end user might encounter Windows Media content is by browsing the Windows Media Showcase site (http://www.windowsmedia.com/). To obtain the music of The Trumpets, however, the end user goes to the group's Web site and clicks a link to download the clip. After saving the clip, the end user finds the file and double-clicks it to play the music. The default browser opens, and a Web page for The Trumpets fan club is displayed. The Web page explains that the end user must submit an e-mail address and Zip code to play the clip. After the end user enters the information and clicks **Submit**, another page displays a link to play the content. At this point, the license has been issued and saved on the end user's computer and the end user's information has been recorded. The end user clicks the link to play the downloaded clip.

Corporate communications

The Windows Media Technologies components are optimized to deliver low bit-rate streaming content over the Internet. However, many corporations and organizations have implemented Internet-style Web sites on their internal networks. Intranets bring the flexibility and simplicity of Internet networking to corporate communications. And Windows Media components provide organizations with intranets the ability to stream audio and video directly to the desktops of employees throughout an enterprise.

Windows Media Technologies can be used for many new types of corporate communications. Because most corporate LANs (local area networks) have far greater bandwidth than the Internet, the corporate producer can create far richer multimedia experiences for an end user. You can use the components of Windows Media Technologies to:

- Deliver audio, video, slide presentations, and other data to large numbers of people, either live in real-time or in a stored, on-demand format.

- Create and host live presentations, press conferences, and meetings.

- Archive and re-broadcast corporate communications events, such as speeches and press conferences.

- Conduct seminars.

Corporate communication fictional scenarios

The following fictional scenarios show three ways that Windows Media Technologies can be used in corporate communications.

- **On-demand library.** An online archive of stored media.

- **Event guide.** An intranet guide to live broadcasts.

- **PowerPoint Presentation Broadcasting.** A method of broadcasting using Microsoft® PowerPoint® 2000.

> **NOTE**   The example companies, organizations, products, people, and events depicted herein are fictitious. No association with any real company, organization, product, person, or event is intended or should be inferred.

On-demand library

Corporations, organizations, and institutions have all been created and organized around central stores of information. Most of this information is stored as text and static images. However, much of an organization's communication involves people speaking: demonstrating ideas and concepts. This type of communication can be captured and included as part of the central information store by using Windows Media Technologies.

Just as an organization maintains a library of books, drawings, and papers, it can offer end users access to a library of events such as meetings, talks, lectures, and related audio and video pieces as on-demand .asf files. The organization's intranet can provide end users with the means of locating on-demand files and playing them.

At the Contoso Pharmaceutical Corporation, an end user opens a browser to locate the internal streaming media library page and initiates a search for media using the keywords: bovine and nutrition. An SQL (Structured Query Language) database performs the search and returns four entries: two excerpts from television newscasts, a general staff meeting of the Bovine Health Division, and a lecture by a visiting veterinarian. The end user clicks the link associated with the lecture, and a new page opens containing an embedded

Windows Media Player and a frame for displaying images. As the lecture plays back, the lecturer's face is displayed in the player, and images are displayed in the associated frame. This particular end user is only interested in information about a certain drug that is used for treatment of the disease, so he goes to the table of contents list on the player and clicks an entry labeled "treatment." When he does so, Windows Media Player seeks (changes playback position) to a point 35 minutes into the lecture.

Before Windows Media Technologies, Contoso Pharmaceutical rented a large meeting room at a local hotel, flew in guest lecturers, and bused a hundred or more employees and contractors to the lecture. The cost of such an event forced the company to limit the number of lectures. By streaming the lectures, the company can reach more people and the interruption to work is minimal.

The streaming media library is maintained by the internal IT department. The .asf files are stored on Windows Media servers connected to the intranet. If a presentation, program, or performance requires associated images or other information, such as closed-captioned files and special Web pages, they are stored in folders on a Web server. A naming convention is created for the media. At Contoso Pharmaceutical, the bovine nutrition lecture production is internally titled BNL0399, and all related information is archived using that name: the Windows Media file is named BNL0399.asf, the Web page folder and database is named BNL0399, and all associated filenames are derived similarly. Keywords about BNL0399 are entered into the library SQL database, and the ASP page-based library Web site displays lists of media and descriptive text according to input from end users.

Event guide

The Contoso Pharmaceutical on-demand library was so successful, the company started offering live streaming media broadcasts. The company began with weekly 30-minute state-of-the-company briefings from the CEO, but soon other divisions, departments, and groups were broadcasting weekly meetings. Then, individual teams began broadcasting information concerning new internal tools and research results. Because the media production system was already in place, the cost of broadcasting internally was minimal. For example, a chemist at the CPC division in Oklahoma City could tune in to a briefing by a product group in Phoenix and learn how the drug that his team had developed was being marketed.

Because the broadcast system was so successful, it soon began to fall apart. There was so much information available that no one could find anything. To solve the problem, the library took on the role of aggregator. In addition to on-demand content, the library created an event guide on the intranet that listed upcoming broadcasts by date and time. The end user could then browse for events and search for listings by category or keyword.

A group in the library maintains the event guide and generates the internal work orders to request production support from the in-house production facility. The budget to produce a broadcast comes from the group requesting the broadcast. As the presentation or lecture streams live, the stream is also saved to an .asf file. Immediately after the event, the file is automatically archived in the on-demand system and made available to end users.

PowerPoint Presentation Broadcasting

The task of pulling together all of the graphic elements to build visual aids for corporate presentations has been included in programs like Microsoft PowerPoint. In addition to the functionality and features that have made PowerPoint a great tool for creating powerful presentations, PowerPoint 2000 offers a new way to synchronize a digital media event with presentation slides.

One month before a veterinarian is scheduled to speak on bovine nutrition to interested end users on the Contoso Pharmaceutical streaming media system, pre-production begins. The library streaming media group receives a request from the R&D division to broadcast the veterinarian's lecture. The roles are immediately established. The R&D division will secure the meeting room and handle all dealings with the veterinarian. The library group will coordinate the broadcast part of the event and contract with an in-house producer from the production facility to handle the technical aspects of the event. The library group will also make event information available internally, using the event guide, and archive the on-demand file.

The library group also sets up the broadcast program on the Windows Media server using Windows Media Administrator to remotely create broadcast publishing points and multicast stations, programs, and streams. The veterinarian uploads the completed PowerPoint slides and the PowerPoint project file to an FTP server designated by the library group. The group will then move the slides to the intranet Web server.

On the day of the lecture, the production crew arrives early to install lights, video cameras, and all the other equipment for recording video and audio of the event. They also install the pre-configured computer that will run the PowerPoint presentation. The computer is connected to the video projection system for the audience in the meeting room, and it is connected to the internal corporate network. During the presentation, PowerPoint will display slides for the meeting room audience, as well as encode video, audio, and slide change cues (script commands) for the intranet. The corporate network connection will carry the encoded signal to the Windows Media servers, which will broadcast the stream.

The end user finds out about the broadcast by browsing the listings or searching by keyword in the event guide. Announcements are also e-mailed to potential end users. The end user does not need PowerPoint to view the presentation, just a current version of a popular Internet browser, such as Microsoft Internet Explorer 5, and Windows Media

Player. If an end user comes to the broadcast Web site before the broadcast starts, the event guide provides a lobby page that displays brief presentation information and a clock that counts down to the beginning of the talk.

During the event, the veterinarian's voice and face are streamed live to end users. When a slide changes, the new image is projected in the meeting room, and the slide change cue (script command) is sent to the end users' computers. When an embedded Windows Media Player receives a slide change cue, it instructs the browser to open a particular slide. The file for this slide is downloaded from the intranet Web server to a frame adjacent to the embedded player on the presentation Web page. The result is that anyone on the intranet can receive the complete PowerPoint presentation. As soon as the broadcast ends, the .asf file is immediately available. This .asf file contains the audio, video, and slide change cues for the PowerPoint presentation. An end user can play the file in the associated Web page and receive the complete presentation.

When using the Presentation Broadcasting feature of PowerPoint 2000, the slides can be updated and published to a Web server minutes before a scheduled presentation, if necessary. The presentation station can be pre-configured so a person giving a presentation can convert the slides to HTML and post them on a Web server. The result is that an online presentation can be developed and delivered using standard tools in PowerPoint, with little or no specific knowledge of Windows Media Technologies or media production. Slides can be built, transitions can be used, and the audio/video components of the presentation can be broadcast live. These components can also be provided afterward, on demand, to end users.

NOTE The Contoso Pharmaceutical example demonstrates a full production. However, a presentation can be greatly simplified. A speaker can run an entire presentation from an office using a microphone or clip-on video camera plugged directly into a capture card. For more details on PowerPoint presentations using Windows Media Technologies, see Chapter 8, "Streaming PowerPoint Presentations."

Distance learning

Home study and distance learning have been used for many years as alternatives to traditional classrooms. People who want to learn and receive credit but are not able to attend school in person, can read books, view an instructor on television, and take tests in their homes, on their own time. The greatest disadvantage of this type of learning is that there is no interactivity. All communication, except for the mail-in test, is one way. The Internet and intranets provide the framework for an interactive global classroom.

End users can attend a virtual classroom on any computer that is connected to the Internet. Static text and graphics can be downloaded from the school's servers. The end user can interact with an instructor by sending e-mail, by responding through the classroom's chat server, or by submitting information to the school's Web server, using ASP pages. The classroom experience comes to life by adding the real-time voice and face of the instructor, using Windows Media Technologies.

The following elements can be used to create interactive distance learning courses:

- **Broadcasting.** With Windows Media Technologies you can stream a classroom session live. Live streaming allows an instructor to engage students interactively. For example, an instructor can poll students to see what percentage of them has finished reading a chapter in the textbook. He can receive the information, using any of a variety of Web technologies, almost instantly, and adjust his instruction on the fly.

- **On-demand archive or library.** Students who cannot attend the live session can play back the on-demand file and experience every aspect of the instruction, excluding the live interactivity. Students can also search a database and replay archived sessions. For example, a live instructor can suggest students replay a special session featuring a guest lecturer.

- **PowerPoint presentation.** As described earlier in this chapter, with PowerPoint 2000 you can integrate PowerPoint slides with a live presentation. Also, by using the Windows Media® Publish to ASF for Microsoft® PowerPoint® 97 plug-in, PowerPoint slides can be synchronized with narration and encoded in an .asf file. For more details, see Chapter 8, "Streaming PowerPoint Presentations."

- **Synchronized multimedia.** Using an embedded Windows Media Player and script commands, you can control other elements on the Web page in synchronization with an ASF stream. For example, you can control DHTML elements on a Web page. You can also encode text in a script command, which can then be printed to a text box on a page. For example, when an instructor changes topics or makes a point, bold text can be printed in a text box positioned at the top of the page. For more details, see Chapter 9, "Designing and Developing Using Windows Media Technologies."

- **Pay-per-view.** You might think of pay-per-view in the context of a sports event or movie. However, Windows Media pay-per-view functionality can just as easily be used to restrict entry to an Internet classroom. You may choose to restrict access based on payment of tuition or to keep the classroom membership contained. For more details, see the Windows Media Technologies SDK, which can be installed from the Welcome page of the JumpStart CD included with this book. For additional information about pay-per-view, see the Windows Media Web site (http://www.microsoft.com/windows/windowsmedia/).

NOTE	The example companies, organizations, products, people, and events depicted herein are fictitious. No association with any real company, organization, product, person, or event is intended or should be inferred.

Distance learning fictional scenario

This fictional scenario describes the creation of an end-user experience for distance learning.

State University has extended its reach to the Internet, offering courses in indigenous wild animal veterinary medicine. An end user in Australia, for example, can sign up for a course on treating moose diseases. To bring immediacy and interactivity to the courses, the university decided to use Windows Media Technologies.

A developer at State University created Windows Media server plug-in software for authenticating and authorizing end users to receive their classroom streaming media content. The developer used information in the Windows Media Technologies SDK to design the pay-per-view plug-ins that meet the specific requirements of the college. Without authentication, an end user coming to the classroom site can only see parts of the page. Without authorization, the end user cannot receive the ASF stream or participate in the class.

When an end user is accepted into the online course, the end user's name is added to a database. This database is accessible by the Web server and Windows Media server. Prior to the beginning of the class, the end user receives e-mail containing the URL of the class Web site and a password. On the first day, minutes before the start of class, the end user goes to the Web site and receives a log-on prompt. The end user enters a name and password.

The database recognizes the student and connects the embedded Windows Media Player to the broadcast stream. Before the class starts, a lobby page appears in one of the frames on the container page. The lobby page displays information about the class and a countdown clock; Windows Media Player displays a graphic on the screen and plays music so the student knows he has connected successfully. When class starts, a script command is sent with the broadcast stream that changes the lobby page to the first slide, and the professor appears in the player.

As the class progresses, the professor occasionally displays large images in the frame adjacent to the player. Because the images are large, the professor allows enough time for them to download. One image shows the moose anatomy, another shows a diseased moose. The professor also uses script commands to change text in a banner describing the current topic and highlighting certain words.

At several points during the lecture, the professor takes time for interactivity. For example, he polls the students to see how many of them are practicing veterinarians. A script command sent in the live stream flips the image frame to an ASP page containing a small questionnaire. After the student submits the page, an Internet Server Application Programming Interface (ISAPI) filter on the Web server tallies the results and presents them to the professor on a secure Web page. During another part of the lecture, the professor opens the floor to questions. Again, a script command flips the image frame to another ASP page containing a form for submitting questions. The student enters a question: "When do moose molt, or do they?" The class size has been limited to 15 students, so the professor is not overwhelmed by the number of questions that appear on her private Web page.

At the end of class, the image page flips to an ASP page containing a quiz. The results of the quiz, which are graded by using the ISAPI filter, are entered into the database and become part of the student's final grade in the course.

Windows Media Technologies rovides a rich set of tools that can integrate with many other Web tools. With all of these tools, you can create an infinite variety of rich end-user experiences involving streaming media. For current information about Windows Media Technologies and many related subjects, see the Web sites listed in Appendix B, "Getting Help."

Summary

Windows Media Technologies is a set of tools, services, protocols, and file formats you can use to create, deliver, and play digital media content. You can use Windows Media Tools to capture and encode content, convert existing content to an .asf file, and edit stored media files in a variety of ways. You can use Windows Media Services to distribute live or on-demand content, and you can use Windows Media Player to play it.

To understand Windows Media Technologies, you must understand the underlying streaming media technology. Streaming media consists of source audio and video that has been digitized and assembled into data packets for transmission over a network, using either the unicast or multicast transport method. The digital media content can be delivered as a passive broadcast event or as an interactive on-demand event.

Windows Media Technologies is used in the entertainment field, for communicating information and news to a mass global audience, in corporate communications, and for distance learning. Pay-per-view Web sites can be created using the Windows Media Services SDK, music can be encrypted using Windows Media Rights Manager, live slide shows can be broadcast using PowerPoint Presentation Broadcasting, and elements of a Web page can be synchronized with a Windows Media stream using script commands.

Chapter 2, "Creating and Improving Multimedia Content," builds on the information provided in this chapter and discusses issues to consider when you create or edit multimedia content for streaming.

Chapter

2

Creating and Improving Multimedia Content

There are many issues to be aware of when you create or edit multimedia content for streaming. Regardless of the type of source material you are using—live music, pre-recorded film, or a home video—the quality of the streaming media can be no better than the quality of the source. Before you delve into how to use the Microsoft Windows Media Technologies components (Chapters 3, 4, and 5), here are some tips about how to create, improve, and archive your audio and video—helping ensure that you have the best possible source before you start streaming your content. After reading this chapter, you'll be able to answer the following questions:

- How does the background affect the compression of video?

- What is the best type of lighting to use for streaming video?

- How can I compensate for flaws in existing video?

- What video recorder and formats should I use?
- What are some ways to improve the quality of an audio recording?
- What should I be archiving?

Creating and improving video

Creating high-quality streaming video requires the use of standard video production techniques. While not intended to be the definitive source, this section provides basic information about improving the quality of your video. For more information about video production techniques, consult your local bookstore.

It is important to know that some traditional production techniques will have an adverse effect on streaming video technology. For example, when you stream video that contains rapid cuts or fast pans at dial-up connection speeds with a large frame size, you may end up streaming at an unacceptably low frame rate.

Because of the small frame size and large pixel size of streaming media, fine detail can be lost, and you may need to place your subjects closer to the camera than when shooting for television. In addition to practicing standard production techniques, selecting the right background, lighting, clothing patterns and colors, and video formats will help improve the quality of your streaming video.

Backgrounds

Selecting the right background before you begin shooting your video can help significantly improve the quality of your content after it is compressed. The compression techniques used to create streaming media work by selectively removing repetitious data from the source video.

To determine what data to keep or what data to remove, the compression software used by Windows Media Encoder analyzes each frame in the video clip. If there are areas of each frame that stay constant over time, there is no need to store a duplicate copy of the same data for every frame. This method can produce compression ratios great enough to allow smooth video streaming. However, the compression works best if the frame-to-frame differences are minimal.

By eliminating as much movement in your background as possible, many of the differences from one frame to the next are eliminated and greater compression can be achieved. With less compression, the bit rate rises, and the only way Windows Media Encoder can contain the bit rate within the set bandwidth is by lowering the frame rate or reducing the image quality.

One example of a background that is difficult to compress is a wide-angle shot of the crowd at a football stadium just after a touchdown is scored. In this shot thousands of tiny objects are in random motion throughout the background. When viewing this scene after it is compressed, you will notice that the frame rate and quality decrease as the background movement increases.

To minimize background interference as you create content for streaming media:

- **Always try to use a solid, unchanging background, such as a professional photo studio backdrop.** A moving background can compromise streaming video quality. If you need to create content with a moving background, you may have to compromise streaming video quality and frame rate.

- **If you have to shoot against a moving background, try reducing the depth of field to help reduce the amount of detail in the background.** Depth of field is the measurement of the area in front of and behind the subject that is in focus. Reducing the depth of field or shortening the area in focus softens the background and helps reduce the amount of data that changes from frame-to-frame.

  To help reduce depth of field, use a lower level of light and move the subject closer to the lens to help the background go out of focus. Also, moving the subject farther away and using a telephoto lens to zoom in may shorten the depth of field.

Lighting

The primary job of lighting is to bring the level of light up to a point where an image can be produced on a piece of film or digital video camera chip. Lighting is also used to create aesthetic beauty. When creating video for streaming, it helps to think of streamed video as a new medium. Light is used one way for news video, another way for portrait photography, another way for dance sequences in a music video, and another way for streaming video.

When implemented properly, the following lighting guidelines will help produce better streaming video:

- **Provide adequate lighting for your subject.** A television is capable of displaying a poorly lit image, but the lossy video compression codecs used in streaming video may not produce a useful image if the subject is poorly lit. For the definition of lossy and lossless codecs, see Chapter 10, "Principles of Digital Compression and Encoding." Although most camcorders can produce an acceptable image in low light, professional studio lighting will help produce images with sharper edges, lower contrast, richer color, and less video noise. Images that have these qualities are more likely to compress well.

- **Use soft, diffuse light.** Use a diffusion sheet or reflective umbrella to soften the light source, remove heavy lighting contrasts, and reduce harsh shadows. Add light to the background if necessary, and focus a backlight at the back of the subject to help separate the subject from the background and improve edge definition.

- **Avoid direct high-contrast lighting.** Hard, intense lighting sources, such as sunlight or a spotlight, create high-contrast video images. High-contrast lighting creates video images with very bright and very dark areas and not many areas in the middle. High-contrast lighting also creates heavy shadow lines. Although film is capable of capturing a wide range of light levels, video cameras have a far more limited range, and compressed video is even more limited.

  A certain amount of contrast is necessary for lighting a subject, but the light-to-dark ratio should be limited when shooting for streaming video. For example, when shooting a face lit by strong sunlight from the side, the facial features may be sharp and distinguishable on film; however, if the scene is shot with a video camera and then compressed, all detail in the shadow areas may be completely lost.

- **Use consistent light levels.** Windows Media Encoder sees changes in the light level as a change in the image that will reduce the compression rate. Strobe lights, light wheels, and other rapidly changing light effects will cause the same problem. The more movement there is in a scene, the higher the bit requirement is to reproduce it.

Clothing patterns and colors

A person's clothing can affect the quality of the compressed video image. Bright colors, such as white, reflective orange, and fire-engine red tend to bleed or spread outside an object. Stripes may cause Moiré patterns, especially when the person is moving slowly. *Moiré patterns* are video artifacts that occur when shooting an object that has many thin parallel lines; the lines appear to move or crawl and can be distracting.

Clothing colors should complement the skin tone of the person and should be sufficiently different from the background and other overlapping objects. When video is compressed, resolution is lost and edges and forms can change in unexpected ways. Color can be used to help define and recover lost resolution and to help create a compressed image that is much more pleasing to the eye. For example, so much detail may be lost when compressing an image of a person wearing a dark blue suit against a dark blue background that the person may seem to disappear. Unless that is your goal, you may be better off placing the person against a lighter, contrasting background.

Videotape recording formats

With videotape recording formats, the basic rule is that you get what you pay for. A $50,000 Betacam SP camcorder will produce better images than a $450 Hi-8 camcorder. However, with the proper conditions, an inexpensive camcorder can produce acceptable images. Betacam SP produces higher resolution, clearer, cleaner, less noisy, and more detailed images overall. However, with enough light and some extra care in adjusting focus and color, a Hi-8 camcorder can produce video that is acceptable—and for many thousands of dollars less.

The quality difference between formats is more noticeable when shooting in low or poorly lit scenes. The circuitry, CCD imaging device (the computer chip that captures the image), lens, and videotape recording system are much higher quality in the Betacam SP camcorder. When shooting a poorly lit subject, Hi-8 video circuits and processors can be pushed beyond their limits, which result in more video noise, washed-out colors, and loss of detail. The videotape writing speed, which is far slower in a Hi-8 camcorder, accentuates flaws.

Selecting a video camera or recorder

Many factors go into the selection of a video format. However, video noise, color definition, resolution, and on-board processing are particularly important to recording video that will be delivered as streaming media.

■ **Video noise.** The electronic circuitry and the videotape record/playback system of a camcorder or deck introduce video noise. Noise is visible in the image as fast-moving specks, similar to the grain in film. The snow that you see when you tune a TV to a channel with no station is 100 percent noise. Higher quality video formats introduce less noise while recording and playing. When encoding a noisy video, the codec sees the noise as frame-to-frame change and attempts to faithfully reproduce the noise by increasing the bit rate. Although you may have produced a textbook streaming video scene with little on-screen movement, noisy video produced by an inexpensive camera is seen by Windows Media Encoder as full-screen changes on every frame. A digital format camera, in theory, eliminates most of the common sources of noise in the signal chain.

■ **Color definition.** Color definition is determined by the quality of the CCD imaging device and by the color processing components of the camcorder. Color definition represents how faithfully the video format reproduces the color of the original scene. Consumer camcorders typically have two CCD chips; professional Betacam SP camcorders typically have three. Because the professional camcorder has an additional CCD chip, the color rendition is truer. Also, in a Betacam SP there is a lot more circuitry that can discern differences in luminance, saturation, and hue. A 2-chip camera may be able to reproduce two overlapping orange and blue objects; however, the definition between the two orange objects with a different shade may be blurred, and when the video is compressed for streaming, the definition may disappear completely.

■ **Resolution.** The camera lens, the CCD imaging device, the electronics, and the videotape system, determines resolution. The lines of resolution that make up the image determine the sharpness of the image. A professional camera can produce more than 700 vertical lines of resolution; an inexpensive camera can produce less than 300 vertical lines of resolution. Low-resolution cameras may not reproduce detail well. The resolution of a video is drastically reduced when it is compressed for streaming, so it is important to start with a sharp image.

■ **On-board processing.** On-board processing refers to the electronic circuits on a camcorder that correct and enhance color and resolution, reduce noise, and perform special tasks, such as increasing video gain for extreme low-light conditions. Higher priced cameras, in general, have superior processing electronics that create better images. The automatic color balancing components of some inexpensive cameras may not interpret the color of a scene correctly. In situations where sunlight is mixed with warm incandescent light, faces can end up looking gray, and compressing a poorly processed signal makes the problem worse.

Recommended formats

Video formats include Betacam SP, DVCam, Hi-8, S-VHS, and VHS. Betacam SP tends to produce a more professional-quality image, while VHS tends to produce a consumer-quality image.

■ **Betacam SP format.** Betacam SP is a professional-quality format that is used widely at television stations and production companies around the world. Betacam SP decks usually include a variety of audio and video outputs, which makes them easy to connect to your computer. Many have time code and remote control capabilities that are useful for an encoding station. Higher quality formats, such as Digital Betacam, are available; however, the improvement in content quality for streaming media is minimal when compared to the difference in cost of standard Betacam SP.

■ **DVCam format.** Like Betacam SP, DVCam is a professional format. DVCam has the advantage of being digital, which means it produces less noise. Before purchasing a DVCam, however, make sure the video output connections are compatible with your video capture card.

■ **Hi-8, S-VHS, and VHS formats.** Video noise is the main disadvantage of using Hi-8, S-VHS, and VHS formats. As explained earlier, noise is seen by Windows Media Encoder as movement in the video. Because noise is most visible when the light level is low and the camera's on-board processor is forced to increase gain, it is very important to have adequate light when shooting a scene using S-VHS, VHS, or Hi-8 camcorders.

More video tips

Most videotape players have composite video outputs. The connector is usually a single RCA jack that is labeled "video" on the back of the player. Another popular output type is S-video, which has a round connector with four small pins. A composite video image is usually a bit noisier and has lower resolution than an S-video image because the composite video signal has been routed through more processing and conversion electronics. Composite video is acceptable if you capture video directly from your original tape. If you plan to edit the tape or work from copies, using S-video throughout the entire process will help reduce noise.

Firewire (IEEE 1394) connections from digital cameras and DVCam tape players are becoming more popular. Firewire delivers high quality video plus audio and enables a computer to control the playback operations. When buying a firewire card, select one that has a hardware codec. Hardware codecs operate much faster than software codecs, which cannot keep up with the speed of firewire.

Use brand name, high quality videotapes for recording, and whenever possible, capture the video from the original tape. A tape copy always has lower video quality than the original—similar to a photocopy of a photocopy. A copy of digital videotape, in theory, should be identical to the original; however, the processing and amplifying electronics can introduce noise and artifacts.

Video file formats

If video editing is required, it is recommended that you capture and archive video files in the AVI format. After an .avi file has been edited, it can be encoded directly into an .asf file for streaming. Although there are numerous codecs available for compressing .avi files, use **Full Frames (Uncompressed)** as the compression setting in your AVI capture software. The internal format of the video is also important. The Microsoft MPEG-4 video codec compresses best if content is captured in the following formats, in the priority given: RGBT, RGBH, IYUV (I420), YV12, and YUY2.

To maintain the aspect ratio of your video image (the proportion of height to width), capture video to the same frame size that you will use when you encode the AVI for streaming. We recommend using the following standard sizes (in pixels):

- **160×120**
- **176×144** (QCIF)
- **320×240**
- **352×288** (CIF)
- **640×480** (this is only recommended for slide shows or screen captures at low frame rates)

For detailed information about video file formats, see Chapter 10, "Principles of Digital Compression and Encoding."

NOTE	Many AVI editors only accept frame sizes that are evenly divisible by 16.

Compensating for flaws

Ideally, video producers have complete control over production elements such as shot selection, lighting, and video format. However, in many cases video producers have to shoot in harsh sunlight using an inferior video format. Or, producers may just be handed a tape that is either inadequate or unsuitable for streaming media. This section discusses some common flaws and offers tips on how to deal with them.

Over saturation

When viewing a scene shot with a consumer-quality camcorder or a copy of a tape, you may notice that the colors are so intense that they bleed outside the edges of objects or smear when an object moves. This is called *over saturation* and can often be fixed before capturing by adjusting the computer capture card's saturation setting to a lower level. Saturation is the amount of color in the image. Too little saturation produces images that can appear black and white. Too much saturation produces colors that appear artificially bright. For example, someone wearing a red shirt can appear to be wearing a neon-red life vest. If you use a professional-quality video switcher or processor, certain video levels, such as saturation, hue (or color phase), video (or luminance), and setup (or pedestal), can be adjusted before being sent to the capture card.

Low or clipped video

If a picture is extremely dark or bright, the recording may be beyond repair. However, a picture can often be recovered by adjusting:

- **Brightness**, to raise or lower the video level.
- **Contrast**, to optimize the number of shades of gray or levels of luminance, also known as the grayscale.

A dark picture can be corrected by raising the video brightness setting and optimizing the grayscale. Doing so, however, increases video noise because noise is most noticeable in dark areas of an image. It is possible to partially hide the noise by increasing the contrast.

A video camera has a limited range of contrast that it can reproduce. For example, when shooting a dark, poorly lit subject against a very bright background, only one or the other is correctly reproduced. If the background looks correct, the subject is in silhouette. If the subject looks correct, the background is so bright it appears washed out and detail that should be present in brighter areas are completely white. When part of an image appears like this, it is said to be "clipped." Clipping is a mechanism built in to video cameras to keep video levels that are too high from overloading the camera and the tape recording.

Video that has been clipped is usually not correctable because detail in the white areas that was lost cannot be recovered. On professional format camcorders, video gain is often not automatically adjusted. In such cases, an extremely high video level can result in a distorted recording on the tape—white areas of the picture are covered with flashing black lines and specks—making it completely unusable. However, if there is a small amount of detail left, raising the contrast can sometimes bring the detail back partially.

Out-of-focus image

An out-of-focus picture cannot be corrected by adjustments on a capture card or processor. Some high-end editing programs and hardware offer image enhancement, which can be used to sharpen edges in a soft or low-resolution video image. However, the image enhancer can also sharpen video noise and create edges where there were none before.

Software tools for editing video

No tool is currently available to edit video after it has been encoded into an .asf file. Therefore, it is recommended that you record and archive content in the AVI format and convert it to ASF after it has been edited. Several programs allow you to edit video in the AVI format and encode directly from finished AVI to ASF.

Adobe Premiere is an AVI editing package with many professional quality features. A plug-in is available that you can use to convert .avi files to .asf files. Many video capture cards include a free copy of the LE (light edition) version of Premiere. For more information, see the Adobe Web site (http://www.adobe.com/).

Ulead Media Studio Pro 5.2 is another AVI editing package that comes bundled with several hardware packages. Media Studio Pro 5.2 can also convert .avi files to .asf files.

Terran Interactive Media Cleaner Pro 4 is an AVI processing package that you can use to make color, brightness, hue, saturation, and a variety of other corrections to captured video. For more information, see the Terran Interactive Web site (http://www.terran.com/).

Creating and improving audio

As with video, the quality of your source content will affect the quality of the final compressed audio stream. Audio has been around longer, so there are more and better tools for editing and repairing audio than for video. There are many commercial audio editors (digital audio workstations) for the PC that you can use to cut and paste sections, process the sound, and even add special effects. The processing functions of audio editors can filter out hiss, pops, hum, and other annoying background noises and can adjust the overall audio level. As with video, there are currently no tools for editing and processing audio after it has been compressed and encoded. It is recommended that you save and archive uncompressed audio using the WAV format.

Audio hardware

When capturing audio on the computer, the make and model of the sound card is very important. An inexpensive sound card with properly adjusted input levels may be adequate for a voice-over on a video. However, if you are capturing high-quality music, invest in a quality card that has a digital input. A consumer card not only generates its own noise, it can pick up noise from disk drives and other devices in the computer. Noise can be hard to detect when listening to audio on small speakers that are next to your noisy computer. However, when you play the audio on a quality sound system, you will not only notice the noise, you will probably notice a lack of fidelity in general. For the highest quality, use digital audio from start to finish.

When recording audio for video, if lip synchronization is not required, consider recording the audio separately on digital audiotape (DAT) or some other digital audio equipment. You can then capture it to the hard disk of your computer using a S/PDIF (consumer digital) or optical input. A digital capture makes an exact copy of the audio data from the DAT onto your hard drive, without adding any noise or distortion. There are several consumer cards available that offer digital-in and digital-out. If you must use the analog inputs, be sure to capture at the 44.1-kilohertz (kHz) sampling rate and 16-bit sampling depth.

Studio recording

Sound reflects off hard surfaces, such as walls and windows. Computers, air conditioning, and traffic from the street outside can create additional ambient noise. Noise and reverberation that are introduced by using a typical office space for recording audio add complexity to the audio wave that makes it difficult to compress without adding artifacts. The steady hiss from an air conditioner, for example, may become an annoying swirling sound after compression. Using a professional sound studio can eliminate these problems; however, using a professional studio might not always be feasible.

If you cannot use a professional studio, you can convert an office into a better audio recording environment by:

- **Softening hard surfaces by hanging curtains or tapestries on the walls.** Large rugs make excellent sound dampeners.

- **Turning off computers, fans, and other machines in the room.** If you can, also turn off the heating, ventilation, and air conditioning (HVAC) system.

- **Using an interior room that is isolated from street noise.** If the room has a persistent low rumble, you can reduce it to some extent by using equalization on an audio mixer. You can also use the roll-off switch, if your microphone has one.

Microphone skills

This section discusses four guidelines that can help you record better sound using a microphone: pointing the microphone at the source, reducing or eliminating background noise, eliminating microphone noise, and monitoring the recording.

Pointing the microphone at the source

A small clip-on or lavaliere microphone is a good way to record a person who is speaking. When attaching a microphone, be sure the microphone is facing out, away from the person's clothing. Make sure that the clothing is not covering or rubbing against the front of the microphone. If you use a lavaliere microphone, you should put it as close as possible to the speaker's mouth.

Middle to low frequency sounds enter a microphone from almost any angle, but the higher frequencies that add definition to speech enter a microphone only from the front. When a microphone is not aimed properly, the source sounds muddy, distant, and can make it more difficult to understand what a person is saying. If the microphone is aimed at another person that is talking, a noisy computer, or a hard surface that is reflecting the voice, the recorded audio can have a hollow sound.

Reducing or eliminating background noise

There are two ways to attack background noise: eliminate the source of the noise and move the microphone closer to the sound source. If you cannot stop background noise, block it off by closing windows and doors, hang heavy furniture blankets, or move behind a wall. Point the microphone away from the source of the background noise. Reposition the source, so that the front of the microphone faces the source and the back of it faces the noise. Move the microphone as close as possible to the source. If the source is a voice, the microphone should be six- to twelve-inches from the speaker's mouth.

If possible, use a separate microphone to record someone being videotaped with a camcorder. If there is microphone mounted on or built into your camcorder, it is most likely a poor quality microphone, and it is probably too far from the speaker.

Eliminating microphone noise

Microphone noise is an artificial sound that is introduced when an object comes into contact with the microphone. When placing a microphone, be sure that it will not be bumped. Remind a speaker who will be holding a microphone not to tap pencils and rings against it or play with the cable. Leave the front of the microphone exposed. Holding the head of a microphone introduces noise and can cause feedback if the microphone is used in a public address system.

Creating and Improving
Multimedia Content

Be sure that the microphone isn't too close to the speaker's mouth. High velocity air from a person exhaling or speaking the letter "P" can cause loud pops in microphones that do not have pop filters built into them. Small lavaliere microphones are designed to be clipped to a tie and have little or no protection against pops and wind.

Monitoring the recording

A recording should be monitored in two ways: by listening on headphones or a speaker and by watching the record meters. The only way you can be sure that clean sound is being recorded to tape or hard disk is by listening to it. Most tape recorders have headphone jacks; you can also use the output jack on a sound card. If you are recording in separate room from the source, you can monitor the audio using speakers.

To ensure that the proper signal is going to tape or hard disk, watch the record meters. Many consumer tape recorders and camcorders do not have meters because the record gain is adjusted automatically. It is important to adjust the microphone input on a sound card by reading the record meter and ensure that it never goes into the red.

Audio file formats

Windows Media Technologies accepts WAV and MP3 audio formats for encoding into compressed .asf files. As with video, you can save disk space by capturing directly to a .asf file using Windows Media Encoder. When capturing to WAV, it is recommend that you capture full CD-quality audio: uncompressed, 16-bit sampling depth, and 44.1-kHz sampling rate. If you have a choice, choose Pulse Code Modulation (PCM) audio.

Software tools for editing audio

Dozens of good audio editing tools are available. Among the most popular is Sonic Foundry's Sound Forge. You can use Sound Forge to edit, process, and add effects to audio files and the audio tracks of video files. You can also save audio and video directly to the Windows Media format. Sound Forge also provides batching, which you can use to process and encode multiple files automatically. For details and demonstration software, see the Sonic Foundry Web site (http://www.sonicfoundry.com/).

Cool Edit Pro by Syntrillium Software includes noise cancellation routines that can help improve audio quality. For more information, see the Syntrillium Web site (http://www.syntrillium.com/).

Rippers are software tools that provide a way to transfer tracks from an audio CD to .wav files on a hard disk. Some of them also convert .wav files to the MP3 format. Many rippers can also access the CDDB (the global CD database), which encodes the artist name, album title, and track title into each track. Before using a ripper to convert someone else's work, read Appendix C, "Using Content Legally." To find out more about rippers, search for *rippers* on the Internet.

Archiving content

Often a production ends up with boxes of unlabeled tapes and a hard disk filled with a variety of unknown media files. A little organization in the beginning, carried through production, can save you a great deal of hassle and wasted time and money later. For example, it is much easier to save and label a small tape than it is to reshoot an interview or pay to retransfer a tape to a file that was erased to save space.

As you plan a production, consider what elements you will keep and how you are going to keep them. For example, if you think you may have to re-edit a piece, be sure to label and save all of your camera tapes and edit decision lists. Many times all you will need to save is the original edited tape. In any case, it is recommended that you save at least the *master* .avi file. A master is the final edited piece from which the .asf file is encoded. If you only save your .asf file, you will not be able to re-edit a piece or re-encode it to another format. There are many inexpensive hard disk and removable media products available for storing large files.

Summary

The best way to ensure the quality of your streaming media is to start with well-produced source content and to use good equipment. Because media is compressed when it is encoded, you should take into account any factors that reduce compression, such as a busy background or noise. If you're working with existing material, there are adjustments you can make to compensate for some flaws. After you have created your content, archive the master .avi file and any other important source material. The .avi file is the final edited piece from which the .asf file is encoded.

Chapter 3, "Using Windows Media Tools," shows you how to install, configure, and use the components that make up Microsoft Windows Media Tools to prepare your multimedia content for streaming.

Creating and Improving
Multimedia Content

Section

II

Using Windows Media Technologies Components

This section describes the components of Microsoft Windows Media Technologies: Windows Media Tools, Windows Media Services, and Windows Media Player. It describes how to use Windows Media Tools to create digital media content, how to use Windows Media Services to set up and administer your content, how to use and customize Windows Media Player to render content, and how to use all of the components together. Chapters in this section include:

Chapter 3—Using Windows Media Tools. This chapter shows how Windows Media Tools can be used to create content and encode content into Advanced Streaming Format (ASF).

Chapter 4—Using Windows Media Services. This chapter introduces Windows Media Services, shows how to install Windows Media Services, and then describes how to configure and administer a Windows Media server.

Chapter 5—Using Windows Media Player. This chapter describes how to install, use, and configure Windows Media Player to receive and render streams from a Windows Media server, play clips from a movie, render a music video hosted on a Web site, play a corporate presentation, and much more.

Chapter 6—Putting It All Together. This chapter brings the information from Chapters 1 though 5 together and provides information that will help you make an important primary decision—whether to produce a live event or create stored content. This chapter also walks you through some of the ways you may want to use Windows Media Technologies.

Chapter

3

Using Windows Media Tools

Microsoft Windows Media Tools includes a variety of tools you can use to create content and encode content into Advanced Streaming Format (ASF). Once content is in ASF format, it can be sent to a Windows Media server, saved as an .asf file, or both can be done simultaneously. This chapter describes how to install, configure, and use the tools available for Windows Media Technologies. After reading this chapter, you'll be able to answer the following questions:

- What tools are included in Windows Media Tools, and what does each tool do?

- How do I install Windows Media Tools, and how do I use them?

- How can one .asf file target different bandwidths?

- How can I encode a file to accommodate multiple bandwidths?

- Are there other tools I can use with Microsoft Windows Media Technologies, and where can I find third-party tools?

Introducing Windows Media Tools

Windows Media Tools includes the content creation and editing components of Windows Media Technologies. Windows Media Tools has components for authoring both live and on-demand content and for converting other file formats (such as WAV, AVI, QuickTime 2.0 or earlier, and MP3) to ASF. This section describes what each tool does, and recommends tools for live and on-demand content production as well as post-production editing.

Content creation tools

The components of Windows Media Tools that you can use to create ASF content include:

- **Windows Media Encoder.** This tool turns content into an ASF stream or file. Content can include stored media files or live input from a microphone or video camera. Windows Media Encoder converts and compresses audio content, video content, and script commands into ASF content, using state-of-the-art compression technologies.

- **Windows Media On-Demand Producer.** This tool, developed for Microsoft by Sonic Foundry, Inc., simplifies the creation of streaming media content. You can use Windows Media On-Demand Producer to encode existing digital content, synchronize markers and script commands, and enhance video. The Publish Windows Media Wizard automatically creates all of the necessary ASF Stream Redirector (.asx) and .htm files for publishing content on the Web or on an intranet.

- **Presentation Broadcasting.** This feature of Microsoft PowerPoint 2000 integrates with Windows Media Technologies to make it easier to create and publish Windows Media content. With Presentation Broadcasting, you can broadcast streaming PowerPoint presentations, in real time, to network users. In addition to broadcasting PowerPoint slides, presenters can broadcast video and audio simultaneously to deliver a live multimedia show online, and then store their presentations for on-demand playback. For more information about creating PowerPoint 2000 presentations for streaming, see Chapter 8, "Streaming PowerPoint Presentations."

- **Windows Media Plug-In for Adobe Premiere.** This tool compresses and converts your video files into ASF from within Adobe Premiere.

- **Windows Media Author.** This tool provides a graphical interface for combining and synchronizing audio and image files. Windows Media Author can display a simulation of your .asf file before you create it. Windows Media Author supports multiple target bandwidths and script commands.

- **Windows Media Presenter for Microsoft PowerPoint 97.** This add-in tool, along with Windows Media Encoder, helps you convert a PowerPoint presentation to an ASF stream.

- **Windows Media Publish to ASF for Microsoft PowerPoint 97.** This add-in tool combines PowerPoint presentations with narration.

- **VidToASF.** This command-line utility converts .avi or .mov files into .asf files. You can use a command-line option to specify script files that add markers, invoke URLs, and execute script commands.

- **WavToASF.** This command-line utility converts .wav or .mp3 files into .asf files. You can use a command-line option to specify script files that add markers, invoke URLs, and execute script commands.

Content editing tools

In addition to content creation tools and utilities, Windows Media Tools includes the following components to help manage and edit your .asf files:

- **Windows Media ASF Indexer.** This graphical tool is used to edit .asf files. Use Windows Media ASF Indexer to add indexes, properties, markers, and scripts to an existing .asf file, and to trim the beginning and ending portions of an .asf file.

- **ASFChop.** This command-line utility edits .asf files. Use ASFChop to add markers, scripts, and properties to an .asf file or to delete time periods from an .asf file.

- **ASFCheck.** This command-line utility verifies .asf file formats. ASFCheck can identify problems within an .asf file and repair some of the identified problems.

Tables 3.1, 3.2, and 3.3 list recommended tools for performing a variety of common authoring and editing tasks.

Table 3.1. Recommended tools for live content production.

Task	Recommended tool	Tool features
Convert and compress live audio and video into Windows Media format file.	Windows Media Encoder	• Template-based encoding options. • Controls for scaled encoding. • Ability to insert script commands and URL flips on the fly.

Using Windows Media Tools

Convert and compress live audio and video into a live stream.	Windows Media Encoder	• Template-based encoding options. • Controls for scaled encoding. • Ability to insert script commands and URL flips on the fly.
Create live audio and video synchronized with PowerPoint 2000 slides.	Presentation Broadcast (a feature of PowerPoint 2000)	• Archives for on-demand access. • Slide changes are synchronized with presenter's audio and video. • Only the presenter needs to have PowerPoint 2000. • Clients need Windows Media Player and a Web browser.
Create live audio and video synchronized with PowerPoint 97 slides.	Windows Media Presenter for Microsoft PowerPoint 97	• Slide changes are synchronized with presenter's audio and video. • Only the presenter needs to have PowerPoint 97. • Clients require Windows Media Player and a Web browser.

Table 3.2. Recommended tools for on-demand content production.

Task	Recommended tool	Tool features
Convert audio and video files to ASF format.	Windows Media On-Demand Producer, Windows Media Encoder	• Basic media trimming (mark in and out points). • Fade-in and fade-out settings. • Insert script commands, URL flips, markers, and text/captions. • Simple batch processing.

Task	Recommended tool	Tool features
Create slide-show style presentations.	Windows Media Author	• Low-bandwidth content authoring. • Project-based authoring of multiple bit rate presentations. • Basic HTML template support.
Create .asf files directly from Adobe Premiere.	Windows Media Plug-in for Adobe Premiere	• Easy .asf file creation. • Common stream formats template. • Easy ASF testing and editing.
Create live or on-demand audio and video synchronized with PowerPoint 2000 slides.	Presentation Broadcast (a feature of PowerPoint 2000)	• See "Create live audio and video synchronized with PowerPoint 2000 slides" in Table 3.1.
Convert PowerPoint 97 presentations into ASF.	Windows Media Publish to ASF	• See "Create live audio and video synchronized with PowerPoint 97 slides" in Table 3.1.

Table 3.3. Recommended tools for post-production editing of .asf and .asx files.

Task	Recommended tool	Tool features
Edit existing .asf files.	Windows Media ASF Indexer	• Adds indexing to video files (scroll/fast forward/rewind). • Adds properties, markers, and script commands to .asf files. • Imports and exports script files.
Detect and fix problems commonly found in ASF version 1.0 files.	ASFCheck	• MS-DOS command-line tool. • Has batch capabilities.

Using Windows Media Tools

Hardware and software requirements

Table 3.4 shows the minimum, recommended, and optimal hardware and software requirements for Windows Media Tools.

> **NOTE** All of the tools in Windows Media Tools will function if the minimum hardware and software requirements are met. The recommended and optimal columns in Table 3.4 are designed to enhance the Windows Media Encoder computer.

Table 3.4. Windows Media Tools requirements.

Component	Minimum required	Recommended	Optimal
Processor	Intel Pentium 90 megahertz (MHz)	Intel Pentium II 266 MHz or later	The fastest processor available; a dual-processor configuration is ideal
Memory	32 megabytes (MB)	64 MB	128 MB or more
Network card	10-megabit TCP/IP Ethernet card	10/100-megabit TCP/IP Ethernet card	100-megabit TCP/IP Ethernet card
Available hard disk space	5 MB for Windows Media Tools	5 MB for Windows Media Tools; enough disk space for content creation and editing	500 MB for content creation and editing
Audio card	Sound card compatible with Creative Labs Sound Blaster 16	High-quality card, compatible with Creative Labs Sound Blaster 16	High-quality card, compatible with Creative Labs Sound Blaster Live
Video capture card	Video capture card that supports Video for Windows	ViewCast, Osprey 100, or Winnov Videum video capture card	Osprey 100 video capture card

Component	Minimum required	Recommended	Optimal
Software	Microsoft Windows 95 (real-time encoding of audio only)	Windows 98 or Microsoft Windows NT Server or Windows NT Workstation version 4.0 with Service Pack 4 or later	Windows NT Workstation 4.0 with Service Pack 5

Installing Windows Media Tools

After setting up a computer with at least the minimum hardware and software requirements, install Windows Media Tools from the JumpStart CD included with this book.

To install Windows Media Tools

1. Install and configure the audio and video capture devices you are using.

2. If you have an Intel Pentium III processor, and you want your encoder to use the Windows Media codecs that have been optimized for the Pentium III Streaming SIMD Extensions, complete one of the following procedures:

   ■ If you are using the Windows NT operating system version 4.0 with Service Pack 4, download and install the Intel Streaming SIMD Extension Driver from the Intel Web site (http://support.intel.com/support/processors/pentiumiii/ntdriver.htm).

   –or–

   ■ Install Windows NT Service Pack 5 (http://www.microsoft.com/NTServer/all/downloads.asp), which includes the Intel SIMD Extensions driver.

> **NOTE** For more information about the Intel Pentium III SIMD Streaming Extensions, see the Intel Web site (http://support.intel.com/support/processors/pentiumiii/ntdriver.htm).

3. Insert the Windows Media JumpStart CD into the CD drive. The CD should automatically start and open to the default HTML page.

4. When the JumpStart HTML page opens, point to **install it**, point to **Content Creation Tools**, and then click **Windows Media Tools**. Select the appropriate processor and click **wmtools.exe**.

Using Windows Media Tools

5. Read the End User License Agreement. If you agree to the terms of the agreement, click **Yes** to accept it, and then click **Next**.

6. Choose an **Installation Option**, and then click **Next**.

   Choose **Complete Installation** to install all the components of Windows Media Tools and documentation, including the PowerPoint add-ins. Choose **PowerPoint Add Ins Only** if you want to install the add-ins but you don't want to install Windows Media Tools and the documentation.

7. Choose the directory in which you want to install Windows Media Tools, and then click **Finish**.

Windows Media Tools is installed in the specified directory, and a program group is created on the **Start** menu. This program group includes:

- Windows Media Encoder
- Windows Media Indexer
- Windows Media Author

The PowerPoint add-ins and Adobe Premiere plug-in are available within the target applications.

NOTE	The command line tools are installed in the \Windows or \winnt directory and can be run from the command prompt.

After installation is complete, you can begin using Windows Media Encoder and Windows Media Tools to create Windows Media content.

Using Windows Media Encoder

Windows Media Encoder is an authoring tool that produces media content in ASF. The processes supported by Windows Media Encoder include acquiring the content from a capture card or a stored file; compressing it by using both audio and video codecs; encapsulating it into ASF format, which includes a timeline with synchronized audio, video, and script commands streams; and then sending it to a Windows Media server, to an .asf file, or to both.

When creating ASF content, Windows Media Encoder can operate in either live capture mode or in file transcoding mode. This section discusses using live capture mode, using file transcoding mode, configuration basics, creating and saving the configuration, viewing statistics and monitoring, and encoding a multiple bit rate stream.

Using live capture mode

When operating in live capture mode, Windows Media Encoder is configured to create content in real time using input from a sound card and, optionally, from a video capture card. After the content is created, it is sent to either a Windows Media server, an .asf file (for archiving), or to both simultaneously.

Live capture mode is used to broadcast content, such as a training session throughout a corporate intranet. In this scenario, a presenter conveys material from one location and the audience watches the presentation from another (remote) location. The audience watches the broadcast of the presentation as it happens in real time. Windows Media Encoder can simultaneously archive the session to an .asf file that can be made available for on-demand viewing after the live event.

Using file transcoding mode

Using the file transcoding mode, you can transcode .avi, .wav, and .mp3 files into ASF. During the process of transcoding, the content is read from the source file, uncompressed, recompressed by using the configuration parameters you select, and then packetized into ASF.

Windows Media Encoder configuration basics

Windows Media Encoder includes a configuration wizard to help you start encoding quickly. The configuration wizard contains configuration templates that have predefined settings for common encoding scenarios. To build the best configuration based on your specific content, you may get better results by using the custom configuration option in the configuration wizard. The information in this section will help you determine which options to select while creating a custom configuration. For more information about using the configuration wizard and templates, see "Creating the configuration" later in this section.

With Windows Media Encoder, you can create .asf files that contain only audio, audio with video, audio with scripts, or audio with video and scripts. Video-only configurations are not available because Windows Media Encoder uses the audio track as a reference for timing.

> **TIP**   If you need to use a video-only configuration, you can simulate it by setting the configuration of the audio stream to near-zero bandwidth. To do this, select **0 Kbps** for the Windows Media Audio codec on the **Compressions and Formats** screen of the custom configuration wizard.

As part of the configuration process, you must specify the following settings:

- The location and type of source content

- The target bandwidth for the content

- The codecs to use for audio and video compression

- The type of encoder output

These steps are described in the following sections.

Selecting the source content

The first step in configuring Windows Media Encoder is to select the location and type of source content. Windows Media Encoder can be configured to receive source content directly from audio and video devices that support Video for Windows. Source content can also come from files that are saved in AVI, WAV, and MP3 formats.

In addition to including audio and video content, a Windows Media Encoder custom configuration can include script commands. Script commands are useful for sending URLs or closed-caption data to the client computer. For example, a radio disc jockey may create a configuration that encodes audio content and script commands. When the disc jockey talks about a specific song or event, she could send a URL to a Web page that provides listeners with more information. When the client computer receives the URL, the Web browser on that computer displays the associated Web page.

Selecting the bandwidth

Windows Media Encoder can be configured to generate ASF content that is appropriate for either a single bandwidth or multiple bandwidths. Bandwidth is the amount of data that can be transmitted in a fixed amount of time. On computer networks, a higher bandwidth indicates a faster rate of data transfer. Network bandwidth is expressed in bits per second (bps).

Windows Media Encoder can produce content for a single target audience. For example, you can specifically target people who use 28.8-kilobits-per-second (Kbps) modems. If you look at the details section of the QuickStart wizard after selecting the configuration template, you will notice a discrepancy between the target audience bandwidth (28.8 Kbps) and the encoded bandwidth (20 Kbps). This discrepancy is a built-in safety measure to enable additional network traffic to access the client computer. If all of the bandwidth is consumed by the ASF stream, the client will not be able to send or receive commands over the network or maintain its network connection if the bandwidth fluctuates.

> **TIP**   To increase the quality of your audio stream, you can create a custom configuration. When selecting the compression, choose the Windows Media Audio codec, and specify a sample rate of 22 Kbps stereo. This gives you an additional 2 Kbps of data while still maintaining adequate overhead bandwidth for more network activity.

Windows Media Encoder can also produce content suitable for multiple audiences using multiple bit rate encoding. For example, if a college professor wants to provide a lecture to students at home, the students could have modems that range from 28.8-Kbps to ISDN (Integrated Services Digital Network).

Multiple bit rate encoding enables Windows Media Player and the server to use intelligent streaming to switch between the available streams, depending on network bandwidth availability. The intelligent streaming features in Windows Media Technologies ensure that end users will receive the highest quality media possible, regardless of Internet connection speed or network congestion. Because Windows Media Technologies is an end-to-end, client/server system, the server and the client can communicate with each other. By communicating before and during data transmission, the server and the client can establish actual network throughput and make necessary adjustments to the stream to maximize quality.

Windows Media Encoder creates ASF content that has a variety of video streams at variable bandwidths (for either low- or high-bandwidth target audiences) and a separately encoded audio stream. When creating multiple bit rate video content for low-bandwidth audiences, the video streams can range from 18 Kbps to 300 Kbps. When creating multiple bit rate content for high-bandwidth audiences, video streams can range from 81 Kbps to 10 megabits per second (Mbps).

When encoding multiple bit rate video content using a custom configuration, you can select up to five different bit rates. One other video stream, called an insurance stream, is also encoded. The bandwidth of the insurance stream is based on a percentage of the lowest selected bandwidth. After receiving the multiple bit rate stream, the server determines which bandwidth to use to stream to a client. This determination is based on the available network bandwidth.

> **NOTE**   Multiple bit rate video is not supported on generic HTTP servers. In addition, only the highest bandwidth video stream and audio stream are used with a multicast distribution.

Compressing the content

Windows Media Encoder installs a number of audio and video codecs onto your computer. The primary recommended video codec is the Microsoft MPEG-4 video codec. This video codec is a low to high bit rate video codec. Version 3 of this codec is optimized for use with multiple-bandwidth and high-bandwidth encoding.

The most popular audio codecs include Windows Media Audio and Sipro Labs ACELP.net. The Windows Media Audio codec is a high-quality lossy codec that is capable of producing CD-quality sound. Windows Media Audio produces quality sound when the source content contains mixed media types and music-based content. ACELP.net is a codec that provides excellent voice compression at very low bit rates, primarily in the 5-Kbps through 8.5-Kbps range. The ACELP.net codec is best suited to low-bandwidth, voice-only content, such as that of a podium speaker or an anchor desk correspondent.

Selecting the destination

As mentioned earlier, ASF content that has been created with Windows Media Encoder can be sent to a Windows Media server, to an .asf file, or to both simultaneously. When .asf files are generated, they can then be played back directly by Windows Media Player, or they can be placed on a Windows Media server and be streamed on demand. When connecting Windows Media Encoder to a server, it can be configured by way of an alias to a Windows Media Station service or sent to a specific set of ports and protocols.

Windows Media Encoder supports two connection protocols: MSBD and HTTP. The Media Stream Broadcast Distribution protocol (MSBD) is a protocol used to reference the Windows Media Encoder, such as msbd://*encoder_name,* that is the source of a stream. The default port that Windows Media Encoder uses with the MSBD protocol is 7007. The MSBD protocol is also used when streaming from the Windows Media Station service to a content-storage server or for server-to-server distribution. When streaming through a firewall is important, the HTTP protocol is used. The default port for the HTTP protocol is 80, but other ports can be used.

Creating the configuration

When configuring Windows Media Encoder, you can choose to use the configuration wizard, or you can open a previously saved configuration. The configuration wizard is displayed in the **Welcome** dialog box when Windows Media Encoder is launched for the first time or when you select **New** on the **File** menu. The configuration wizard provides the following configuration options:

- **QuickStart.** The QuickStart configuration assumes that you are encoding from a live source and delivering the content to a Windows Media server. With QuickStart, you choose the bandwidth and type of ASF stream you want to create. All other configuration settings are automatically chosen for you, based on the template you select.

- **Template with I/O Options.** When you select **Template with I/O Options**, you specify the audio and video input and the output options. The output options include the IP port or Windows Media server that receives the ASF stream and whether you want Windows Media Encoder to output the ASF stream to an .asf file. The template sets the other configuration options including the target bandwidth, the ASF stream types, and compression.

- **Custom.** When you select **Custom**, you have full control of Windows Media Encoder settings. This is for users with advanced knowledge of bandwidth capacity, media settings, and codec usage. You must identify the bandwidth of the network you are using, the media that make up the ASF stream, the codecs that you use to make your media fit within the network bandwidth, and other details of the encoding process. Custom configuration options include:

  - **Input.** This specifies whether the content source is from a device (such as a sound card or a video capture card) or from an .avi, .wav, or .mp3 file.

  - **Bandwidth.** This specifies the target bandwidth of the ASF output (a stream or a file).

  - **Compression.** This specifies the audio and video codecs that are used to compress the content. For audio, you can specify the bandwidth, frequency, and number of channels. For video, you can specify advanced settings for image size, number of frames per second, number of seconds per I-frame, pixel format, delay buffer, and image quality.

  - **Output.** This specifies the destination .asf file and/or whether the ASF stream will be sent to a Windows Media server.

> **NOTE** When using a custom configuration with video, select the default pixel format. This enables Windows Media Encoder to automatically negotiate a pixel format with the device that will match the codec to produce the best quality video. In addition, setting the image quality to zero, with the MPEG-4 version 3 video codec, enables the codec to automatically determine the smoothest, most crisp algorithm to apply.

Saving the configuration

After defining a Windows Media Encoder configuration, it is helpful to save the configuration for reuse at a later time. With Windows Media Encoder, you can save any number of different configurations. The encoder configuration is saved to an ASF Stream Descriptor (.asd) file.

The .asd files are portable across computers that are running Windows operating systems (Windows 95, Windows 98, and Windows NT Server or Windows NT Workstation 4.0). Certain aspects of a given configuration may cause conflicts when the .asd file is moved to another computer and loaded by another instance of Windows Media Encoder. For

Using Windows Media Tools

example, if the source content of a configuration is from a file that only exists on the original computer, the second instance of Windows Media Encoder will fail to load the configuration successfully, and you will be asked to change the source location.

Viewing statistics and monitoring

To evaluate the effectiveness of your encoding, you can view statistics about the session. The statistics can help you to achieve optimal rendering of content by analyzing the effect of changes to codecs and bit rate settings. Available statistics include:

- **ASF statistics.** ASF statistics include the amount of data sent, the amount of padding sent, and the bit rate used to transmit the data.

- **Audio statistics.** Audio statistics include the amount of data sent and the bit rate used to transmit the data.

- **Script commands.** Script commands provide a measure of the number of script command bytes that have been sent and the number of script commands.

- **Video statistics.** Video statistics provide a measure of the amount of data sent and the amount of data lost. They also provide summary statistics about the bit rate and the number of frames per second transmitted.

- **Current connections.** Current connections display the IP addresses of computers that are currently connected to Windows Media Encoder.

Encoding a multiple bit rate stream

This section describes two methods of encoding a multiple bit rate stream. The first method uses a predefined QuickStart template. The second method uses a custom configuration.

From **QuickStart** in Windows Media Encoder, there are three predefined templates that make it easy to produce multiple bit rate streams. Table 3.5 describes each template. To encode a multiple bit rate stream by using QuickStart, select an appropriate template and answer the questions on each screen of the wizard.

Table 3.5. Multiple bit rate templates.

Template	Description
Dial-up Modems - ISDN Multiple Bit Rate Video	Creates one ASF stream or file for multiple target audiences. Use this template to encode multiple bandwidths that support client connections over dial-up modems and single-channel ISDN using

Template	Description
	speeds between 28.8 Kbps and 56 Kbps. This multiple bit rate stream contains target bit rates of 22 Kbps, 27 Kbps, 32 Kbps, 37 Kbps, and 42 Kbps, and has a total live bandwidth distribution requirement of 151 Kbps.
Intranet – High Speed LAN Multiple Bit Rate Video	Creates one ASF stream or file for multiple target audiences. Use this template to encode multiple bandwidths that support client connections ranging from dial-up modems to high-speed corporate Internet connections. This multiple bit rate stream contains target bit rates of 150 Kbps, 300 Kbps, 500 Kbps, and 700 Kbps, and has a total live bandwidth distribution requirement of 1,637 Kbps.
28.8, ISDN, and 100 Multiple Bit Rate Video	Creates one ASF stream or file for multiple target audiences. Use this setting to encode multiple bandwidths that support client connections ranging from 28.8-Kbps dial-up modems to corporate intranet connections. This multiple bit rate stream contains target bit rates of 22 Kbps, 42 Kbps, and 100 Kbps, and has a total live bandwidth distribution requirement of 151 Kbps.

To create custom multiple bit rate encoding settings

1. Start Windows Media Encoder.

2. In the **Welcome** window, select **Custom**.

Using Windows Media Tools

3. On the **Input Settings, Input Source** screen, select either **Live Source** or **AVI/WAV/MP3 File**.

   ■ If you select **Live Source**, the **Input Settings, Capture Source & Media Types** screen appears. The capture devices are determined automatically by your preferred devices. To use different capture devices, click **Custom**, and then click the device in the list. Select the **Script Commands** check box if you want to include script commands in your ASF stream.

   ■ If you select **AVI/WAV/MP3 File**, the **Input Settings, Source File** screen appears. Under **File name**, type the name of your source file, or click **Browse** to locate it on your computer. Leave this box blank to create a generic configuration for use with many different input files.

> **NOTE**   Video content cannot be streamed in real time due to the transcoding that occurs. When transforming the video from AVI to ASF format, you must create an .asf file if you are transcoding content from a file.

4. On the **Configure Stream, Bandwidth Selection** screen, select **Use multiple bit rate video**.

5. Select either **Low Bandwidth** or **High Bandwidth** target audiences.

   You can change the **Target Audience** list and the **Target Audience** settings in the following ways:

   ■ Click **Edit** to change the selected target audience. The Edit Item window appears. From this window, you can change the **Target Audience** description and the video stream bit rate.

   ■ Click **Remove** to remove the selected target audience. The target audience is removed from the list, and the **Add** button is activated.

   ■ Click **Add** to insert a new target audience to the list. From the **Add Item** window you can select the **Target Audience** description and the video stream bit rate.

6. Click **Next**.

7. On the **Configure Stream, Compression & Formats** screen, for each type of content, choose the compression algorithm (or codec) that you want to use from the list. Most audio codecs have multiple formats. Choose the audio format you want in the list.

8. Under **Video**, click **Advanced** to specify additional video settings.

9. On the **Output Settings, Output Options** screen, specify the destination of the ASF stream. Click one of the following options:

  ■ **To Windows Media server(s) over a network.** Click this to deliver the ASF stream to a Windows Media server for unicasting or multicasting.

  -or-

  ■ **To a local ASF file.** Click this to save the stream as an .asf file for on-demand unicasting.

  -or-

  ■ **To both.** Click this to deliver the ASF stream to a Windows Media server and to save it as an .asf file.

10. Choose one of the following options:

  ■ Output to a Windows Media server. From the **Output Settings, Transmission** screen, select the method that Windows Media Encoder uses to transmit the ASF stream to the Windows Media server. Use either a fixed IP port, or initiate the connection to the Windows Media server. If you choose the fixed port method, you can also select an HTTP port. If you choose to initiate the connection to the Windows Media server, specify the name of the server to which you want to connect in **Station Manager**, and name the ASF stream coming from the encoder in **Stream alias**.

  -or-

  ■ Output to a local .asf file. On the **Output Settings, Output File** screen, specify a file name for the output file. You also can limit the .asf file by file size and encoding duration. By selecting the **Automatic Indexing** check box, you can index your .asf file so that end users can fast-forward and rewind while viewing the file. On the **File** menu, click **Save** or **Save as**, and type in a file name to save the .asd file. If you are sending this stream to a Windows Media server, make sure to provide this .asd file to your Windows Media system administrator.

Producing content with other Windows Media tools

This section describes how to use Windows Media On-Demand Producer, Windows Media Author, Windows Media Plug-In for Adobe Premiere, Windows Media Publish to ASF for Microsoft PowerPoint 97, and Windows Media ASF Indexer to accomplish a specific task.

Using Windows Media Tools

Producing a news clip with Windows Media On-Demand Producer

Windows Media On-Demand Producer (developed for Microsoft by Sonic Foundry, Inc.) is designed for Web authors—from the novice who is putting video on a Web site for the first time, to the technically savvy video producer who is ready to encode sophisticated AVIs for Web presentations. This section steps through the process of taking an existing AVI video clip and creating a news presentation with closed-captioned text in a Web page.

To create the news presentation, there are four primary tasks. Complete each task in the following order:

1. Add script commands containing the closed-captioned text.

2. Save as a Windows Media file. Encode a file in the Windows Media format.

3. Publish Windows Media files. Create template Web pages that contain an embedded Windows Media Player control and play the content.

4. Test the playback. Play the file, and see if it looks and sounds right.

To add script commands for closed-captioned text

1. On the **File** menu in Windows Media On-Demand Producer, click **Open/Add**.

2. Locate an .avi file to which you want to add a caption and then click **Open**. If **Audio Waveform** is selected in the **View** menu, a waveform display is calculated and appears in **Audio Display**. The first frame of the video appears in **Video Display**.

3. Play the file and press the C key to add a script command where you want the caption to occur (for example, at the beginning of each sentence). Alternatively, you can click the **C** button on the **Script Command** bar.

4. Right-click the first script command icon, and then click **Edit** in the shortcut menu.

> **NOTE** If the **Script Command** bar becomes too crowded with icons, you can locate a command by using the **Edit Command** dialog box. On the **Edit** menu, click **Commands**. Click a command in the list, and then click **Edit**.

5. Type the caption text for the script command in **Parameter**.

6. In **Type**, click **WMClosedCaptionTEXT**, and then click **OK**.

7. Repeat steps 4, 5, and 6 for each script command.

> **NOTE** If necessary, adjust script command timing by dragging the icons to new positions along the **Script Command** bar. You can also enter times manually by using the **Script Command Properties** dialog box or by opening the **Edit Command** dialog box on the **Edit** menu.

8. On the **File** menu, click **Save Project**.

To save as a Windows Media file

1. On the **File** menu in Windows Media On-Demand Producer, click **Save as Windows Media**.

2. On the **Introduction** screen, click **Encode current file**, and then click **Next**.

3. Select an encoding template. In **Template**, click a suitable template, and then click **Next**.

4. On the **ASF Destination** screen, enter a path designating where you want the encoded file to be saved on your Windows Media server, such as *ServerName*\asfroot*tutorial*, and then click **Finish**.

Windows Media On-demand Producer automatically names encoded files with the same file name as the current .avi or .wav file. For example, if the current file is Pickle.avi, Windows Media On-Demand Producer names the encoded file Pickle.asf.

To publish a Windows Media file

1. On the **File** menu in Windows Media On-Demand Producer, click **Publish Windows Media**.

2. On the introduction screen of the wizard, click **Next**.

3. On the following screen, select the **Generate Redirector file** check box.

4. In **Enter the target ASF File Name**, enter the name of the .asf file you just encoded.

5. In **ASF Server Path**, enter the URL of the .asf file on your Windows Media server, omitting the .asf file name, for example, *mms://WindowsMediaserver/Tutorial/*.

> **NOTE** To help organize your Web server, create a folder named ASX into which you can place the .asx files you create using Windows Media On-Demand Producer.

6. In **Destination directory for ASX file**, enter a path designating where you want the .asx file to be saved on your Web server, such as *Webserver*\Inetpub\Wwwroot*ASX*.

> **NOTE**   When you open a Windows Media On-Demand Producer wizard, the initial settings are carried over from the last time you used the wizard.

7. On the following screen, select the **Generate HTML file** check box.

> **NOTE**   **Enter target ASX File Name** contains the name of the .asx file created on the previous screen. The .asx file is named using the file name of the .asf file. Normally, this name does not need to be changed.

8. In **URL to ASX file**, enter the URL that points to the .asx file you created on the previous screen, omitting the file name, for example, *http://WebServer/ASX/*.

9. In **Select HTML Template**, click **WMClosedCaption**.

10. In **Destination directory for HTML file**, enter a path designating where you want the folder containing HTML elements to be saved on your Web server, such as *\\WebServer\Inetpub\Wwwroot\Odp*.

> **NOTE**   An HTML folder that is created using the Publish Windows Media Wizard contains Default.htm and any other required elements, including HTML files used in frames, applets, and any image files. The name of the HTML folder is composed of the .asf file root name, followed by an underscore character, and ending with an abbreviation of the HTML template that is used. For example: *SampleFile_WMCC.*

To test playback

Open your Internet browser and enter the URL of the Default.htm, for example, *http://WebServer/Odp/SampleFile_WMCC/default.htm*. When the Web page opens, the embedded Windows Media Player control connects to the .asf file on your Windows Media server, using the .asx file. As the file plays, script commands display closed-captioned text in the area to the right of the Windows Media Player control. An applet, which is included in the HTML folder, is used to display the text.

This method can be used to display closed-captioned text in a Windows Media On-Demand Producer template. You can display the text directly in the closed-captioned text display panel of Windows Media Player by using the *TEXT* type when editing script command properties.

Authoring slide shows with Windows Media Author

Windows Media Author, developed by Microsoft and Digital Renaissance (http://www.extendmedia.com/), is a tool that produces illustrated audio content for Web streaming. Windows Media Author was designed to help you synchronize images, text, and audio. This section describes how to synchronize a set of digital pictures with a sound track.

To author slide shows with Windows Media Author, there are four primary tasks. Complete each task in the following order:

1. Set up a new Windows Media Author project. A project contains all of the source files.

2. Build and view a project. Add audio and images to the timeline, and determine how they are synchronized.

3. Convert images on the timeline. Compress images that are too large.

4. Publish a project. Create Web page elements.

To set up a new Windows Media Author project

A project is a folder containing all of the content files, published files, and the project file. The project file contains most of the settings from a project. You can revisit the project at another time by opening this file.

1. On the **File** menu, click **New**.

2. On the **Edit** menu, point to **Bit Rate**, and then click to make a selection. To add a custom bit rate, on the **File** menu, click **Properties**, click the **Project Bit Rates** tab, and then click **Custom**.

3. On the **Insert** menu, click **Insert media** to add image and .wav files that you will use in your project.

4. Locate the folder containing the content. Click a file name, or press the CTRL key and click multiple file names, and then click **Open**.

> **NOTE**   Windows Media Author works best with JPEG (.jpg) images.

5. Save the settings that you make in a Windows Media Author project. On the **File** menu, click **Save**. The **Save as** dialog box opens. Locate the folder you want to save the project in. To create a new folder, click the **Create new folder** button on the toolbar. Click **Save**. All files in the **Content** window are copied to the new project folder.

To build and view a project

1. Drag a .wav file from the Content window to **Time Line**. Rest the mouse pointer on the **Time Line**. A cursor appears on the audio bar, next to the text **Drop Time:** and **a time value**. While still holding the mouse button, move the mouse left or right until the **Drop Time** value is **00.2**. Then release the mouse button. The audio can be moved to a new position later. (If the **Drop Time** value is 00.0, the .wav file does not move to **Time Line**.)

2. Click **OK** when prompted to convert the image to fit the current bit rate.

3. In the **Audio Conversion** dialog box, click one of the first four conversion types, such as **Internet 28.8kb/s Voice**, and Windows Media Author compresses the .wav file, using the default codec and settings. Or, click **Other Compression** and choose your own. Click **OK** to compress the .wav file, and a green bar representing the audio appears on **Time Line**. If you add more .wav files to **Time Line**, they are automatically compressed, using the same settings.

4. Play the audio track and note timings. On the **File** menu, point to **Preview**, and then click **Media**. The **Test Playback** dialog box opens and plays the media. Using the **Current time** indicator, note the times when you want images to change.

> **NOTE**   Windows Media Author calculates image presentation according to the file size of the image, bandwidth selected, and bit rate of the compressed audio. The bandwidth of a project may be too small to accommodate the time it takes to download the images and play the audio concurrently, if images are too close together. Therefore, you may have to adjust the timings you note in this step later, or compress the image further.

5. Add the first image to **Time Line**. Drag the image to **Time Line** and, using the **Drop Time** value, drop it at the point where you want the image to appear. A blue bar appears representing the download time of the image.

   As you play the .asf file that you create from the project, the image will start downloading at the time coinciding with the left edge of the image bar, and appear at the time coinciding with the right edge. If the image size is smaller or a higher bandwidth is selected, the image bar will be shorter.

6. Repeat step 5 to add more images to **Time Line**.

> **NOTE**   If the image bars overlap, a red section appears. This means that you have not given one image sufficient time to download and appear before starting to download the next image. Windows Media Author does not display images that overlap. Change the positions of the images to remove overlaps.

7. **Save** the project.

8. After images and audio tracks are in place on **Time Line**, you can preview the project. On the **File** menu, point to **Preview**, and then click **Media**.

9. You can also create and view an .asf file. On the **File** menu, point to **Preview**, and then click **Converted media**.

10. A message appears: "The .asf file must be built before it can be played. Build now?" Click **OK**. The .asf file is encoded from the project, and Windows Media Player opens and plays the file.

To convert images on the timeline

To fit more images on **Time Line**, you can decrease their download times by converting them. The image file conversion process enables you to compress the images and change their display sizes.

1. Click the image on **Time Line** to highlight it.

2. On the **Edit** menu, click **Convert**. The **Convert** dialog box opens.

3. Change the settings to convert the image file to a smaller size. The following list describes the settings:

    ■ **JPEG type.** Choose either to have the image saved as a Loss-Tolerant JPEG or a standard JPEG. A Loss-Tolerant JPEG is slightly larger but will stream better on lossy networks.

    ■ **Size.** Enter new dimensions, and the image size is converted.

    ■ **Colors.** Enter a new value, and the color depth is converted.

    ■ **Quality.** Enter a lower percentage value, and the quality and file size are decreased.

4. Click **OK**, and a temporary image file is converted.

5. Repeat steps 1 to 4 for all image files that need to be reduced in size.

To publish a project

When Windows Media Author publishes a project, an .asf file and Web page templates that play the file in an embedded Windows Media Player control are created.

1. On the **File** menu, click **Publish**, and then the **Publish** dialog box opens.

2. To generate an .asf file, type a name for the file and enter a path if necessary in the **ASF file** box. Verify other items in the dialog box, and enter file names and paths to configure the template Web pages, or accept the default settings.

3. Click **Finish** to create the .asf file and template Web pages.

For more information on the settings available on the **Publish** dialog box, see Windows Media Author Help.

Using Windows Media Plug-In for Adobe Premiere

With Windows Media Plug-In for Adobe Premiere, you can edit your media and create effects and transitions in Adobe Premiere, and then export the resulting AVI to ASF.

To create a Windows Media file with the Adobe Premiere plug-in

1. After you have finished editing your Adobe Premiere project, export it as an .avi file. On the **File** menu, point to **Export**, and then click **Movie**.

2. View the settings that Adobe Premiere will use to create the .avi file. To modify them, click **Settings** to open a series of dialog boxes. For the best quality, export .avi files using the highest quality settings that you can. If possible, audio should be saved uncompressed and at a **Rate** of at least 22 kilohertz (kHz) and **Format** of 16 bits. If video compression is used, the quality setting should be as high as possible.

3. Enter a file name and click **Save**. After the .avi file is made, it opens in a separate window in Adobe Premiere.

4. Click the final .avi file to make it the active window.

5. On the **File** menu, point to **Export**, and then click **Windows Media (.ASF)**. The **Export to ASF** dialog box opens.

NOTE	This menu item is only available if Windows Media Tools is installed after Adobe Premiere is installed.

6. Select an encoding template in the **Template** list, or click **Custom** to create a template using your own settings.

7. In **Properties**, type title, author, copyright, description, and ratings text.

8. In **Destination,** type a path and file name, or click **Browse**.

9. To encode the .asf file, click **Create**. A dialog box opens that shows encoding progress. When the .asf file is finished, a dialog box opens giving you a choice of three items. Select one.

   - **Preview ASF File.** Windows Media Player opens and plays the finished file.

   - **Edit ASF File.** Windows Media ASF Indexer opens with the file, enabling you to add script commands and markers.

   - **Back to Premiere.** This returns you to Adobe Premiere.

Creating on-demand presentations with Windows Media Publish to ASF for Microsoft PowerPoint 97

Although you can use PowerPoint 2000 to make rich presentation broadcasts, there is also a need for creating presentations for on-demand viewing that are contained in a single, portable Windows Media file. The Windows Media Publish to ASF for Microsoft PowerPoint 97 add-on was designed to help you use the narration feature to prepare audio tracks for each slide and then publish to an .asf file to create a synchronized slide show in a single file.

To create an on-demand presentation, there are four primary tasks. Complete each task in the following order:

1. Set up to record a narration. Connect a microphone to your sound card and adjust audio levels. Use the Sound Recorder program that comes with Windows if necessary.

2. Record the narration. Narrate the slides as you go through them.

3. View the finished slide show with narration.

4. Convert the presentation to an .asf file.

To set up to record a narration to slides

Before recording the narration, plug a microphone into your sound card, make sure it is working properly, and adjust record levels. There is also a utility in the **Record Narration** dialog box of PowerPoint for adjusting levels. If the mixer software that comes with your sound card does not enable you to adjust line or microphone input levels unless a recording is being made, you can use the Sound Recorder program that comes with the Windows operating system. Sound Recorder is located in either the **Multimedia** or **Entertainment** folder of the **Accessories** folder in the **Start** menu.

1. Open the mixer program that comes with your sound card and make sure the microphone input slider and record meter are visible.

2. To start the test recording, click the **Record** button on Sound Recorder. While Sound Recorder is recording, the record meter on the mixer is active.

3. Speak into the microphone and adjust the microphone slider on the mixer so that the level is as high as possible without distorting. The meter goes into the yellow or red areas if the signal from the microphone is distorting.

4. To stop the recording, click the **Stop** button. Close Sound Recorder, and do not save the file.

To record narration to slides

1. Open the PowerPoint presentation that you want to add narration to.

2. On the **Slide Show** menu, click **Record Narration**.

3. If you are using PowerPoint 2000, click **Set Microphone Level**, and follow the directions to set your microphone level.

   For a more polished presentation and to avoid having to do re-takes while recording live with the slides in PowerPoint, you can write a script and pre-record the narration on a tape recorder. Then you can play the tape back through the line input of your sound card, instead of using the microphone, while recording narration in PowerPoint.

Using Windows Media Tools

4. To start recording, click **OK**.

5. Advance through the slide show, and add narration as you go. Press the spacebar to change slides.

6. At the end of the show, a message appears. Click **Yes** to save the timings along with the narration.

To view a finished narration

1. On the **Slide Show** menu, click **View Show**. The show plays with narration.

2. Repeat the steps in the preceding section, "To record narration to slides," to redo the narration track if necessary.

To create a Windows Media file from a PowerPoint presentation

1. Save your presentation.

2. On the **Tools** menu, click **Publish to ASF**. Follow the instructions in the wizard to set the target bandwidth and destination for the .asf file.

3. On the final screen of the wizard, you can play the finished file, click **Back** to revise the file, or click **Details** to view a list of the slides and audio timings for each.

Using Windows Media ASF Indexer

Typically, Windows Media files are highly compressed and then encoded. There are many challenges to editing encoded audio and video. Multimedia editing tools edit uncompressed and unencoded audio and video. When the editing is complete, the content is compressed and encoded. However, sometimes the original uncompressed content is not available. For this reason, Microsoft created Windows Media ASF Indexer. With this tool you can do basic editing of a Windows Media .asf file by trimming the beginning and the end of the file, editing markers and script commands, and setting file properties such as the title, author, and copyright information.

You can use Windows Media ASF Indexer to perform two main tasks:

■ Trim a file. Remove a portion of the beginning and end of an .asf file.

■ Edit script commands and markers. Add, edit, or remove script commands and markers.

To open an .asf file in Windows Media ASF Indexer, on the **File** menu, click **Open**. When the file opens, properties already in the file appear in the **Properties** dialog box, and markers and script commands appear as red or green icons on the **Timelines**.

To trim a file

1. Play the file.

2. Click **Mark in** at the point where you want the new beginning to be. Click **Mark out** at the point where you want the file to end.

3. To save the new settings, on the **File** menu, click **Save**. Because you cannot preview the new beginning and end points, you can use **Save as** to create a new file rather than replace the original file. Settings that you enter in Windows Media ASF Indexer are not part of the file until you save the file.

To edit markers and script commands

1. Click **Edit Markers** or **Edit Script Commands**.

2. Click **New**, or select an item in the list and click **Remove** or **Edit**.

3. In the **Properties** dialog box, enter time and other information.

4. You can also change the time of a script command or marker by dragging it to a new position on **Time Line**.

Finding third-party tools for Windows Media Technologies

There are many third-party companies that have developed tools for Windows Media authoring, audio processing, audio and video production, and Web media authoring. These companies have taken Windows Media content creation and authoring to new levels of power and simplicity by incorporating direct support for Windows Media Technologies.

Sonic Foundry (http://www.sonicfoundry.com/) specializes in digital audio editing and processing for all audio applications, including Internet, mastering, sound design, and audio for video. Tools include:

- **ACID (Pro, Music, DJ, Rock).** This is a loop-based production tool for producing royalty-free, professional-quality music.

- **Sound Forge.** This is professional sound editing software for the Windows operating system that includes an extensive set of audio processes, tools, and effects for manipulating audio.

- **Stream Anywhere.** This is the all-in-one solution for authoring streaming media to the Web, and represents an advance in digital multimedia development applications. Stream Anywhere is designed for both novice and experienced Web developers.

- **Vegas.** This is a multitrack media editing system. It is a Windows-based, non-linear, hard-disk recording system for nondestructive, multitrack audio/media editing.

Using Windows Media Tools

Terran Interactive (http://www.terran.com/) produces Media Cleaner Pro for Windows and the Macintosh operating systems. Media Cleaner Pro lets you compress the highest-quality audio and video for CD-ROM, kiosk, DVD-ROM, intranets, and the Web. If you are new to desktop video, an on-board wizard makes it easy to deliver video that will look and play its best. If you are a professional, you can take advantage of powerful features such as batch processing of up to 2,000 movies, crop and scale, advanced data rate control and noise reduction, image adjustments, and more.

We have listed a few key tools here. For a full list of all the third-party products supporting Windows Media Technologies, see the Windows Media Web site (http://www.microsoft.com/windows/windowsmedia/en/partners/tools/).

Summary

Windows Media Tools includes a set of content creation tools and a set of content editing tools. You can use the content creation tools to convert live or existing content into ASF streams or files, combine and synchronize audio and image files, synchronize markers and script commands, broadcast streaming PowerPoint presentations, and compress and convert video files into ASF from within Adobe Premiere.

Windows Media Encoder encodes multiple bit rate streams that accommodate different bandwidths. Multiple bit rate streams combined with intelligent streaming enable the server and client to communicate to preserve continuous playback and maximize the quality of streams.

You can use the content editing tools to edit .asf files and to identify and repair problems in .asf files.

Chapter 4, "Using Windows Media Services," shows you how to install, configure, and use Windows Media Services to distribute your ASF content.

Chapter

4

Using Windows Media Services

This chapter introduces Microsoft Windows Media Services, shows how to install
Windows Media Services, and then describes how to configure and administer
a Windows Media server. Windows Media Services is made up of the Windows Media
component services and Windows Media Administrator. After reading this chapter, you'll
be able to answer the following questions:

- What is Windows Media Services, and what are its components?

- What is a publishing point?

- What is a station?

- What is a program?

Introducing Windows Media Services

Windows Media Services is used to send audio and video content, by unicast and multicast, to clients. The Windows Media Services that enable your Microsoft Windows NT Server to stream audio and video over a network include:

- **Windows Media Unicast service.** This service provides the ability to stream content to a specific client and enables on-demand streaming. On-demand streaming is the playback of a stream that is controlled by the client.

- **Windows Media Station service.** This service is used by the Windows Media server to send a stream to multicast-enabled routers. This enables the Windows Media server to provide a single stream to multiple end users.

- **Windows Media Program service.** You can use this service to control how many times a group of streams is played. This service is used when you are serving a Windows Media station.

- **Windows Media Monitor service.** You can use this service to monitor clients connected to publishing points. You can also use this service to monitor other servers that are connected to your Windows Media server.

Hardware and software requirements

Table 4.1 shows the minimum and suggested hardware and software requirements for Windows Media Services, which includes the Windows Media component services and Windows Media Administrator.

Table 4.1. Windows Media server requirements.

Component	Minimum required	Recommended	Optimal
Processor	Intel Pentium 90 megahertz (MHz)	Intel Pentium II 266 MHz or better	Intel Pentium III 450 MHz in a dual-processor configuration
Memory	64 megabytes (MB)	256 MB	512 MB

Component	Minimum required	Recommended	Optimal
Network card	10-megabit TCP/IP Ethernet card	10/100-megabit TCP/IP Ethernet card	100-megabit TCP/IP Ethernet card
Available hard disk space	21 MB for Windows Media Services; enough disk space for content storage	21 MB for Windows Media Services; 500 MB or more disk space for content storage	4 gigabytes (GB) or more SCSI RAID 0 (Redundant Array of Inexpensive Disks, Level 0)
Software	**Server components:** Microsoft Internet Explorer 5.0 or later; Microsoft Windows NT Server version 4.0 with Service Pack 4 (SP4) **Administrator only:** Microsoft Windows 95 with DCOM95 or Windows NT Workstation 4.0 with SP4	Internet Explorer 5.0 or later; Windows NT Server 4.0 with SP4 or later	Internet Explorer 5.0 or later; Windows NT Server 4.0 Service Pack 5 (SP5)

Installing Windows Media Services

Use the Web-based Windows Media Administrator to control the Windows Media
component services. Windows Media Administrator is installed as part
of the Windows Media Services installation. When you install Windows Media Services,
you can select **Complete Installation** to install Windows Media Services and Windows
Media Administrator. If you want to remotely administer a Windows Media server, you

Using Windows Media Services

can select **Administration Components Only** when you install Windows Media Services. Selecting this installation option installs only the Windows Media Administrator on the computer. For more information about running Windows Media Administrator, see "Administering Windows Media Services" later in this chapter.

To install Windows Media Services

1. Insert the Windows Media JumpStart CD (included with this book) into the CD drive. The CD should automatically start and open to the default HTML page.

2. When the JumpStart default HTML page opens, point to **install it**, point to **Windows Media Server Components**, and click **Windows Media Services**. Select the appropriate processor and click **wmserver.exe**.

3. During setup:

   a. Choose **Complete Installation (Requires Windows NT Server)**.

   b. Use the default path for the Installation Directory.

   c. Accept the default Windows Media Content Directory, C:\asfroot. Let Setup create the directory for you.

   d. Choose **Do not enable HTTP streaming**.

   e. Choose **Create "NetShowServices" Account**.

   f. Click **Finish**.

To install Windows Media Administrator on a remote computer

1. Insert the Windows Media JumpStart CD (included with this book) into the CD drive. The CD should automatically start and open to the default HTML page.

2. When the JumpStart HTML page opens, point to **install it**, point to **Windows Media Server Components**, and click **Windows Media Services**. Select the appropriate processor and click **wmserver.exe**.

3. During setup:

   a. Choose **Administration Components Only**.

   b. Use the default path for the Installation Directory.

Administering Windows Media Services

If the Windows Media server is a member of a domain, a user can log on to any remote computer in the domain (or any fully trusted domain) using a domain user account and administer Windows Media component services on the Windows Media server. Windows Media Administrator must be installed on the remote computer, and the domain user account must be a member of the NetShow Administrators group or the Administrators group on the Windows Media server.

You can also create a domain group account for administering Windows Media component services, and add the group to the NetShow Administrators group on the Windows Media server. You'll then be able to administer the Windows Media server both locally and remotely. To do so, log on to the domain with an account that is a member of a domain group account belonging to the local NetShow Administrators group.

Making a domain user or group account a member of the NetShow Administrators group does not mean a user has full control of the Windows Media server. The NetShow Administrators group only grants the rights necessary for Windows Media Services tasks. These include creating publishing points for on-demand unicast streams, enabling or disabling authentication packages, and managing stations. Domain users who do not have Write privileges to a physical directory on the Windows Media server cannot create directories and define them as publishing points.

If the Windows Media server or the remote computer is not a member of a Microsoft Windows domain, you can still administer the Windows Media server from the remote location. To administer Windows Media component services from a remote computer, you must create an administrator account, including a password, on the remote computer that is identical to an account on the Windows Media server. You must also be able to access the Windows Media server (for example, both computers must be connected to the Internet if you want to perform remote administration over the Internet). You must install Windows Media Administrator on the remote computer and connect to the server where Windows Media Services is installed by supplying the IP address of the Windows Media server.

You can use the Distributed Component Object Model (DCOM) for remote administration of Windows Media component services. If you want to use DCOM for remote administration through a firewall, you must enable ports on the firewall that allow DCOM packets to pass through.

Consult your firewall vendor to decide if you need to adjust your firewall to allow DCOM traffic for remote administration of Windows Media Services. For more information about configuring your firewall to allow DCOM communication, see "Using Windows Media Services with firewalls" later in this chapter.

Using Windows Media Services

Understanding publishing points and stations

Windows Media Services uses the terms publishing points and stations to describe how the server provides content to a client. Most end users access content by clicking a link on a Web page. Because users have no idea how they are accessing the stream, the responsibility of deciding how the end users will receive it belongs to the content provider or server administrator. As the content provider or server administrator, you have to decide:

- The number of streams you are going to deliver on one server.

- The number of end users who may be receiving streams simultaneously.

- Whether the source of the stream is going to be a stored file or a live event.

- How you are going to provide access to the stream.

- The stream quality your end users will be able to receive. Will they be satisfied with 28.8-kilobits-per-second (Kbps) streams or will they expect 56-Kbps streams or faster?

- Will end users be able to receive multicast streams?

The answers to these questions will help you determine whether you want to use a publishing point or a station. For example, if your end users cannot receive multicast streams, you must deliver the content by way of a publishing point. If you are on a corporate LAN and end users expect high-quality streams, you may want to deploy a station.

Publishing points

A *publishing point* is used to access unicast content. A publishing point is a virtual directory on your Windows Media server that stores content you make available to clients by unicast. Publishing points on a Windows Media server are analogous to virtual directories on a Web server. As a content provider, you provide the client with a link to your content. This link is an ASF Stream Redirector (.asx) file. The .asx file can be a file sent in e-mail, or it can be used as an HREF link in a Web page.

With Windows Media Services, you can use unicast publishing points to make Advanced Streaming Format (.asf) files and streams available on a Windows Media server, to Microsoft Windows Media Player. You can create and test unicast publishing points on your own, or you can use the QuickStart wizards that are available on the Unicast Publishing Points page in Windows Media Administrator.

There are two types of unicast publishing points:

- **On-demand unicast publishing points.** On-demand unicast publishing points make stored files (.asf, .wma, or .mp3) available to Windows Media Player. On-demand unicast publishing points are directories on a Windows Media server that contain stored media files.

- **Broadcast unicast publishing points.** Broadcast unicast publishing points make live ASF streams available to Windows Media Player. Broadcast unicast publishing points are used to publish live ASF streams that are generated from Windows Media Encoder or from a remote unicast publishing point.

Unicast is a point-to-point connection between the client (Windows Media Player) and the server. What is important about this method of streaming is that each client receiving a stream from the server is using up part of that server's bandwidth. It doesn't matter whether the server is delivering stored content (such as .asf, .wma, or .mp3 files) or a live stream; the streams that the server delivers use the available bandwidth. Why would you stream a unicast? The answer is that many parts of the Internet are not multicast-router enabled. Without multicast routers, ASF streams cannot move from network section to network section. To make sure end users are able to receive the streams they want, set up your Windows Media servers to enable end users to connect to the server and receive a stream.

Creating on-demand publishing points

To establish an on-demand publishing point, use Windows Media Administrator to identify a folder on the Windows Media server as the publishing point. When creating an on-demand publishing point, the folder must already exist on the hard drive. After you create the on-demand publishing point, you can make .asf, .wma, or .mp3 files available for streaming by storing them in the publishing point.

Windows Media Administrator provides a QuickStart wizard to help you create on-demand publishing points. To make it easier for end users to access the files you want them to be able to stream, you can use this wizard to create .asx files that reference the .asf, .wma, or .mp3 files stored in the on-demand publishing point. After you create the pointer to the content in the on-demand publishing point, you can use the wizard to test the .asx file and watch or listen to the streaming media, just as an end user would.

> **NOTE** One of the easiest ways to publish the links to on-demand files is to make the .asx files the object of an HREF link in a Web page. As long as the end user has Windows Media Player installed, the player automatically opens and begins playing the referenced file when the end user clicks the link.

Using Windows Media Services

Creating broadcast publishing points

To establish a broadcast publishing point, use Windows Media Administrator
to create a publishing point that receives a live stream from Windows Media Encoder,
another publishing point, or a Windows Media station.

Unlike on-demand publishing points, broadcast publishing points do not contain files.
Instead, broadcast publishing points are redirectors that point to a location where
Windows Media Player can connect to a server and receive live content.

As with on-demand publishing points, Windows Media Administrator has a QuickStart
wizard that can help you create a broadcast publishing point and publish the .asx file, or
pointer, that links to the stream. Broadcast publishing points are especially useful if you
want to secure a live stream. Because end
users receiving the stream will have to connect to the server, you can secure the
publishing point that end users will use to access the live stream. Although the live
stream does not go through a physical directory on the server, broadcast publishing
points appear in the registry and can be secured.

Stations

A station is the Windows Media mechanism for enabling users to monitor broadcast
multicast content. A broadcast multicast is a stream served over a network to no particular
destination. You can think of broadcast multicast as the streaming media equivalent of
cable television. To watch cable television, you
use your television to monitor a particular chunk of the cable bandwidth. You can think
of this chunk of bandwidth as a television channel. You can monitor any channel by
going to the numerical address of that channel. For end users, the experience of watching
television is analogous to monitoring a multicast broadcast. Instead of using the controls
on the television to switch between available content, Windows Media end users use an
.asx file, provided by the content creator, to find the IP address of the station. Windows
Media Player monitors the IP address and renders the streamed information.

In both cable television and broadcast multicast, the content that is delivered is
independent of the channel or station. The channel or station is the conduit for the
content to get to the end user. This section describes how to create a station, how to
deliver content using that station, and how to enable end users to watch the content.

Creating a station

The easiest way to create a station is to use the QuickStart Wizard in Windows Media
Administrator.

To start the Multicast Station QuickStart Wizard

1. On the Windows Media Administrator, click **Multicast Stations**.

2. Make sure the **Use wizard to create new station** check box is selected.

3. Click **New** on the **Stations** list.

The wizard, shown in Figure 4.1, can be used to create or edit a station.

Figure 4.1.

In the Create a new station dialog box, specify the station name, description, and distribution mode.

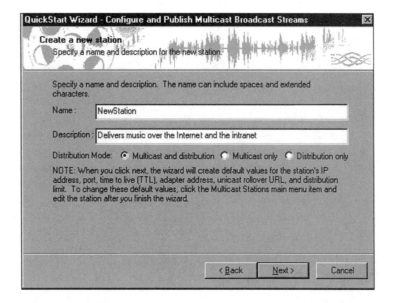

As you work your way through the QuickStart Wizard, one of the first things you must specify is the distribution mode. This identifies the purpose of the stream. You can choose one of the following distribution modes when you are creating a station:

- **Multicast Only.** The stream will be used in a connectionless environment. In this scenario, the stream is sent over the network (by way of an IP address and port) to no particular destination. The stream is available to any Windows Media Player on the network that has been directed to the correct location of the stream. Clients use an .asx file to determine the information that is needed to monitor the stream. The location the client uses is a multicast IP address. The client does not connect to the server. You cannot use the multicast-only method to deliver a stream from one Windows Media server to another.

- **Distribution Only.** The station is used specifically for delivering a stream from one Windows Media server to another. A distribution-only station can help deliver multicast content past network segments that are not connected with multicast-enabled routers. They can also be used to distribute a stream past a firewall. Distribution stations differ from multicast stations by using the Media Stream Broadcast Distribution (MSBD) protocol instead of Microsoft Media Server (MMS) protocol. MSBD is the protocol used for communicating between Windows Media components. Unlike a multicast station, a distribution station does not use an IP address or port and cannot be monitored. A Windows Media server can support up to five distribution stations. If a server is already supporting five distribution clients, it will deny access to any additional distribution clients.

■ **Multicast and Distribution.** The server provides both a distribution and multicast station. When you select **Multicast and distribution**, the server provides a stream the same way it would if you could select **Distribution Only** and **Multicast Only**. In this scenario, the server creates a broadcast publishing point from which the content is unicast; this is the distribution station. The content is also multicast from a station. The name of the station and the alias of the broadcast publishing point are the same. Remote Windows Media servers can receive a distribution stream over MSBD, and Windows Media Players can connect to the server to receive the unicast version of the stream by a broadcast publishing point. The benefit of this is a feature called unicast rollover. Clients who want to monitor the multicast can monitor the stream by way of the station. However, if for some reason clients cannot receive the multicast, the clients can connect to a server and receive the stream. As a content provider, you can create an .asx file that automatically provides this option for the end user. This way, the end user is never prevented from receiving content.

Programs and streams

Programs and streams are the structure and content for a station. A program is a type of container for one or more streams. To understand why there are programs and streams, think of how you would want to deliver content. If you want to simulate the 24-hour-a-day television experience, complete with commercials, news, sports, talk shows, and other varied content, you will need many content sources. Combining all of the sources into one file would create unnecessary duplication, and it would be expensive. Instead, you can combine files and live streams into a single experience by ordering and grouping the files and streams into one program. The following information leads you through the creation of a program and stream.

Creating a program

A program is a server-side device that you use to cluster streams. You create a program so that you can play a stream or streams more than once or to stop the stream if an error occurs.

The program, MyProgram, shown in Figure 4.2, is designed to play its three streams for 10 iterations. The information in the Name, Description, Author, and Copyright areas is for use in Windows Media Administrator. This information is not included as part of the stream. Therefore, it is not visible on Windows Media Player.

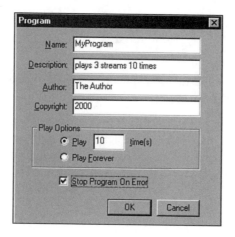

Figure 4.2.

MyProgram plays through 10 times and stops when any error occurs.

You can specify **Play Options** in the **Program** dialog box in Windows Media Administrator because a stream does not give you control over how many times it plays. The number of times specified in the Play Options area applies to all streams associated with that program. In the following section, Figure 4.3 depicts the Multicast ASF Programs and Streams area. In this figure, MyProgram has three streams associated with it. As the program plays, it runs through the list of streams and then starts over. As specified in the program, the list of streams will play 10 times and then the program will end. In Figure 4.2, the **Stop Program On Error** check box is selected. Make this selection if you want the program to stop when it encounters an error. If the check box is not selected, the program attempts to move on to the next stream if it encounters an error.

Understanding streams

Streams are digital media content that can be either a file stored on a server or a live event. Streams do not have to originate on the local sever, they can be pulled from remote servers. Figure 4.3 shows three streams, Sample1, Sample2, and Sample3, that belong to the program MyProgram.

Figure 4.3.

Sample1, Sample2, and Sample3 are part of the program MyProgram.

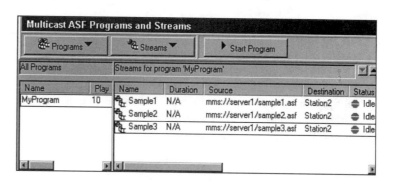

Using Windows Media Services

The Streams section of Windows Media Administrator contains columns for Name, Duration, Source, Destination, and Status that contain the following information about the stream:

- **Name.** The title you assign to the stream when you create it and how you refer to it in the program.

- **Duration.** The length of time you set for that stream to play. If the stream source is a live event, Duration defines the length of the live event. If the stream source is a stored file, Duration specifies the length of time that the stored file will be streamed. If the stored file is part of a server-side playlist, Duration specifies the length of time that the current stored file in the playlist will be streamed before the next stored file in the playlist starts; if the playlist does not contain another stream, the program ends.

- **Source.** The URL to the stored file or the live stream. In the example, all three streams are .asf files. If the source is a live stream, the URL will describe a broadcast publishing point.

- **Destination.** The name of the station that will contain the streams.

- **Status.** The current state of each stream. In Figure 4.3, all streams are Idle because the program, MyProgram, has not yet been started.

Adding streams to a program

To add a stream to a program, click a program in the **All Programs** list, and then click **New** on the **Streams** menu. In the **Advanced Streaming Format** dialog box, specify all the information about the new stream in the General, Source/Destination, and Advanced tabs.

The General tab

On the General tab, type a name and description for the stream.

The Source/Destination tab

Use the **Source/Destination** tab, shown in Figure 4.4, to identify the stream source and the station on which the stream will be delivered.

In the **Source** area of the dialog box, you can specify the path to the source with either a **URL** or an **Alias**. Use **URL** to identify the path, using either the MMS or HTTP protocol, to a file or publishing point.

Use **Alias** when you have created, or are going to create, an alias using Windows Media Encoder. You establish an alias using Windows Media Encoder to provide flexibility because you can constantly change the stream source that defines the alias without changing the name of the alias referenced by the station. For example, suppose three encoders supply live music streams from various concert halls around the country. No two of these encoders are ever in use at the same time. If you establish the alias of all three encoders' streams as MusicAlias, you can define MusicAlias as the source for the station using the alias. In the field, as each encoder turns on and streams the music, the station will receive the stream because the station correctly references the alias. As one encoder stops and the next encoder starts, the station adjusts and picks up the stream. The station does not have to be reset because the alias did not change. This provides a continuous listening experience for the end user. The user has to monitor only one station, and the content switches without the end user having to do anything. It is up to the network administrator to make sure that there are no conflicting stream aliases.

Figure 4.4.

On the Source/ Destination tab, enter a path to the stream and the station on which the stream will appear.

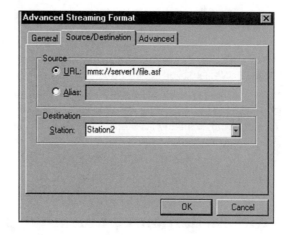

The **Destination** is the station that will receive the stream. Programs are not assigned to stations. When you define a stream, you must specify the station on which the stream will be delivered.

The Advanced tab

Use the options on the **Advanced** tab to define the output or to control the behavior of the output. Select the **Save To ASF** check box to send the stream content to an .asf file. This option is helpful if the stream is being pulled from a remote live source, and you don't know if a local copy is being made. After you check **Save To ASF**, specify the location and file name for the .asf file. To set a limit on the size of the .asf file, you can select **Maximum Size**. If the .asf file reaches the maximum file size, the server stops saving the stream out to a file.

Other properties you can set for the .asf file include **Duration**, **Open Timeout**, and **Ignore Source From Station Stop**. **Duration** specifies the length of time that you want the server to save the stream out to an .asf file. If you use this option to limit the .asf file, specify the maximum length of time you want it to be saved. Specify this information in the format of hh:mm:ss (where hh = hours, mm = minutes, and ss = seconds). You should set either the **Maximum Size** or the **Duration** because one of these characteristics is going to cause the file to close. If you set both, the size of the stream (in Kbps) will determine whether the **Maximum Size** or **Duration** causes the file to close. **Open Timeout** is the time limit for how long the server will wait, when an error occurs, before attempting to play the next stream in the program. Specify this information in the same format as the **Duration**. **Ignore Source From Station Stop** ensures that a stream continues to play, even if the source stream temporarily stops. Select this option if the source for the stream is another station.

Securing the content on the server

Windows Media Services can be configured to restrict access to a stored on-demand .asf file by requiring that end users be authenticated before the file is streamed to the end user. Windows Media Services also uses access control list (ACL) checking in Windows server to set access permissions on individual .asf files stored in on-demand and broadcast unicast publishing points. Access to live streams from a broadcast unicast publishing point can be restricted by applying access permissions to the registry key associated with the publishing point. You can restrict access to a Windows Media station by securing access to the .asx file that references the station. For more information, see "Security for stations" later in this section.

Security for on-demand publishing points

Windows Media Services can be configured to restrict access to a stored on-demand .asf file by requiring that end users be authenticated before the file is streamed to the end user. *Authentication* is the process of proving an end user's identity. This means that when end users attempt to connect to a stream, they are queried for a user name and password. By securing publishing points, Windows Media Services provides security against unauthorized end users accessing on-demand content.

Authentication is not enabled by default when Windows Media Services are installed. However, you can enable one of the following authentication packages, installed with Windows Media Administrator for on-demand unicast streaming:

- **HTTP-BASIC Authentication and Membership Service Account.** Use the HTTP-BASIC Authentication and Membership Service Account to authenticate end users against a database. Typically, this means you need to have the Personalization & Membership features of Microsoft® Site Server version 3.0 installed on the same computer. To play ASF content from a publishing point, the client must supply a user name and password. HTTP-BASIC authentication is ideal for Internet applications.

- **Windows NT® LAN Manager Authentication and Account Database.** Uses an encrypted challenge/response scheme to authenticate the end user who is logged on to the client computer against a Windows NT domain. This form of authentication is best used on an intranet, where all users are part of the same, or trusted, domain.

- **HTTP–BASIC Authentication and NTLM Account Database.** This is the same as an HTTP–BASIC Authentication and Membership Service Account, except that end users are prompted for domain, user name, and password information before they are granted access to the media. This form of authentication is best used for intranet environments that require cross-platform authentication or the Internet.

To activate an authentication mechanism

1. In Windows Media Administrator, click **Server Properties**.

2. On the Server Properties page, click the **Publishing Point Security** tab.

3. From the list of **Authentication Packages**, select a package and click **Apply**. After you change any authentication mechanism, you must restart the computer.

4. If you want to enable **Access Control List (ACL) checking**, select the check box and click **Apply**. You cannot use ACL checking without enabling an authentication mechanism, because unknown end users cannot be authorized.

Security for broadcast publishing points

Broadcast publishing points are not physical folders that you can view in Windows Explorer. To restrict access to a broadcast unicast stream, you must use Registry Editor to apply access permissions to the registry key associated with the broadcast unicast publishing point.

To set permissions for a broadcast publishing point

1. Start Registry Editor (Click **Start**, click **Run**, and then type **regedt32**).

2. In Registry Editor, use the tree view to navigate through the following path:

    HKEY_LOCAL_MACHINE\SYSTEM\CurrentControlSet\Services\
    nsunicast\Parameters\Virtual Roots

    A virtual root exists for all publishing points, including on-demand publishing points.

3. Select the virtual root that contains the permissions you want to set.

4. On the Registry Editor **Security** menu, click **Permissions**.

5. Create the permissions for the broadcast publishing point.

Using Windows Media
Services

Security for stations

End users use .asx files to access publishing points and stations. All the information that a client needs to receive a stream by way of a station is contained in an .asx file. This includes the path to the station (or .nsc file) that provides the IP address of the live stream. Based on this information, you may think that all a client has to do to access a station's live stream is to reference the .nsc file, but that is incorrect. The .nsc file must be referenced from the .asx file for Windows Media Player to be able to read the information. Security for stations should always begin with securing the .asx file that references the station. The .nsc files can be secured via authentication, authorization, or some other type of security. You should feel fairly safe about sharing the directory where the .nsc files will be stored, because an end user cannot click on the .nsc file to access a live stream. Therefore, to secure a station, you should secure access to the .asx file.

Managing server bandwidth

Windows Media Administrator can be used to set system-wide server properties for the maximum number of clients that can connect to the Windows Media server, the maximum aggregate bandwidth, and the maximum file bit rate that the server can stream, ensuring reliable delivery of your content.

When you install Windows Media Services, no server limits are created and the Windows Media server will attempt to support an unlimited number of client connections and stream all the files that are requested. Although the only true limitation is the physical limitation of the network card, establishing limits for bandwidth, maximum file bit rate, and client connections can help ensure a high-quality end-user experience. As a simple limitation, make sure the maximum file bit rate, multiplied by the maximum number of clients, does not exceed the maximum bandwidth. For example, if your network card's bandwidth is 10 megabits (10,000,000) and the maximum file bit rate you want to support is 100 kilobits (100,000), then you must set your maximum clients to 100. This assumes that, at some point, there will be 100 concurrent end users streaming 100-kilobit files. If the server contains files that are smaller (less than 100 kilobits), then the limits can be changed to allow for additional end users.

> **NOTE**   When determining server limits, keep in mind that the sustained effective throughput of a network card is generally lower than its rated line speed. For example, a 10-megabit network card can only sustain approximately 7 or 8 megabits. For more information about sustained effective throughput, see "Effective versus rated network card bandwidth" in Chapter 11.

Determining bandwidth limits

Bandwidth refers to the data transfer capacity that Windows Media Services can use without interfering with other applications or services on the computer. The maximum is restricted to the maximum sustainable throughput of your network card. However, if

Windows Media Services shares a computer with other applications or services that depend on network connections, you will need to factor in the amount of bandwidth required for those applications or services.

Determining the maximum file bit rate

Maximum file bit rate refers to the bandwidth used by one stream. To determine the bit rate required for your content, divide the file size by the time needed to play the content. For example, if a one-minute content file is 4,000 kilobytes (KB) in size, then 4,000 KB divided by 60 seconds equals 66.66. The file bit rate for this content is 66.66 kilobytes per second (KBps).

Determining the maximum number of clients

The *maximum number of clients* refers to the number of end users who can connect to the server and receive a file. This only applies to on-demand connections.

Setting server limits

Under most circumstances, when finding out what your limits should be, it is best to begin with the maximum bandwidth. This is because the limit will be determined by the capacity of your network card. If you have a 100-megabit network card (and Windows Media Services can use all of the bandwidth), you have 100,000 KBps that you can distribute among your end users. The second factor you should be aware of is the file types that are stored on the server. For example, if all the files are 64-KBps audio files, then 1,562 end users (100,000/64) could be simultaneously connected and receiving streaming files. If all files were 1-MBps high-resolution video, then 100 end users (100,000/1,000) could simultaneously receive files.

> **TIP** When determining server limits, keep in mind that the sustained effective throughput of a network card is generally lower than its rated line speed.

When you know how many end users can simultaneously watch streams, it is a good idea to set this limit so the server will not try to deliver a stream when the appropriate amount of bandwidth is not available. If you have files with varying bandwidths, estimate how many clients can connect. Getting the limits exactly correct is more important if Windows Media Services has to share the network bandwidth with other resources. This is because it is not known how the other resources will respond when forced to interact with reduced bandwidth.

Using Windows Media Services

To set bandwidth, maximum file bit rate, and client connection limits

1. In Windows Media Administrator, click **Server Properties**. The Configure Server - Server Properties page appears in the content frame.

2. On the **General** tab, three limits can be set: **Maximum clients**, **Maximum bandwidth**, and **Maximum file bit rate**. If no limits have been established for these properties, each property will be set to **No Limit**. Otherwise, the limits will appear in the **Current value** dialog box. For each property, choose **Limit to** from the **Limit to** menu, and then type a value in the **Current value** dialog box.

3. When you have finished all of your edits, click **Apply**.

Managing server performance

Windows Media Services comes with a set of Windows NT Performance Monitor counters for monitoring streaming server performance. To start Windows Media Performance Monitor, click **Start**, point to **Programs**, point to **Windows Media**, and then click **Windows Media Performance Counters**. This loads the file Nsperf.pmc, which contains a customized set of performance counters that are specific to Windows Media Services.

Figure 4.5 shows an example of the Windows Media Performance Monitor. Items that can be monitored include active TCP/UDP/HTTP streams, the number of connected end users, the total send rate, as well as late reads and CPU usage. For a complete list of available performance counters, consult the Windows Media Services documentation (Netshow.chm), which can be installed from the Welcome page of the JumpStart CD included with this book.

Optimizing server performance

Several software optimizations can be performed to a Windows Media server to increase overall network throughput:

- **Change Windows NT server cache settings to *Minimize Memory Used*.** Windows Media Services does not use system memory to cache file system data. Therefore, it is recommended that you configure the server to minimize the memory used by the operating system to increase the memory available for handling client connections.

- **Set the foreground application performance boost to *none*.** This provides more CPU time to background services, such as Windows Media Unicast service.

- **Disable non-essential Windows NT services.** Non-essential services, such as spooler, license logging, alerter, and messenger, can be disabled to release more CPU resources to serving streams. If Microsoft® Internet Information Server (IIS) is installed on the Windows Media server, you can also disable the content indexer, FTP, and SMTP services if they aren't needed. Disabling some of these services may affect other computer functions. If you are not completely aware of the consequences of disabling a service, consult the Windows NT Server product documentation.

Figure 4.5.

The Windows Media Performance Monitor

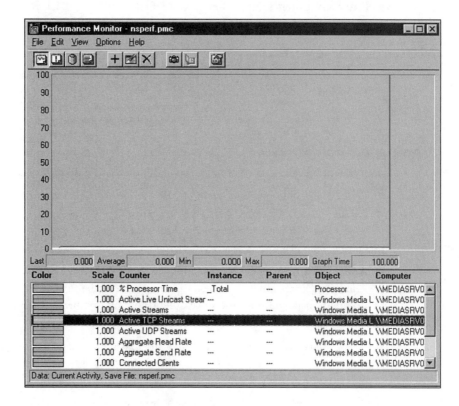

Monitoring server activity

Windows Media Administrator contains a variety of monitors that you can use to track your sources and to administer your streams. A Windows Media server can be the originator of a stream, the hub in a route that a stream uses, or the final destination for a stream. The various monitors in Windows Media Admin-istrator can help you configure and manage the traffic that moves through your server.

Monitoring clients

Windows Media Administrator provides a monitor that can be used to view the clients connected to the server, to disconnect clients from the server, and to configure the monitor's refresh interval. To open the monitor, click **Publishing Point Clients** in Windows Media Administrator. By default, the client monitor is turned off. If you want to monitor the unicast clients that connect to the server, check **Enable client monitoring** on the Publishing Point Clients page. When you turn on the client monitor, the monitor does not immediately refresh. Either click **Refresh** or wait for the Auto-refresh time to update the list. By default, Auto-refresh is selected and set for 30 seconds. You can adjust the time limit that is used, or you can turn off Auto-refresh. If you turn off Auto-refresh, the monitor will refresh only if you click **Refresh**.

Monitoring events

The event monitors in Windows Media Administrator are used to display overall system activity, including client connections, server status and limits, and administrative functions.

Monitoring unicast events

Four types of unicast events can be monitored with the Windows Media Unicast Event Monitor:

- **Client events.** Windows Media Administrator reports client events when Windows Media Player connects to, or disconnects from, a server or when the client starts playing, fast-forwarding, or rewinding a file.

- **Administrator events.** An example of an administrator event is Windows Media Administrator terminating a client's connection. Another example is setting maximum bandwidth for the server, the maximum number of clients, or the maximum file size.

- **Alert events.** Alert events occur when the maximum number of clients a server can support is exceeded, or when the maximum bandwidth that the server can stream is exceeded.

- **Server events.** An example of a server event is the server going offline or one of the Windows Media component services stopping or starting.

To open the Windows Media Unicast Event Monitor, click **Publishing Point Events** in the Windows Media Administrator. In the monitor window, separate icons identify the different events. For a key to the event icons, click **Properties**. You can also use this dialog box to choose the type of events you want to monitor. By default, all events are selected. The monitor updates events as they occur. To view the events, you must be a member of the NetShowServices group or an administrator on the local computer.

To aid in monitoring several servers, you can open a monitor for one Windows Media server while you are connected to several other servers. To open a separate monitor window, click **New Window**. The Windows Media Unicast Event Monitor window opens. Drag that window into a corner of the screen so you can see Windows Media Administrator again. You can now connect to another server by adding it and then selecting it from the list of servers in Windows Media Administrator. You can create a separate monitor window for as many servers as you want. All monitor windows will be updated individually as events occur.

Monitoring station events

Three types of station events can be monitored with Windows Media Station Event Monitor:

- **Station events.** Windows Media Station Event Monitor can monitor station status on the Windows Media server. For example, an event is generated when a station is added to or deleted from the Windows Media Administrator or when a station property is changed.

- **Stream events.** Windows Media Station Event Monitor can monitor stream activity for a station. Eight possible events can occur: activated, deactivated, opened, closed, started, stopped, stream property changed, and stream archive closed.

- **Client events.** Windows Media Station Event Monitor can monitor when a client connects or disconnects. In this case, the client does not refer strictly to Windows Media Player. A client can be any other computer that is going to deliver a stream. The client is referenced by its IP address and port number.

As with the Windows Media Unicast Event Monitor, you can open several instances of this monitor if you want to monitor several servers. Unlike the client events that occur in the Windows Media Unicast Event Monitor, the client events that are monitored in the Station Events monitor are connections between a Windows Media Encoder and the server (or from one server to another, as in a server-to-server distribution). End users who are watching or listening to content streamed over a station from the server cannot be monitored because they are not connected to the server. To have a record of the actions of the end users who are receiving a station, you must configure the server to log the end users' events. To start the Windows Media Station Events Monitor, click **Station Events** in the Windows Media Administrator.

Monitoring station connections

MSBD connections made by a Windows Media server, Windows Media Encoder, and Windows Media Player to a station can be monitored using the Station Connections page in Windows Media Administrator. This page displays all connections to the server, including recent connect and disconnect events. To view the MSBD connections to a station, click **Station Connections** in Windows Media Administrator.

Station connections do not include clients that connect to on-demand or broadcast unicast publishing points. Also, a station connection does not refer to clients that receive a multicast stream.

Each connection to the station is referenced by the IP address and the port number of the connected computer. This information is helpful when a string of computers is distributing streams from server to server. You can also use this monitor to terminate a connection. This can be helpful if a remote server or encoder is sending you unwanted streams. To remove the server from the stream, select the connection and click **Terminate Selection**.

Using Windows Media
Services

Monitoring station streams

The streams that a station uses as its source can be monitored using the Station Streams page in Windows Media Administrator. You can also use this page to terminate the ASF stream connection. To view the streams that stations are using, click **Station Streams** in Windows Media Administrator. The Station Streams page appears and automatically displays the active stations and the streams that are being delivered.

Logging client activity

Windows Media Services stores information about the clients that view streams in information logs. This information can be used to determine a variety of things, including which stream is watched most often, how long a client receives a stream, the IP address of the client receiving an ASF stream, and the Internet service provider (ISP) a client is using.

Clients that view unicast streams are connected to the Windows Media server. Windows Media Services is installed ready to log unicast client information. For more information, see "Logging unicast client activity" later in this section.

Clients that view multicast streams are not connected to the Windows Media server. However, information logs can be generated on clients that receive a multicast ASF stream. The Windows Media server must be configured before a multicast client information log can be generated. For more information, see "Logging multicast client activity" later in this section.

Client information is not entered into a log file if the client uses the MSBD protocol to connect to a unicast publishing point or a multicast station.

The unicast and multicast client information log files are text files that contain fields delimited by a space. If you do not have an application designed to read log files, you can open the log file with Microsoft® Notepad. If you want to arrange the information in rows and columns, you can open the file in Microsoft® Excel. For a description of the content that is stored in a log file, see the Windows Media Services documentation (Netshow.chm), which can be installed from the Welcome page of the JumpStart CD included with this book.

Logging unicast client activity

Windows Media Administrator can log information on activities generated by clients that connect to your unicast publishing points. The log file name is NetShow.*yymmddiii*.log, where *yymmdd* is the year, month, and day when the log file is created and *iii* is a number that starts at 000 and increases by one for every log generated on the current date.

To enable unicast logging

1. In Windows Media Administrator, click **Server Properties**.

2. On the Server Properties page, click the **Publishing Point Logging** tab.

3. To enable logging, select the **Enable logging** check box.

4. Under **Period**, select an interval (Daily, Weekly, or Monthly) or a maximum size for the log file.

5. In **Log file directory**, enter the location where the log file will be stored.

6. Click **Apply** to begin logging unicast client information.

Logging multicast client activity

Logging multicast client information enables you to view information about the client that is receiving a stream and the client connection. Use the Windows Media Internet Server Application Programming Interface (ISAPI) extension (Nsiislog.dll) for logging multicast client information. If Windows Media Services is installed on a computer where IIS is already installed, Nsiislog.dll is installed in both the *SystemDrive*\Program Files\Windows Media Components\Server directory and the *SystemDrive*\Inetpub\scripts directory. If IIS is not installed on the server computer, then Nsiislog.dll is installed in the *SystemDrive*\Program Files\Windows Media Components\Server directory only.

When logging is enabled on a station, a log file is saved to *SystemRoot*system32\logfiles. The log file name is NetShow.*yymmddiiii*.log, where *yymmdd* is the year, month, and day when the log file is created and *iiii* is a number that starts at 0000 and increases by one for every log generated on the current date.

To enable multicast logging

1. Verify that the directory containing the Windows Media ISAPI extension (Nsiislog.dll) is shared as a Web directory. Network clients must be able to access this file.

2. In Windows Media Administrator, click **Multicast Stations**.

3. Under **Stations**, click the station for which you want to create the logging file, click **Stations**, and then click **Properties**.

4. On the Edit Station page, in **Logging URL**, type the URL to Nsiislog.dll and then click **OK**.

5. When you are prompted, save the changes to the .nsc file.

Using Windows Media Services

Using Windows Media Services with firewalls

A *firewall* is a piece of hardware or software that prevents data packets from either entering or leaving a specified network. To control the flow of traffic, numbered ports in the firewall are either opened or closed to types of packets. The firewall looks at two pieces of information in each arriving or departing packet: the protocol through which the packet is being delivered and the port number to which it is being sent. If the firewall is configured to accept the
specified protocol through the targeted port, the packet is allowed through.

If you have problems delivering or receiving Windows Media streams, you may need to open additional ports in your firewall. This section describes how Windows Media Services interacts with firewalls and offers suggested firewall settings.

> **NOTE**   This section is included for advanced users. If you are not familiar with configuring a firewall, it is recommended that you consult with a computer system security specialist or your firewall vendor.

Allocating ports in a firewall for Windows Media Services

Because Windows Media Services does not use any of the standard, well-known ports that would be open by default (except HTTP), you must open special ports. Windows Media Technologies was formerly known as NetShow; many firewalls have a NetShow port setting that can also be used for Windows Media Services.

When you allocate ports for Windows Media files, you must open all of the UDP and TCP ports corresponding to those port numbers. The number ranges in the following sections indicate an entire range of available ports; typically, the actual number of ports allocated is far less.

When deciding how many ports to open, balance security with accessibility by opening just enough ports to allow all clients to make a connection. However, port range restrictions potentially affect all remote procedure call (RPC) and Distributed Component Object Model (DCOM) applications sharing the system, not just Windows Media Services. If the port range is not broad enough, competing services such as IIS will start to fail with random errors. The port range must be able to accommodate all potential applications in the system that will use RPC/COM/DCOM services. The number of open ports is entirely up to the individual corporate security philosophy, but as a starting point, determine how many ports you expect to use for Windows Media Services, then open 10 percent more to account for overlap with other programs. Once you've established this number, watch your traffic to determine if adjustments are necessary.

The recommended firewall allocation for Windows Media Services is described in the following sections:

- Firewall and registry settings for DCOM

- Windows Media server to a client behind a firewall

- Windows Media server behind a firewall to a client

- Windows Media Encoder to a Windows Media server behind a firewall

- Windows Media Administrator to a Windows Media server behind a firewall

- IP multicast

Firewall and registry settings for DCOM

DCOM dynamically allocates one port per process. You need to decide how many ports you want to allocate to DCOM processes, which is equivalent to the number of simultaneous DCOM processes through the firewall. You must open all of the UDP and TCP ports corresponding to the port numbers you choose. You also need to open TCP/UDP 135, which is used for RPC End Point Mapping, among other things. In addition, you must edit the registry to tell DCOM which ports you reserved. You do this with the "HKEY_ LOCAL_MACHINES\Software\Microsoft\Rpc\Internet" registry key, which you might need to create.

The following example tells DCOM to restrict its port range to 10 ports:

```
Named Value: Ports
Type: REG_MULTI_SZ
Setting: Range of port. Can be multiple lines such as:
3001-3010
135

Named Value: PortsInternetAvailable
Type: REG_SZ
Setting:"Y"

Named Value: UseInternetPorts
Type: REG_SZ
Setting: "Y"
```

These registry settings must be established in addition to all firewall settings in the following sections.

Windows Media server to a client behind a firewall

The following firewall configuration allows a Windows Media Player behind a firewall to access a Windows Media server outside the firewall:

> Streaming ASF with UDP
> In: UDP between port 1024–5000 (Only open the necessary number of ports.)
> Out: TCP on 1755
> Out: UDP on 1755
>
> Streaming ASF with TCP
> In/Out: TCP on port 1755
>
> Streaming ASF with HTTP
> In/Out: TCP on Port 80

Windows Media server behind a firewall to client

The following firewall configuration allows a Windows Media Player outside a firewall to access a Windows Media server behind a firewall:

> Streaming ASF with UDP
> In: TCP on port 1755
> In: UDP on port 1755
> Out: UDP between port 1024–5000 (Only open the necessary number of ports.)
>
> Streaming ASF with TCP
> In/Out: TCP on port 1755
>
> Streaming ASF with HTTP
> In/Out: TCP on Port 80

Windows Media Encoder to a Windows Media server behind a firewall

The following firewall configuration allows a Windows Media Encoder outside a firewall to access a Windows Media server behind a firewall:

> Protocol: MSBD
> In/Out: TCP on port 7007

For encoder-to-server communication, you can specify a different port. The default port is 7007, but in the Windows Media Encoder **Output** dialog box, you can choose any other free port; you can also push a button to allow the encoder to select a different port. If you choose a different port, you must specify the same port in the server when you set up the station.

Windows Media Administrator to a Windows Media server behind a firewall

The following firewall configuration allows a Windows Media Administrator outside a firewall to access a Windows Media server behind a firewall:

> Protocol: HTTP
> In/Out: TCP on port 80
>
> Protocol: DCOM
> In: TCP on port 135

You must open TCP and UDP on port 135. This port is used for initial Windows Media server-to-client and server-to-encoder communications, as well as essential processes. The protocol used for these initial communications is DCOM.

IP multicast

The following firewall configuration enables IP multicasting:

> Streaming ASF with Multicast
> IP Multicast Address range: 224.0.0.1 to 239.255.255.255

To enable IP Multicasting you must allow packets sent to the standard IP Multicast address range above to come through your firewall. This IP Multicast address range must be enabled on both client and server sides, as well as every router in between.

Running Windows Media Services and IIS on the same server

Ideally, Windows Media Services should be run on a server that is not hosting any other services for network clients. This is recommended because of the real-time nature of streaming media. Contention for CPU resources between services, such as IIS and Windows Media Services, can result in problems as the CPU load increases. If insufficient CPU resources are available to Windows Media Services, it can fall behind, and ultimately data that is slotted for real-time transmission to clients can be lost. In addition, the asynchronous network traffic generated by a Web server, or by other network applications, can degrade the smooth and constant streaming of data that is required for optimal performance.

If you must run both Windows Media Services and IIS on the same computer, they will coexist when you use their default values. The Windows Media Unicast service binds to port 1755, the Windows Media Station service binds to port 7007, and IIS binds to port 80.

Using Windows Media Services

Enabling HTTP streaming for Windows Media Services that share a server with IIS

So what can you do if you must run IIS on the same platform as Windows Media Services and stream HTTP? One option is to change the default port that IIS listens to for HTTP requests. This is not advisable because most Web browsers are specifically configured to attempt to connect through port 80. Another option is to change the default port that Windows Media Services listens to for HTTP requests. Unfortunately, HTTP is the least efficient protocol for streaming. By changing the port number from 80 to another unused port number, you may no longer be able to penetrate firewalls. The ability to penetrate firewalls is the main advantage of using HTTP streaming in the first place. If firewall penetration is not a concern, then HTTP streaming should not even be used. Instead, MMS is a more appropriate protocol to use. Can anything actually be done to make it possible for both Windows Media Services and IIS to support port 80 HTTP requests simultaneously? The answer is yes!

The Windows Media Unicast or Windows Media Station service must have a separate IP address available on port 80 to stream ASF content over HTTP. Windows Media Services cannot stream ASF content over HTTP when IIS 3.0 or earlier is installed on the server, because IIS binds to port 80 on all available IP addresses. However, with IIS 4.0, you can specify an IP address that IIS can use when it binds to port 80 to serve HTTP streams. The Windows Media Unicast service or Windows Media Station service can then use another available IP address to stream ASF content over HTTP. To enable HTTP streaming for the Windows Media Unicast or Windows Media Station service, Web sites running under IIS 4.0 must not be configured to use all unassigned IP addresses.

To use HTTP streaming when Windows Media Services and IIS 4.0 are installed on the same computer, you must have at least two IP addresses enabled on the server. This is referred to as *multi-homing*. This does not require the use of two network cards. In addition to multiple IP addresses, you may also require a unique Domain Name Server (DNS) entry to reference the Windows Media server IP address and the IIS server IP address. For more information on multi-homing, consult the Windows NT online help.

To enable HTTP streaming for Windows Media Services that share a server with IIS

Although Windows Media Services and Microsoft IIS can co-exist on the same computer, it is not a suggested design for anything other than a test environment. Windows Media Services should be dedicated to serving streams. The overhead required for Web serving is unnecessary. If you do choose to install Windows Media Services, with HTTP streaming enabled and IIS on the same server, see the special configuration notes for these services in the Windows Media Services documentation (Netshow.chm), which can be installed from the Welcome page of the JumpStart CD included with this book.

Step 1: Ensure that the server has at least two IP addresses available

When a server has more than one IP address, it is considered to be multi-homed. This can be done by assigning multiple IP addresses to a single network card. It can also be done by assigning a single IP address to multiple network cards that are installed in the server. The method used will depend on the requirements of the installation. Either method will work.

Step 2: Configure IIS to bind to a specific IP address for each Web site

The following steps are applicable only if you are using Windows Media Services with IIS 4.0.

1. In IIS Administrator, select the Windows Media server computer.

2. Right-click **Default Web Site**, and then click **Properties**.

3. In **Default Web Site Properties**, click the **Web Site** tab.

4. On the **Web Site** tab, in **IP Address**, select the IP address that you want IIS to use. The IP addresses that are available on the server should be displayed in the drop-down menu.

5. Repeat steps 2 through 4 for additional Web sites that you run under IIS, including the administration Web site.

Step 3: Enable HTTP streaming for the Windows Media service you want to use

HTTP streaming can be enabled for either the Windows Media Unicast service or the Windows Media Station service. For more information on enabling HTTP streaming for Windows Media Services, see "Enabling HTTP Streaming" in Chapter 11.

Step 4: Make the Windows Media service that is streaming HTTP dependent on the IIS Web server

To make the Windows Media service that will be streaming HTTP dependent on the IIS Web Server service, you must manually edit the registry. If you do not make the Windows Media service dependent on the IIS Web Server service, it is possible that Windows Media Services will start before IIS and bind to port 80 on all of the available IP addresses. This will result in IIS being unable to bind to port 80 on any IP addresses, making IIS incapable of accepting HTTP requests.

Use extreme caution when you edit the registry. You should back up the system before making any changes. Incorrectly editing the registry can severely damage your system and may even prevent the affected operating system from starting.

The following steps are specific to using Windows Media Services with IIS 4.0. If you use Windows Media Services with a different Web server, check the documentation for that server for instructions on setting dependencies.

Using Windows Media Services

1. Start Registry Editor. In the **Run** menu, type **regedt32** and click **OK**.

2. To update the Windows Media Unicast service, in Registry Editor, use the tree view to navigate through the following path:

   ```
   HKEY_LOCAL_MACHINE\System\CurrentControlSet\Services\
   nsunicast.
   ```

   -or-

   To update the Windows Media Station service in Registry Editor, use the tree view to navigate through the following path:

   ```
   HKEY_LOCAL_MACHINE\System\CurrentControlSet\Services\
   nsstation.
   ```

3. Double-click **DependOnService**.

4. Type **W3SVC** at the end of the list of services. W3SVC is the setting that makes Windows Media Services dependent on IIS.

5. Restart the computer.

Setting up MIME types for Windows Media Services

Multipurpose Internet Mail Extension (MIME) types allow the exchange of different kinds of files on the Internet. For Windows Media files to stream properly, Web browsers and servers must have their MIME types properly configured to recognize .asf, .asx, .wma, and .wax files. Although browsers usually have their MIME types set automatically, in some cases you may need to perform this task manually. This section discusses browser MIME types and provides information about how to set Windows Media MIME types on Web servers.

Browser MIME type considerations

Browser MIME types should be set automatically when Windows Media Player is installed. If you have Internet Explorer 2.0 or later, or Netscape Navigator 3.0 or later, the MIME type is set automatically. This is true even when you install Internet Explorer or Netscape Navigator after installing Windows Media Player. If you are experiencing MIME type problems, reinstall Windows Media Player.

If you are using a browser other than Internet Explorer, AOL, Opera, or Netscape Navigator, or if you have installed a browser after installing Windows Media Player, you may need to set the MIME types. The best way to set the MIME types for a browser is to reinstall Windows Media Player. To change these settings manually, refer to your browser documentation to determine how to add the following settings:

- **MIME types.**   video/x-ms-asf, audio/x-ms-wma, and audio/x-ms-wax

- **Extensions.**   .asf, .asx, .wma, .wax

- **Helper application.**   .mplayer2.exe

For Windows Media Player versions 5.2 and later, reinstalling the player will set the MIME types for newly installed browsers. For Windows Media Player version 6.1 or later, click **Options** from the **View** menu, and then click **Formats** to associate file types. Select all the file types you want to add, then click **OK** or **Apply**. Windows Media Player will register all selected file types in the Internet Explorer, AOL, Opera, and Netscape Navigator Web browsers.

Setting up Windows Media MIME types on Web servers

This section describes how to set up Windows Media Services MIME types for IIS 4.0, IIS 3.0, Apache, NCSA HTTPd, O'Reilly Web site, CERN HTTPd, Roxen Challenger/ Spinner, Netscape, EMWAC, Webstar/Webstar PS, and Glaci HTTPd Web servers.

> **NOTE**   For updated information about setting up MIME types, see the Windows NT Server Streaming Media Services Web site http://www.microsoft.com/ntserver/mediaserv/).

To set up Windows Media MIME types for IIS 4.0

1. Open Microsoft® Management Console (Internet Service Manager).

2. Select **Properties** for the Web site you want to update.

3. Select **HTTP Headers**.

4. Click the **File Types** button.

5. Add the following file extensions with their Associated MIME types:

Extension	MIME type
.asf	video/x-ms-asf
.asx	video/x-ms-asf
.wma	audio/x-ms-wma
.wax	audio/x-ms-wax

6. Click **Apply**, and the Web site will be updated.

To set up Windows Media MIME types for IIS 3.0

If you are running Windows NT Server and IIS and you want to configure the MIME types, you can create a .reg file with the following text by typing it into Microsoft Notepad, or another text editor, and saving the file with a .reg extension.

1. Open Notepad or another text editor.

2. Type the following text:

```
REGEDIT4
[HKEY_LOCAL_MACHINE/SYSTEM/CurrentControlSet
/Services/InetInfo/Parameters/MimeMap]

"video/x-ms-asf,asf,,5"=""
"video/x-ms-asf,asx,,5"=""
"audio/x-ms-wma,wma,,5"=""
"audio/x-ms-wax,wax,,5"=""
```

3. Save the file with a .reg extension.

4. Double-click the file to add the entries to your registry.

5. Stop then restart all IIS services.

To set up Windows Media MIME types for Apache

1. Make sure you have server administration privileges. If you do not have server administration privileges, and cannot get these privileges, relay this information to your server administrator and ask your server administrator to update these MIME type extensions.

2. Change directories to <apache_root>/httpd/conf. Edit the file srm.conf.

3. Add the following lines to the end of the file (or to the same location as the other AddType video/* entries):

```
AddType video/x-ms-asf asf asx
AddType audio/x-ms-wma wma
AddType audio/x-ms-wax wax
```

If you add these lines to the end of the file, make sure the file ends with a blank line.

4. Save your changes, and close the editor.

5. Restart the Web server.

To set up Windows Media MIME types for NCSA HTTPD

1. Make sure you have server administration privileges. If you do not have server administration privileges, and cannot get these privileges, relay this information to your server administrator and ask your server administrator to update these MIME type extensions.

2. Change directories to <httpd_root>/conf. Edit the file mimes.types.

3. Add the following lines to the end of the file (or to the same location as the other video/* entries):

```
video/x-ms-asf asf asx
audio/x-ms-wma wma
audio/x-ms-wax wax
```

If you add these lines to the end of the file, make sure the file ends with a blank line.

4. Save your changes, and close the editor.

5. Restart the Web server.

To set up Windows Media MIME types for O'Reilly Web site

1. Click the ORA Web site yellow gear icon (beside the clock on the Taskbar). Select **Server Properties**.

2. Choose the **Mapping** tab.

3. In the **List Selector** section, choose the **Content Types** radio button.

4. In the **File Extension (class)** field, type **.asf**.

5. In the **MIME Content Type** field, enter **video/x-ms-asf**.

6. Click **Add**.

7. Click **Apply**.

8. Repeat steps 3 through 7 for the following Windows Media Services MIME types:

Extension	MIME type
.asx	video/x-ms-asf
.wma	audio/x-ms-wma
.wax	audio/x-ms-wax

9. Click **OK**.

10. Save your changes, and close the editor.

11. Restart the Web server.

To set up Windows Media MIME types for CERN HTTPD

1. Make sure you have server administration privileges. If you do not have server administration privileges and cannot get these privileges, relay this information to your server administrator and ask your server administrator to update these MIME type extensions.

Using Windows Media Services

2. Change directories to <httpd_root>/conf. Edit the file mimes.types.

3. Add the following lines to the end of the file (or to the same location as the other AddType ... video/* entries):

```
AddType .asf video/x-ms-asf binary
AddType .asx video/x-ms-asf binary
AddType .wma audio/x-ms-wma binary
AddType .wax audio/x-ms-wax binary
```

If you add these lines to the end of the file, make sure the file ends with a blank line.

4. Save your changes, and close the editor.

5. Restart the Web server.

To set up Windows Media MIME types for Roxen Challenger/Spinner

NOTE   Roxen Challenger is the more recent release of Spinner.

1. Make sure you have server administration privileges. If you do not have server administration privileges, and cannot get these privileges, relay this information to your server administrator and ask your server administrator to update these MIME type extensions.

2. Change directories to <webserver_root>/etc. Edit the file Extensions.

   Add the following lines to the end of the file:

```
asf video/x-ms-asf
asx video/x-ms-asf
wma audio/x-ms-wma
wax audio/x-ms-wax
```

3. Save your changes, and close the editor.

4. Restart the Web server.

To set up Windows Media MIME types for Netscape Web Server

1. Make sure you have server administration privileges. If you do not have server administration privileges, and cannot get these privileges, relay this information to your server administrator and ask your server administrator to update these MIME type extensions.

2. Change directories to <netscape-server_root>\config. Edit the file mime.types.

3. Add the following lines to the end of the file (or to the same location as the other type-video/* entries):

```
type=video/x-ms-asf exts=asf,asx
type=audio/x-ms-wma exts=wma
type=audio/x-ms-wax exts=wax
```

If you add these lines to the end of the file, make sure the file ends with a blank line.

4. Save your changes, and close the editor.

5. Restart the Web server.

To set up Windows Media MIME types for EMWAC (NT)

1. Make sure you have server administration privileges. If you do not have server administration privileges, and cannot get these privileges, relay this information to your server administrator and ask your server administrator to update these MIME type extensions.

2. Open the **HTTP server Control Panel** applet.

3. Click **New Mapping**.

4. In the **Extension** field, type **ASF**.

5. In **MIME type**, enter:

   ```
   video/x-ms-asf
   ```

6. Click **OK**.

7. Repeat steps 3 through 6 for the following Windows Media Services MIME types:

Extension	MIME type
ASX	video/x-ms-asf
WMA	audio/x-ms-wma
WAX	audio/x-ms-wax

8. Save your changes, and close the editor.

9. Restart the Web server.

To set up Windows Media MIME types for Webstar/Webstar PS (Mac)

1. Open the WebSTAR Admin application.

2. Open the **Configure** menu and select **Suffix Mapping**.

3. Set Action to **BINARY**. Set File Suffix to **.asf**. Set File Type to *. Set MIME type to **video/x-ms-asf**. Set Creator to *.

4. Click **Add** to add the new suffix mapping.

5. Repeat steps 2 and 3 for the following Windows Media Services MIME types:

Extension	MIME type
ASX	video/x-ms-asf
WMA	audio/x-ms-wma
WAX	audio/x-ms-wax

Using Windows Media Services

6. Click **Update** to apply the changes.

To set up Windows Media MIME types for Glaci HTTPd (NetWare)

1. Make sure you have server administration privileges. If you do not have server administration privileges, and cannot get these privileges, relay this information to your server administrator and ask your server administrator to update these MIME type extensions.

2. Change directories to <glaci_root> (usually sys:\etc). Edit the file mimetype.cdf.

3. Add the following line to the end of the file (or to the same location as the other video/* entries):

```
video/x-ms-asf asf asx
video/x-ms-wma wma
video/x-ms-wax wax
```

If you add these lines to the end of the file, make sure the file ends with a blank line.

4. Save your changes, and close the editor.

5. Restart the Web server.

Summary

Windows Media Services enable your Windows NT Server to stream audio and video over a network. The services include:

- **Windows Media Unicast service**, to stream content to a specific client

- **Windows Media Station service**, to send a stream to multicast enabled routers

- **Windows Media Program service**, to control how many times a group of streams is played

- **Windows Media Monitor service**, to monitor clients connected to publishing points

A publishing point is a virtual directory on your server that stores unicast content. There are two types of unicast publishing points: on-demand unicast for stored files and broadcast unicast for live ASF streams. A station is an IP address, identified by an .asx file that enables users to view or listen to broadcast multicast content. A program is a container you can use to cluster one or more streams. Programs enable you to play streams more than once.

Chapter 5, "Using Windows Media Player," describes how to install and configure Windows Media Player.

Chapter

5

Using Windows Media Player

Microsoft Windows Media Player can receive and render streams from a Windows Media server, play clips from a movie, render a music video hosted on a Web site, play a corporate presentation, and much more. This chapter describes how to install, use, and configure Windows Media Player. After reading this
chapter, you'll be able to answer the following questions:

- What is Windows Media Player?

- What are some of the media formats used with Windows Media Player?

- How can end users control the behavior and appearance of Windows Media Player?

- What is buffering?

Introducing Windows Media Player

Windows Media Player is a universal media player that can:

- Play audio and video in most popular formats. Windows Media Player automatically opens and plays a media file when an end user double-clicks a file icon or clicks a link in a Web page, as long as the file format has been associated with Windows Media Player.

- Read and perform commands scripted in an .asx (ASF Stream Redirector) file.

- Receive script commands, markers, and metadata, such as clip title, author, and copyright.

- Render Windows Media broadcasts and on-demand content for viewing live news updates on the Internet.

- Play movie clips and music videos on a Web site.

Hardware and software requirements

Table 5.1 shows the minimum and suggested hardware and software requirements for Windows Media Player.

Table 5.1. Windows Media Player requirements.

Component	Minimum required	Recommended	Optimal
Processor	Intel Pentium 90 megahertz (MHz)	Intel Pentium 120 MHz or better	Intel Pentium II 266 MHz
Memory	16 megabytes (MB) for Microsoft Windows 95 or Windows 98; 32 MB for the Microsoft Windows NT operating system	32 MB or more	64 MB

Component	Minimum required	Recommended	Optimal
Network card	10 megabit TCP/IP Ethernet card	100 megabit TCP/IP Ethernet card	100 megabit TCP/IP Ethernet card
Audio card	16-bit sound card	Creative Labs Sound Blaster compatible 16-bit sound card	High-quality card compatible with Creative Labs Sound Blaster 16
Video card	16-color display	16-bit color display	16-bit color display with DirectDraw support
Software	Windows 95; a Web browser such as Microsoft Internet Explorer 4.01 or Netscape Navigator 4.0 or later	Windows 95, Windows 98, Microsoft Windows NT Server, or Microsoft®, Windows NT®, Workstation version 4.0 with Service Pack 3; a Web browser such as Microsoft Internet Explorer version 4.01 or Netscape Navigator 4.0 or later	Windows NT Workstation 4.0 with Service Pack 4; Internet Explorer 5

Using Windows Media Player

Installing Windows Media Player

After setting up a computer with the minimum hardware and software requirements, install Windows Media Player from the JumpStart CD included with this book. For the latest version of Windows Media Player, see the Windows Media Web site (http://www.microsoft.com/windows/windowsmedia/).

To install Windows Media Player

1. Install a Web browser, such as Internet Explorer 4.01 with Service Pack 1 or later or Netscape Navigator 4.0 or later.

2. Insert the Windows Media JumpStart CD into the CD drive. The CD should automatically start and open to the default HTML page.

3. When the JumpStart HTML page opens, point to **install it**, and then click **Windows Media Player**.

4. Select **Media Player for i386** or **Media Player for Alpha**, and then follow the on-screen instructions.

Using and Configuring Windows Media Player

End users use Windows Media Player to play a variety of media files, either as a stream or a stored file. You can also use Windows Media Player in your multimedia presentations; for example, you can embed Windows Media Player in a Web page to play media directly from your Web site. For more information about how you can use Windows Media Player, see Chapter 9, "Designing and Developing with Windows Media Technologies."

End users can also configure Windows Media Player to control its behavior. For example, end users can control the display size and volume. The following sections describe the ways in which Windows Media Player can be configured.

Setting the view

By selecting options from the **View** menu, end users can set the view for Windows Media Player.

■ **Select a view.** End users can select one of three predefined viewsfrom the **View** menu: **Standard**, **Compact**, or **Minimal**. The view determines which components appear in the Windows Media Player window. The **Standard** view is not customizable and displays all of the components available. For more information, see "Customizing the Compact and Minimal views" later in this chapter.

- **Turn on closed-captioned text.** End users can turn on closed-captioned text by selecting **Captions** from the **View** menu. If a parti-cular media file is accompanied by a Synchronized Accessible Media Interchange (SAMI) closed-captioned support file, closed-captioned text appears in a space below the video area when the file is played. For more information about authoring content for closed-captioned text, see the Windows Media Player Control Software Development Kit (SDK), which can be installed from the Welcome page of the JumpStart CD included with this book.

Customizing playback

End users can customize playback options by clicking **Options** on the **View** menu and then clicking the **Playback** tab, shown in Figure 5.1.

- **Adjust volume and balance.** Under the **Audio** section, end users can change the volume levels and balance.

- **Set the number of times to play a media file.** Under the **Playback** section, the end user can specify whether to loop playback or set the number of times to play a clip.

- **Set the display size.** The end user can specify the size to play back media files by selecting a zoom value.

- **Disabling hardware acceleration.** The hardware acceleration slider is new in Microsoft Windows Media Technologies 4.0. With this option, end users can disable hardware video acceleration for Windows Media Player. Disabling hardware video acceleration can be useful for computers that exhibit video-rendering problems, which appear as color distortion or as artifacts and distorted patches in the video. If video playback problems are experienced, the slider can be moved one notch to the left, toward **None**. End users can continue decreasing the hardware acceleration for maximum compatibility with older video drivers. This option only applies to video being rendered by Windows Media Player; this is not the same option as the Windows 98 system-wide option by the same name.

Figure 5.1.

*The Playback
tab.*

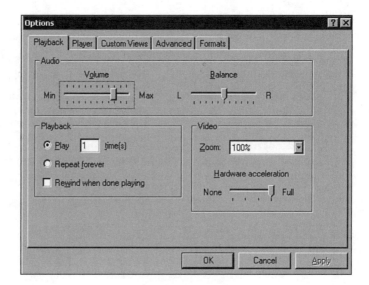

Setting the default behavior of Windows Media Player

End users can control the default behavior of Windows Media Player by clicking
Options on the **View** menu and then clicking the **Player** tab, shown in Figure 5.2.

- **Specify how to display new clips.** By setting options in the **Open options**
  section, end users can specify whether to open a new Windows Media Player
  window for each clip that is played or to play the clip in an existing window. If the
  end user chooses to open a new window for each clip, the performance might
  decrease if multiple clips are viewed simultaneously over a slow connection.

- **Set the default view.** End users can select a default view for the Windows Media
  Player window in the **View** list. The views can be customized with the options on
  the **Custom Views** tab, described later.

- **Keep the player window on top of other windows.** To always keep the
  Windows Media Player window above other windows, the user can select the
  Always on top option. This option lets the end user view other applications, such
  as a Web browser, while playing media content.

- **Set the default display size.** When the **Autozoom player** option is selected, a
  clip is displayed using the default zoom level, which is set on the **Playback** tab.
  When the **Autozoom player** option is disabled, Windows Media Player uses the
  settings from the previous playback.

- **Show controls when viewing a clip in full screen.** End users can specify
  whether the player controls are displayed when a clip is viewed in full screen by
  selecting or clearing the **Show controls in full screen** option.

Figure 5.2.
The Player tab.

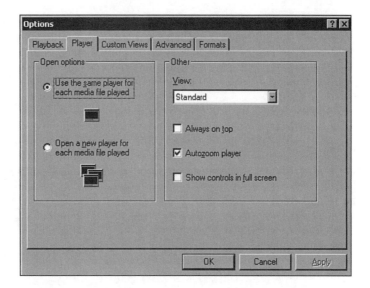

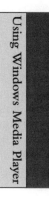

Customizing the Compact and Minimal views

The Windows Media Player window contains various components that can be displayed or hidden. The Windows Media Player components are shown in Figure 5.3.

Figure 5.3.
Windows Media Player components.

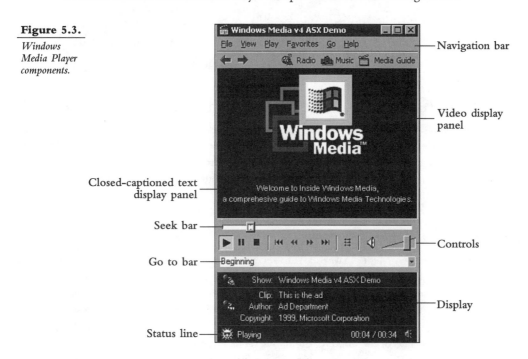

End users can choose which components to display in the Compact and Minimal
views by clicking **Options** on the **View** menu and then clicking
the **Custom Views** tab, shown in Figure 5.4. Programmers can also define the
components to display; when embedding the Windows Media Player control
in a Web page, use HTML scripting to set the appropriate properties of the
control. For more information about the Windows Media Player control, see
the Windows Media Player Control SDK, which can be installed from the Welcome
page of the JumpStart CD included with this book.

Figure 5.4

*The Custom
Views tab.*

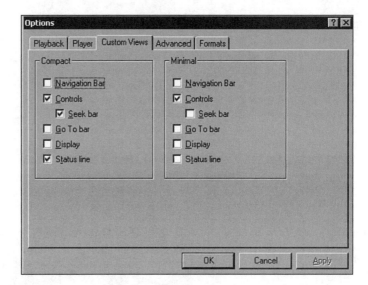

Configuring the way streaming media is received

End users can change settings for receiving Windows Media content by clicking **Options**
on the **View** menu, clicking the **Advanced** tab, selecting **Streaming Media (Windows
Media)**, and then clicking **Change**. On the **Advanced playback settings** tab, shown in
Figure 5.5, end users can view and set options for buffering, protocols, and proxy settings.
The following sections describe these settings.

Configuring the buffer

When Windows Media Player starts to receive a stream, Windows Media Player fills a data
buffer on the client computer before rendering the media. Filling a data buffer provides a
surplus amount of data for rendering during brief periods of network congestion. When
network congestion occurs, causing bandwidth to fall below the bit rate of a stream, data
in the buffer ensures continuous playback. If network bandwidth improves and is greater
than the bit rate of the content, the buffer refills. If network congestion is heavy and the
buffer becomes depleted, the player enters a buffering state, and rendering stops until the
buffer refills.

Figure 5.5.

*The Advanced
playback settings
tab.*

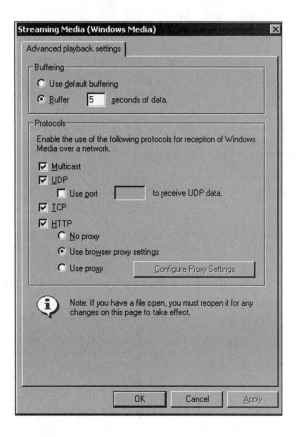

An end user can change the amount of time that Windows Media Player buffers by selecting **Buffer** and entering a different value in **seconds of data**. A higher value increases the tolerance to network slow downs. A lower value decreases the time it takes to begin rendering content. The default buffering time of three seconds is suitable for most applications, and end users should not have to change it unless frequent re-buffering occurs during playback, in which case the value should be increased by a few seconds.

Configuring protocols and the proxy

Windows Media Player supports several TCP/IP protocols including IP Multicast, UDP, TCP, and HTTP. These protocols can be used to send Windows Media streams across networks. End users can enable or disable these protocols, set custom port values for UDP, and configure proxy server settings for HTTP streams.

The proxy options, shown in Figure 5.5, are related to proxy server configurations for the HTTP protocol:

■ **No proxy** is used for a direct Internet connection, such as through a modem or DSL. This setting is also used with Microsoft Proxy Server's Winsock proxy.

- **Use browser proxy settings** is used when the client computer is behind a firewall controlled by a proxy server. This default setting con-figures Windows Media Player to use the same settings as those of the installed Web browser.

- **Use proxy** lets end users specify the name of a proxy server and a port number.

Associating file formats with Windows Media Player

End users can specify the file formats to play in Windows Media Player by clicking **Options** on the **View** menu and then clicking the **Formats** tab, shown in Figure 5.6.

The Windows Media Player installation uses passive file-association rules, which means that if another player has already assumed a default file format, Windows Media Player will honor this rule and not take over playback of the file format. However, the end user can manually select the file formats to associate with Windows Media Player. If a check box appears gray, Windows Media Player only partially owns the file format and may not play back files of this type.

Windows Media Player can play the following types of media files:

- **Microsoft Windows Media formats.** File extensions include .avi, .asf, .asx, .wav, .wma, .wm, and .wax.

- **Moving Pictures Experts Group (MPEG).** File extensions include .mpg, .mpeg, .m1v, .mp2, .mp3, .mpa, and .mpe.

- **Musical Instrument Digital Interface (MIDI).** File extensions include .mid and .rmi.

- **Apple QuickTime®, Macintosh® AIFF Resource.** File extensions include .qt, .aif, .aifc, .aiff, and .mov.

- **UNIX formats.** File extensions include .au and .snd.

Understanding Windows Media formats

The following list describes some of the file formats used by Windows Media Technologies. ASF and WMA are media formats. ASX, WAX, and NSC are metafiles that contain information about the location of media, metadata such as title, author, or copyright data, and stream format data.

- **ASF.** Files in this format are multimedia content files that can contain audio or video tracks along with other data and script commands.

- **WMA.** Files in this format are generally audio-only files that are produced by applications that use the Windows Media Audio codec. This codec provides CD-quality music, while compressing audio files to about half the size of those created with conventional codecs (like MP3).

- **ASX.** Files in this format are redirector files, which are text-based files containing tags you can use to perform various tasks, such as creating playlists. These files can contain references to any of the supported media types that Windows Media Player can play, including both audio and video formats.

- **WAX.** Files in this format are redirector files that contain references to Windows Media Audio files.

- **NSC.** Files in this format are station configuration files, which are used by a Windows Media server to configure a station (a station is a reference point for connecting to a stream). This file is also used to configure Windows Media Player for receiving a multicast stream from the station. When you create a multicast station on a Windows Media server, an announcement .asx file is generated. The .asx file contains a reference that points Windows Media Player to the .nsc file.

For more information about ASF and WMA, see Chapter 10, "Principles of Digital Compression and Encoding." For more information about redirector files, see Chapter 9, "Designing and Developing Using Windows Media Technologies."

Figure 5.6.

The Formats tab.

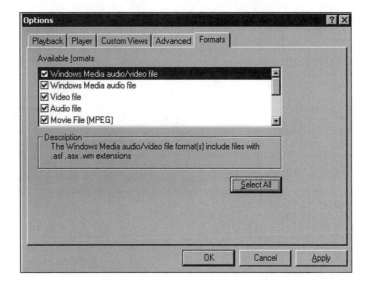

Summary

Windows Media Player can render audio and video in most formats, can read and perform script commands, and can play media right in a Web page. You can use Windows Media Player by including it with your media presentations. End users can use Windows Media Player to play media files in a wide variety of popular formats.

End users can configure all aspects of Windows Media Player, such as its display, playback, default behavior, and protocol settings. In addition, end users can customize the way Windows Media™ Player buffers data.

Chapter 6, "Putting It All Together," contains procedural information that shows you how to use the components of Windows Media Technologies to perform some common tasks—from start to finish.

Chapter

6

Putting It All Together

Chapters 1 through 5 introduced Microsoft Windows Media Technologies, offered advice on creating and improving content, and explained how to install, configure, and use Microsoft Windows Media Tools, Microsoft Windows Media Services, and Microsoft Windows Media Player. This chapter brings all of that information together and provides information that will help you make an important primary decision—whether to produce a live event or create stored content.

This chapter also walks through some of the ways you may want to use Windows Media Technologies. These end-to-end procedures include how to:

- Add audio clips to your Web site
- Put your radio station signal on the Web
- Convert your VHS tapes to Advanced Streaming Format
- Put your television signal on the Web

The final section of this chapter provides additional tips and tricks for producing live events.

> **NOTE**   To understand the procedures in this chapter, you must be familiar with bandwidth and data rates, setting up a server, and capturing and editing content.

Streaming live versus stored content

The decision whether to stream live or on-demand content is one of the first you will have to make. There are many different uses for streaming media and each use has its own set of reasons for going one way or the other. For example, offering an important one-time news story as a live event is a far more effective use of streaming media than offering the event later as a stored file. However, the cost involved in producing a music concert, which doesn't necessarily have to be live to be appreciated, may make on-demand the best choice.

It is disappointing to put together a first-rate event with dazzling production values and impressive technology, only to have very few viewers actually tune-in during show time. Make sure your live event is timely and that you do all you can to make your event known to your audience well in advance. In addition, send a reminder the day before the event. Internet streaming is a new medium with new challenges and many yet undiscovered rewards. The methods you use to market and produce a television broadcast are going to be different than those used for a live Internet event.

This section discusses some advantages and disadvantages of producing live streaming content.

The advantages of producing live content

You should consider streaming an event live for the following reasons:

■ Live communicates a sense of urgency to end users. It encourages them to tune in to your Web site so they won't miss something.

■ Some events are more effective, possibly only effective, if they are live. The live stream from a traffic camera showing current highway conditions would be pretty useless to most end users as an on-demand file.

■ The experience of a live event is entirely different from that of playing an on-demand file. When viewing a live event, an end user is comfortable as a passive observer. There are certain situations when an end user simply does not want to be in control of the experience, such as when viewing a linear story, like a movie.

■ There are also times when you want control of the experience, such as when playing back commercials. An end user can fast-forward past content if the content is on demand.

- Producing a live event for streaming can be very easy and inexpensive, and the process of setting up the stream can be very simple. For example, a live production can entail nothing more than patching your radio signal or a locked-down camera into an encoding computer.

The disadvantages of producing a live event

On-demand may be a better choice for the following reasons:

- Producing some live events can be complex and costly. Live streaming events that are produced as one would produce a live event for broadcast may not generate enough return to justify the expense. To cover a live event, you may need a production crew, including an engineer to attend to the encoding station and monitor the stream. You may also need one or more technicians to monitor the ISDN (Integrated Services Digital Network) or T-1 line carrying the signal and the remote Windows Media server. The expense can be prohibitive; however, there are companies that specialize in producing Windows Media events that can be employed to help.

- A data link is required between the event location and the Windows Media server to carry the encoded signal. Sometimes ISDN or T-1 lines are not available at certain venues, or they may have to be ordered months in advance.

- Similar to live television broadcasts, live events can be risky due to unforeseen problems.

- Recording an event instead of streaming it live gives you time to edit and process the media. This is not a new concept; it is why tape recorders were invented. Editing a show prior to broadcasting it or offering it as an on-demand file not only allows you to fine-tune the audio and video, post-production time also allows you to add elements to the Web page, script commands that change images in a Web page frame, and markers. For example, a live feed may just be a talking head video. However, if you edit the video after the event, you can turn it into a complete interactive online training application.

Putting It All Together

Completing end-to-end procedures

This section provides overview procedures for completing some common tasks. These are high-level, conceptual procedures—they do not tell you what button to push—however, they are designed to provide you with enough information to get started.

- **Adding audio clips to your Web site.** This section discusses how to create high-quality audio clips for use on Web sites.

- **Putting your radio station signal on the Web.** This section describes how to encode a radio station signal and distribute it on the Internet. The section also describes how to create Web pages to incorporate live feed into a Web page.

- **Converting your VHS tapes to ASF.** This section explains how to encode VHS tapes for use on the Internet and how to prepare a Windows Media server to play them.

- **Putting your television signal on the Web.** This section describes how to put a live television signal on the Web and how to create on-demand television clips and put them on a Web page.

Adding audio clips to your Web site

Many different types of audio can be used to add value and interactivity to HTML, for example, music, lectures, radio bits, background effects, and narration. The following section is an overview of the steps for adding audio clips to a Web page.

To prepare for creating streaming content

1. Determine the bit rate of the content you will offer end users. Will you offer on-demand files at only 28.8 kilobits per second (Kbps), for example, or more than one file of the same content encoded at different bit rates? You can offer a file encoded at 28.8 Kbps and a higher quality video at 56 Kbps for end users with high-speed modems. To make this determination, you must define your target audience. Are you targeting end users during the workday who are connected with T-1 lines, or are you targeting home users with 28.8-Kbps modems?

2. Calculate how much bandwidth you'll need by estimating the total number of concurrent connections you expect at each bandwidth. Your Web server logs can help you determine how many people are on your site at a given time and their connection rate. Also, take into account the amount of advertising and promotion that may add spikes to your site's popularity. To calculate the total bandwidth:

```
Total for each bandwidth = number of concurrent connections at a
given
bandwidth * the given bandwidth
Total bandwidth required = sum of total for each bandwidth

For example:
25 concurrent users at 28.8 Kbps
25 concurrent users at 56 Kbps

(25*28,800 bps)+(25*56,000 bps)                                    =
720,000 bps + 1,400,000 bps
= 2,120,000 bps or 2.12 Mbps
```

```
Now that you know how much bandwidth you will need, make sure that
you have enough "pipe" to accommodate those users:
T-1 line = 1.5 megabits per second (Mbps) or approximately 50
concurrent 28.8-Kbps streams
T-3 or DS-3 = 45 Mbps or approximately 1500 concurrent 28.8-Kbps
streams
```

To capture and process audio

You can either record to tape first and then capture from tape to a .wav file through the sound card on your computer, or you can record directly to a .wav file. In the following procedure, content is recorded to tape first.

1. To record to tape, connect an audio source, such as a microphone or mixer, to your tape recorder, and adjust the audio levels.

2. Record the audio. Tape is far less expensive than hard drive space. Therefore, record all of the raw audio on tape, leaving in bad takes and excess sound, then capture only the good sections.

3. Capture audio to your hard drive. Connect the tape recorder to the *line in* of your capture card (see your capture card's documentation). Then prepare your audio capture program for recording. Click the record button on your capture program, and press play on the tape recorder.

   It's important to use high quality source audio. Capture at the 44.1-kilohertz (kHz) sampling rate, 16-bit sampling depth, in mono, and uncompressed. A higher sampling rate and bit depth means that the compression algorithm has more data to work with. With more data, the codec can produce compressed audio that sounds more like the original. For more information about compression, see Chapter 10, "Principles of Digital Compression and Encoding."

   To record the audio to a .wav file on your computer's hard drive, you can use a simple program like Sound Recorder, a program that automatically installs with Windows. You can also use the software that came with your sound card; most cards include good programs for capturing audio. The best solution, though, is to use a quality, digital audio-editing program such as Sonic Foundry's Sound Forge, which can also be used for editing, processing, and creating the final encoded file.

4. Optional: Finesse the audio. You can improve the sound by editing and processing the file with an audio-editing program prior to encoding the final Windows Media files. You can edit out noises and remove extraneous sound from the beginning and end, even cut and paste sections from different takes. Then you can use processing functions such as equalization, audio dynamics (audio compression), and normalization to clean up the sound quality. These functions are available on most audio workstations such as Sound Forge. The following list describes how you can use some basic processing functions to improve your audio file:

- **Equalization.** Boost or lower certain frequency ranges in an audio file. For example, prominent air conditioning rumble can be reduced by lowering frequencies below 100 hertz, and definition can be added to a muffled voice by boosting frequencies around 2,500 hertz.

- **Audio dynamics.** Audio compression (not the same as the compression used by a codec) can be used to reduce the dynamics of an audio file. *Dynamics* refers to the contrast between the loudest and the quietest parts of a piece of audio. Audio compression automatically brings the quiet parts up and the loud parts down, so that the loudness level throughout a file is more even.

- **Normalization.** After you have equalized and audio-compressed a file, you can normalize it. Normalization maximizes the audio level of a file without changing the dynamics. By using audio compression and normalization, you can even out the level differences between files. z

To encode and deliver streaming content

1. Convert the WAV format file to ASF. You can use Windows Media Encoder, Windows Media On-Demand Producer, or a third-party product (like Sound Forge from Sonic Foundry) to perform the conversion.

2. Configure the Windows Media server or publish to a hosting provider's server. When you engage the services of an ISP (Internet service provider), the company provides you with a procedure for publishing your content to their servers.

3. Create an .asx (ASF Stream Redirector) file. For more information, see Chapter 9, "Designing and Developing Using Windows Media Technologies."

4. Add the content to your Web page or application by either linking to the .asx file directly or embedding the Windows Media Player control in the Web page and configuring it to play the content.

Putting your radio signal on your Web site

Streaming your radio station live over the Internet extends the reach of your signal to a global audience. The cost to do so can be minimal compared to the potential benefits down the road.

To put your radio signal on your Web site:

1. Determine the bit rate of the content you will offer end users. Step 1 of the earlier procedure "To prepare for creating streaming content" in "Adding audio clips to your Web site" describes how to determine the bit rate of each live stream.

2. If you encode the signal at a remote location, such as an ISP, select a good radio with digital tuning to capture the content. Digital tuning accurately locks in the station frequency. Also, make sure the radio is placed where the signal is always strong and clear. If the encoder is at the radio station, patch the on-air program feed to the *line in* jack of the sound card in the encoding computer.

3. Configure Windows Media Encoder. Select the audio capture device that will be used to input the sound to the encoder. Then choose the bandwidth, your favorite audio codec, and the port over which you will send the live stream. The QuickStart or Template with I/O options wizards can also be used.

   You can offer the end user a choice of bit rates by encoding multiple streams. To do so, you can split the audio signal into multiple computers, each encoding one stream, or you can open multiple instances of Windows Media Encoder on one computer. Encoding multiple streams on the same computer is far less expensive and takes up less space than using multiple computers. However, doing so requires some special considerations.

   A basic consumer sound card has only one stereo input. When you assign this type of sound card to the input of one instance of the encoder, the next Windows Media Encoder that you open cannot use that input. To encode multiple streams on one computer, you can either install multiple sound cards or use a professional sound card that has more than one input. There are a variety of sound cards available today with four or eight inputs. When you configure Windows Media Encoder on a computer with a multiple-input sound card, each input appears as a separate item in the audio input list. You configure the encoders by assigning a different sound card input to each instance.

4. Start Windows Media Encoder.

5. Configure the Windows Media server components, and create a publishing point for your radio station. Open Windows Media Administrator. Under **Unicast**, select **Set Publishing Points**. In the Set Publishing Points Wizard, make the following selections:

   - Set up a publishing point to the Windows Media Encoder live stream. If you are encoding multiple streams on one computer, create publishing points to each one.
   - Specify aliases for your publishing points (for example, RadioABCD56).
   - Specify a path to the Windows Media Encoder stream, for example, msbd://*Computer:port*. *Computer* is the IP address or computer name of the encoding computer, and *port* is the port address you specified when you set up the encoder.

6. To verify that your publishing point has been set up correctly, click **View Publishing Points**.

7. Create an .asx file.

8. Add the live stream to your Web page or application.

Converting VHS tapes to ASF

Many companies have libraries of video content stored on VHS tape that can be made available to end users on the Internet or over a corporate network. The following steps describe the process of converting those tapes into streaming media files.

To convert VHS tapes to ASF

1. Before capturing any content, make sure you have the right tools:

   - Use a good quality VCR, preferably a hi-fi, stereo, 4-head model. Although you will not be using any editing features for simple capturing, machines that are capable of editing often have advanced video processing and a higher-grade tape handling mechanism, which reproduces a steadier, sharper image than non-editing VCRs do.

   - Use a good quality capture card. You can use any video capture card that is compatible with Video for Windows. You can also use a Motion-JPEG card, but that will cost considerably more.

   - Use a good computer video-editing program. A program such as Adobe Premiere 5.0 will meet most of your needs.

2. Determine what VHS content is appropriate for streaming over the Web. If you have a choice, pick video clips that are best suited for compression. High-motion clips that contain a lot of movement from frame to frame are difficult to compress and can result in a low frame rate, jerky motion, and poor image quality. Low-motion clips that contain smaller changes from frame to frame result in higher quality compressed video.

   For example, a high-action basketball game is very difficult to watch when streamed over a 28.8-Kbps connection on the Internet. When compressing the video for the low bandwidth, so much detail can be lost that the game might not be viewable.

3. Capture the video, and save it as an .avi file.

4. Edit the video, if necessary. A program such as Adobe Premiere allows you to combine pieces from different AVIs, cut and paste sections, edit the audio, and add visual effects. If you are working from a finished piece, you can use Windows Media On-Demand Producer. With this program, you can remove parts of the beginning and end of a file, add fades, process the video and audio, and add script commands and markers.

5. Determine the bandwidth of each stream. Step 2 of the earlier procedure "To prepare for creating streaming content" in "Adding audio clips to your Web site" describes how to determine the bandwidth of each feed.

6. Encode the video. You can use Windows Media Encoder, Windows Media On-Demand Producer, the Adobe Premiere Plug-in, or any of several third-party products. The method you use to convert AVI content to ASF is determined by the video card that was used to capture the AVI content.

   If you used a Video for Windows card, such as the Osprey 100, you can convert directly to ASF. If you used a motion-JPEG card to capture your AVI content, you must save your AVI using some other compression scheme because Windows Media Encoder does not support motion-JPEG.

7. Configure the Windows Media server or post the .asf file to your hosting provider's server.

8. Create an .asx file.

9. Add the file to your Web page or application.

Putting your television signal on your Web site

Many television stations, cable broadcasters, networks, and other television program distributors have discovered the Internet as a vehicle for extending their reach or message to a global audience. There are two primary ways to use streaming media on your television Web site:

- **Creating on-demand content from selected clips.** This is a common approach for companies with many hours of video content. News clips, program segments, and promotional clips of any length can be offered as on-demand files on a Web site.

- **Offering a live signal on a continuous basis.** This is a good approach when a company wants to extend its reach to end users who aren't near a television, such as people at work. Office workers can, for example, tune-in on their office computers to watch late-breaking news during lunch.

To create on-demand content from selected clips

1. Gather the raw media. Decide what clips you would like to make available to end users on the Internet. The clips can be edited pieces on tape or captured live.

2. Capture the video. Play the tape and record to your hard drive using video and audio capture cards. You can also capture directly to the ASF format with Windows Media Encoder, if there is not enough time to convert AVI content. To capture directly to an .asf file, you must use a capture card that is compatible with Video for Windows.

3. Edit and save the video as an .avi file, using a video-editing program such as Adobe Premiere. If you used a Video for Windows card, such as the Osprey 100 to capture the AVI, you can encode an .asf file directly from the AVI. If you used a motion-

JPEG card to capture your AVI, you must save your AVI using some other compression scheme before you can encode an .asf file from it.

4. Determine the bandwidth of each feed. Step 2 of the earlier procedure "To prepare for creating streaming content" in "Adding audio clips to your Web site" describes how to determine the bandwidth of each feed.

5. Encode the AVI to targeted bandwidths. You can use one of several tools to convert AVI to ASF. Windows Media Encoder, Windows Media On-Demand Producer, Sonic Foundry's Sound Forge, and the Adobe Premiere Plug-in are all products that can be used.

6. Configure the Windows Media server, or post the .asf files to your hosting provider's server.

7. Create .asx files.

8. Link to the files from your Web page or application.

To offer your signal on a continuous live basis

1. Connect the audio and video program feed to your capture cards, and make sure that the cards are functioning properly.

2. Determine the bandwidth of each feed. To do this, see Step 2 of the earlier procedure "To prepare for creating streaming content" in "Adding audio clips to your Web site."

3. Configure the encoding computer. If you plan to offer end users a choice of bit rates, you can use one of two methods: multiple instances of Windows Media Encoder or multiple bit rate encoding.

   To implement the first method, you can install more than one capture card on a single computer and configure multiple instances of Windows Media Encoder for different bit rates. However, because video compression requires so much processing power from a computer, you might have to encode each stream on a different computer.

   With the second method, you only need one instance of the encoder on a single computer with one video capture card. Then you configure Windows Media Encoder for multiple bit rate encoding. Not only is this method far less expensive and complicated, it allows the Windows Media server to use intelligent streaming to dynamically adjust the bit rate of the stream to the prevailing bandwidth while the end user plays the content. For more information on configuring Windows Media Encoder for multiple bit rate encoding, see Chapter 3, "Using Windows Media Tools."

4. Open Windows Media Encoder, and select one of the QuickStart templates. Several use multiple bit rate encoding.

5. Start the encoder.

6. Set up the Windows Media server components, and create a publishing point for your television stream. Go to your Windows Media Services, and open the Windows Media Administrator. Under **Unicast**, select **Set Publishing Points**. In the Set Publishing Points Wizard, make the following selections:

   ■ Set up a publishing point to Windows Media Encoder. Only one publishing point is required for a multiple bit rate stream. If you are using separate instances of Windows Media Encoder, a publishing point must be created for each one.

   ■ Specify an alias for your publishing point. Use the call letters of your station, for example.

   ■ Specify a path to the Windows Media Encoder stream, for example, msbd://*Computer:port*. *Computer* is the IP address or computer name of the encoding computer, and *port* is the port address you specified when you set up the encoder.

7. To verify that your publishing point has been set up correctly, click **View Publishing Points** in Windows Media Administrator.

8. Create an .asx file.

9. Link to the stream from your Web page or application.

More tips and tricks

The following suggestions can help you create better live events:

■ Integrate chat with audio/video. Integrating Microsoft® Chat and Windows Media Services is a great way to add interactivity to your Windows Media Services event. Adding Chat allows your end users to interact with the speaker in a live Windows Media Services event. You can use any chat server and client you want to. There is nothing special that you have to do to use Windows Media Services and chat. All you have to do is include both the Windows Media Player control and a chat control.

Listing 6.1 provides an example of the Microsoft Chat version 1.0 j client code.

Listing 6.1

```
<applet code=MSChat archive=mschat.jar
codebase=http://irc.msn.com/Java width=100% height=300>
<param name=cabbase value=mschat.cab>
<param name=port value=6667>
<param name=autodisconnect value=true>
</applet>
```

For more information on Microsoft Chat, download the Microsoft Chat 2.0 SDK found on http://msdn.microsoft.com/.

Putting It All Together

■ Live event feedback mechanisms. During a live event, be prepared for possible glitches, for example, someone unplugging the cord to the encoder. It is highly recommended that you have contingency plans at hand in case of emergency, such as trouble slides, and a spare encoding computer.

■ Add branding with a pre-roll ASF. Before launching end users into your live event or even into your stored content, first use the playlist feature of the .asx file to play a branded piece. For example, add a five-second audio ASF to announce your radio station (call letters and tagline) before the end user joins the live stream in the middle of the song. For more information about playlists, see Chapter 9, "Designing and Developing Using Windows Media Technologies."

■ You can run multiple instances of Windows Media Encoder on one computer. In this scenario, using Microsoft Windows 98 is recommended because the Windows 98 Plug and Play architecture makes configuring multiple sound cards easy. In addition, more device drivers are available for Windows 98.

■ If you run Windows Media Encoder on a Microsoft Windows NT computer, be sure to lock the workstation while the encoder is running to prevent other users from logging off the original user. If the user who starts an encoder session is logged off, the encoder session will stop and so will the radio station feed.

■ You should restart the computer encoding a live stream on a weekly basis. The Windows Media Encoder program can run non-stop; how-ever, because encoding requires so much continuous processing by a CPU, minor problems, such as brief power surges, can degrade encoding performance. Simply restarting the computer on a weekly basis will ensure performance is at its best.

■ Be sure to put the encoder on the same network segment as the Windows Media server.

■ For capacity planning purposes, it has been found that a Pentium II 400 megahertz (MHz) computer with a 100-Mbps network card can accommodate up to 2,000 simultaneous 28.8-Kbps connections or 1,700 simultaneous 56-Kbps connections.

Summary

To start using Windows Media Technologies, one of the first decisions you may have to make is whether to produce a live event or create stored content. This chapter shows the steps you must perform to add audio clips to your Web site, put your radio station signal on the Web, convert your VHS tapes to ASF, or put your television signal on the Web. It also offers additional tips and tricks for producing live events.

Chapter 7, "Packaging Media Files Using Windows Media Rights Manager," explains how you can control the distribution of the digital media content you make available on the Internet.

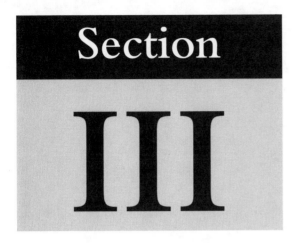

Section

III

Advanced Uses of Windows Media Technologies

This section explains how to encrypt content using Microsoft Windows Media Rights Manager, how to stream Microsoft PowerPoint presentations, and how to customize Web sites by using applications and scripts. Chapters in this section include:

Chapter 7—Packaging Media Files Using Windows Media Rights Manager. This chapter describes how you can use Windows Media Rights Manager to help control the distribution and preserve the rights of digital media you put on the Internet.

Chapter 8—Streaming PowerPoint Presentations. This chapter shows you how to stream PowerPoint presentations using Presentation Broadcasting, a feature of PowerPoint 2000.

Chapter 9—Designing and Developing with Windows Media Technologies. This chapter provides advanced information about ways you can use and customize components of Windows Media Technologies by developing your own applications and scripts. Advanced topics include:

- How to create synchronized multimedia
- How to use Microsoft Windows Media Player in a Web page
- How to use .asx files to implement playlists and event switching
- How to add script commands to an .asf file
- How to program Windows Media Player
- How to automate Windows Media Encoder

Chapter

7

Packaging Media Files Using Windows Media Rights Manager

Downloading songs and other digital media over the Internet is one of the hottest trends today. Accompanying this trend are the issues of piracy, audio quality, and media distribution. This chapter describes how you can use Microsoft Windows Media Rights Manager to help control the distribution and preserve the rights of digital media you put on the Internet. After reading this chapter, you'll be able to answer the following questions:

- What is a packaged media file?

- How do I package my media files?

- How can I distribute packaged media files?

- How are licenses used to deter piracy?

- How can I customize the way Windows Media Rights Manager works?

- How can I gather information about the people who download my media files?

Using Windows Media Rights Manager, you can distribute packaged copies of your digital media over the Internet with superior audio quality. Packaged copies require the people who play your media to acquire licenses before they play it. With this technology, it is easier for end users to legitimately acquire digital media than it is for them to pirate it.

Introducing Windows Media Rights Manager

Windows Media Rights Manager helps you control your digital media, such as songs and videos, by packaging your media files. A *packaged* media file contains a version of your media file that has been compressed, encrypted, and bundled with additional information. The result is a smaller file with high sound quality that can only be played by someone who has obtained a license to play it. The packaged media file is separate from the license needed to play it. This separation, which is a unique feature of Windows Media Rights Manager, means that distribution and licensing can be thought of in new ways.

The basic Windows Media Rights Manager process works in the following manner:

- **Packaging.** Windows Media Rights Manager packages a media file by encoding it, encrypting it with a key, and optionally signing it with a digital certificate (if you have a digital certificate that you'd like to include). Other information is added to the file, such as its title, the artist's name, a copyright statement, a banner image, a URL where a license can be acquired, and other URLs. The resulting packaged media file is saved in Windows Media Audio format (.wma extension) or Advanced Streaming Format (.asf extension) and can be played by any media player that supports these formats, such as Microsoft Windows Media Player.

- **Distribution.** Because a packaged media file is separate from the license that is required to play it, you and your end users can distribute the packaged media file in different ways. Figure 7.1 shows an example of how you can place packaged files on a Web site for download, distribute them on a CD, e-mail them to end users, and so on. Because end users must acquire a license to play packaged media files, files can be shared and copied.

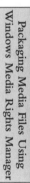

Figure 7.1.

A Web site where end users can download packaged media files.

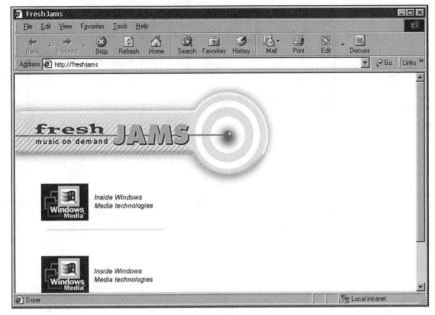

- **License acquisition.** To play a packaged media file, the end user must acquire a license that contains the key to unlock the content. The process of acquiring a license begins automatically when the end user plays a packaged media file for the first time. When a license is not detected on the end user's computer, the Web browser opens a registration page, shown in Figure 7.2, where the end user must complete a transaction before acquiring the license. This transaction might be paying for the right to play the media file or might simply be providing some personal information, such as an e-mail address. The license is then issued and the end user can play the media file.

  After the end user has registered, a license is issued and the end user can play the media file. From this point on, the end user can play the media file according to the rights that are included in the license. Default rights allow the end user to play the media file on the computer that was used to acquire the license and to copy the file to a portable device. Licenses can also have an expiration date. However, licenses are not transferable. If an end user copies a packaged media file for a friend, the friend must acquire a license to play the media file.

- **Piracy and security.** Media files are encrypted so they cannot be played without licenses; licenses, in turn, cannot be shared or copied. Although it is still possible for determined hackers to access the content, Windows Media Rights Manager makes it more difficult to pirate media files than to acquire them legitimately.

Figure 7.2.

After the end user registers, a license is issued and the end user can play the media file.

The process described here is the basic scenario for Windows Media Rights Manager, but you can customize it in many ways to suit your situation and requirements. For example, you may want to collect different registration information from end users, set an expiration on licenses, or collect payment before issuing licenses.

> **NOTE** The example companies, organizations, products, people, and events depicted herein are fictitious. No association with any real company, organization, product, person, or event is intended or should be inferred.

Windows Media Rights Manager components

Windows Media Rights Manager includes the following components:

■ Windows Media™ Packager, the tool you use to package your media files.

■ Windows Media License Service, the service that registers end users and issues licenses.

■ An SQL database, the database that stores information about media files, transactions, licenses, and registration.

■ The Windows Media Rights Manager Web site, a Web site with ASP pages that contain all the functionality of Windows Media Rights Manager. This Web site provides your packaged files for download, registers end users, and issues licenses.

Hardware and software requirements

Windows Media Rights Manager requires the hardware and software listed in Table 7.1. For more information about the software listed and to download it, see the Windows Media Rights Manager Requirements and Installation Guide on the Windows Media Web site (http://www.microsoft.com/windows/windowsmedia/en/support/drm.asp).

Table 7.1. Windows Media Rights Manager requirements.

Component	Minimum required
Processor	Pentium class processor or better.
Available hard disk space	5 megabytes (MB) for Windows Media Rights Manager, plus additional space for other required software components and content storage.
Software	• Microsoft Windows NT Server version 4.0 with Service Pack 4.★★ • Microsoft®, Windows NT®, version 4.0 Option Pack with Service Pack 1. • Microsoft Internet Explorer 5 (preferred), or Microsoft Internet Explorer version 4.01 with Service Pack 1. • Microsoft®, SQL Server version 7.0. • SQL Server Client Network Utility must use TCP/IP rather than named pipes. • You must have a SQL Server logon account that uses SQL Server authentication and has privileges to create databases. • Microsoft Windows Media Tools version 4.0. • Microsoft Windows Media Player version 6.4 or later.

Packaging Media Files Using Windows Media Rights Manager

continues

Table 7.1. Continued.

Component	Minimum required
Optional	• If you want to stream media items, you must install Microsoft Windows Media Services version 4.0. • If your SQL Server is on a different computer from Windows Media Rights Manager, you must install Microsoft®, Data Access Components version 2.0.

**It is strongly recommended that you run the Web server on an NTFS file system partition. When you install Windows Media Rights Manager on an NTFS partition, access control lists (ACLs) are set up to restrict access to Windows Media Packager, the tool you use to administer your Windows Media Rights Manager Web site. When you run Windows Media Packager, you log on using the same account as the one that was used during installation.*
If you set up Windows Media Rights Manager on a FAT partition, anyone who can access the Web server computer can administer the Web site.

Installing Windows Media Rights Manager

When you install Windows Media Rights Manager, the Setup application performs the following tasks:

■ Installs Windows Media Rights Manager server and administration components to the directory you specify.

■ Installs your Web site pages in the directory you specify.

■ Requests the domain name for your Web site, such as http://www.*mysite*.microsoft.com, where *mysite* is your domain name.

■ Requests a name for your Web site, such as *My Music Site*.

■ Creates an SQL database for Windows Media Rights Manager data. You must provide the name of a database (for example, *Music*) and the name of your SQL Server. You must also provide the logon name and password of a SQL logon account; this account must use SQL Server authentication and have privileges to create databases.

Using Windows Media Rights Manager

To begin, you must prepare your media files and then package them. Windows Media Rights Manager places the packaged files on the downloads page of the Windows Media Rights Manager Web site. Before you put your site into production, you can customize the way the site works and looks. After people visit your site and download your files, you can analyze the traffic to your site and generate a mailing list from the end-user registration information. This section includes information about:

- Preparing and packaging media files

- Customizing how the Windows Media Rights Manager Web site looks

- Customizing the way the Windows Media Rights Manager Web site works

- Analyzing site traffic and end user information

Preparing and packaging media files

Regardless of how you want to distribute and license your media files, you need to package them. The first steps are to gather and prepare the media files that you want to package and distribute and to prepare any graphics you want to include.

Preparing media files

Windows Media Packager accepts .wav, .mp3, and .asf files. If you provide .wav or .mp3 files, Windows Media Packager encodes them into ASF format.

Before you decide which format to use as the source for your media files, you need to decide whether you want to schedule Windows Media Packager to periodically repackage your media files. When a file is repackaged, it receives a new key. This reduces the risk of unauthorized licenses because each packaged copy of a media file in circulation requires a different license. However, encoding .wav and .mp3 files requires a significant amount of system resources. If Windows Media Packager is running on your Web server, the Web server will
be slow to respond to HTTP requests while the files are being packaged. If you want to repackage your files frequently, you should pre-encode your .wav and .mp3 files to ASF format. Then, Windows Media Packager will not have to encode your files each time the file is repackaged.

Before packaging your media files, you also need to decide whether you want to display images with the media file. For example, you can display an album cover or pictures of the artist in the player while a song is being played. To include JPG images with a media file, you must pre-encode them in ASF format—you can use Windows Media Author included with Windows Media Tools version 4.0.

> **NOTE** Windows Media Packager can accept additional file formats, such as AVI, if you create a configuration file to handle these different formats and then specify the new configuration file in the Windows Media Packager batch file. For more information, see "Creating a batch file" in the Windows Media Rights Manager documentation, which can be installed from the JumpStart CD included with this book.

Preparing graphics

You can use graphics for banner images and still images.

- A banner image is a small image that is packaged with the media file and displayed when the media file is played. The banner image is linked to a URL that you specify. When you click the banner image, the URL is opened in your Web browser. Banner images must be in BMP, JPG, or GIF format, and the display size can be up to 194 pixels wide × 32 pixels high. When the packaged media file is played, the player may stretch smaller images or crop larger images to fit the banner area, so it is best to use banner images that fit in a 194- × 32-pixel area.

- A still image, such as an album cover, is an image that is displayed next to the download link for a particular media file in the Windows Media Rights Manager Web site. Because still images are part of the Windows Media Rights Manager Web site, these images must be located within the Web site's directory. Copy the still images you want to use to the Content\Images directory of the Web site. By default, the root directory is C:\Inetpub\Wwwroot\WM\Content\Images. A still image must be in BMP, JPG, or GIF format and will be resized to 100 pixels × 100 pixels when displayed. To prevent images from being distorted when resized, use images that have the same aspect ratio.

Packaging media files

When you've collected and prepared the media files and graphics you want to use, you are ready to package your media files.

> **NOTE**   This procedure is based on the assumption that you have already installed Windows Media Rights Manager and are using the computer on which you installed it.
>
> The first time you run Windows Media Packager, you are prompted to acquire a certificate from Microsoft to run Windows Media License Service and issue licenses. Follow the on-screen instructions. After you accept the agreement, Microsoft will send you an e-mail message containing a link from which the new certificate is automatically installed. You must repeat this process periodically; Windows Media Packager prompts you to acquire a new certificate 10 days before your current one expires.

To package a media file

1. On the **Start** menu, point to **Programs**, point to **Windows Media**, point to **Rights Manager**, and then click **Windows Media Packager**.

   If you installed Windows Media Packager on an NTFS file system partition, you must log on using your Windows NT account.

2. On the **Content** tab, click **Add**.

3. Click **Browse** next to the **Input filename and path** box, locate the media file you want to package, and then click **Open**.

4. In the **Output filename** box, type a name for the packaged file (end users will see this file name), and use a file extension such as .wma or .asf. If you don't specify a file extension, .wma is used.

5. In the **Title** box, type the title of the media file. This title is displayed in the Windows Media Rights Manager Web site as the download link and is displayed in the **Clip** field in Windows Media Player when the media file is played. (The sample image to the right of the Windows Media Packager window shows how information is displayed.)

6. The following items are optional:

   ■ In the **Artist** box, type the artist name. This information appears in the **Author** field in Windows Media Player (see the image on the right of the Windows Media Packager window).

   ■ In the **Artist URL** box, type the URL of a Web site that you want to link to the Title, Artist, and Copyright information (the **Clip**, **Author**, and **Copyright** fields in Windows Media Player—see the image on the right of the Windows Media Packager window). When the end user clicks any of these fields while playing the media file, this URL is opened in the Web browser. For example, you could specify the URL to the artist's Web site.

   ■ In the **Copyright notice** box, type a copyright notice that you want to display when the media file is played. To type the copyright symbol ©, press and hold **ALT**, then type **0169** using the numeric keypad.

   ■ In the **Genre** box, select a genre that best describes this media file. This information is only used if you choose to organize your Windows Media Rights Manager Web site by genre; end users visiting the Web site can choose the genre they are interested in, rather than finding media files according to title.

   ■ In the **Still image** box, select the image you want to display with the download link for this media file. This list only displays the images that you have moved to the Content\Images directory of the Web site.

   ■ Click **Browse** next to the **Banner image** box. Locate the banner image you want to use, and click **Open**. Then, in the **Banner URL** box, type the URL that you want to link to the banner image. For example, if the banner image is a company logo, type the URL to the company Web site.

7. To see advanced settings, click **Advanced Options**. All items in the **Advanced Options** section are optional.

- Specify the key to use for this media file. By default, **Generate a new key** is selected and is the correct option for most situations. However, if you want to group several media files with one license (for example, to group songs from one album or to set up a subscription), you will need to use key groups. For more information about setting up subscriptions, see "Setting up a subscription" later in this chapter.

- If you want to create a packaged copy of the media file, but you do not want to have a download link for it on the Windows Media Rights Manager Web site, clear the **Available for download** box.

- If you want to periodically create new packaged copies of this media file with new keys, select **Regenerate content on Packager schedule**. If you want to create only one packaged copy, for example to reduce the impact on system resources, clear this check box. For information about setting the Packager schedule, see "Generating new packaged copies of media files on a schedule" later in this chapter.

- If you want to sign your media files with a digital certificate, select **Sign with a certificate**. Signing your media files makes them tamper proof; signed media files are indicated by a legitimacy icon in Windows Media Player. To use this feature, you must have already acquired a certificate from a Certificate Authority and set it up in Windows Media Packager. For more information about certificates, see the Windows Media Rights Manager documentation, which can be installed from the JumpStart CD included with this book.

- In the **Batch file** box, you can specify a different batch file to use. Batch files run the commands that encode, protect, and sign your media files. Unless you have written a new batch file for this purpose, you should accept the default setting.

- In the **License acquisition URL** box, you can specify the URL that starts the license acquisition process. You should accept the default setting unless you have separated the license acquisition process to a different host Web site or have created a new license acquisition page. For more information, see "Hosting Windows Media License Service separately" in the Windows Media Rights Manager documentation, which can be installed from the JumpStart CD included with this book.

8. Click **Save**, and then click **OK** to confirm.

Editing properties of a media file

After you've packaged a media file, you can edit its properties to change the title, for example, or to add information such as genre or copyright.

To edit properties of a media file

1. In Windows Media Packager, on the **Content** tab, click the media file for which you are editing properties, and then click **Edit**.

2. Enter the information for the media file. An icon indicates the information that is required.

3. Click **Save**.

Customizing how the Windows Media Rights Manager Web site looks

After you've created packaged copies of your media files, you can start thinking about how you want to distribute them. Windows Media Rights Manager includes a Web site that you can use almost immediately to put your packaged media files on the Internet for downloading, registering end users, and issuing licenses. Before you use the Web site, you should edit placeholder text on two pages. Then, it's up to you to determine how much you want to customize the site before publishing it.

The Web site is located in the directory that you specified during installation. The default location for this directory is C:\Inetpub\Wwwroot\Wm. The directory contains pages with ASP and HTML code, images, and packaged copies of the media files. Although you can edit the .asp and .htm pages, you should not move or delete files or change the directory structure.

You can edit .asp and .htm files using a text editor, such as Microsoft Notepad, or an HTML editor, such as Microsoft FrontPage. The benefit of using an HTML editor such as FrontPage is that you don't have to work with HTML tags. If you use an editor that requires you to work with the HTML code directly, be careful not to alter or delete any ASP script (located between <% %> tags). As a precaution, it is recommended that you make backup copies of the Web site pages in case you want to revert to the original version.

Editing the placeholder text

The following pages must be edited before you publish the Web site:

- **Regusage.htm.** This page is a placeholder for your *privacy policy*, which is an explanation to end users stating how you will use the registration information you collect from them. For example, if you plan to sell the e-mail addresses you collect, you should state this clearly on the Regusage.htm page.

  Open Regusage.htm and type over the text *This page is a placeholder for a privacy statement to be provided by the administrator of this Web site.* You can find examples of how to write this policy by looking at other sites on the Internet, or you can use the Privacy Wizard (http://privacy.linkexchange.com/) to create a privacy statement.

- **Recovery.htm.** This page is a placeholder for your *license recovery policy*, which is an explanation of the conditions for reissuing licenses to end users. By default, the Web site allows unlimited license recovery, but you can disable the feature, or, if you are familiar with ASP scripting, you can modify the ASP script to create a new policy.

  Open Recovery.htm and type over the text *This page is a placeholder for the recovery statement to be provided by the administrator of this Web site.* For more information about license recovery, see "Customizing and disabling license recovery" later in this chapter or see the Windows Media Rights Manager documentation, which can be installed from the JumpStart CD included with this book.

Changing the appearance and layout of the Web site

You'll probably want to change the way the Web site looks, such as the font, colors, background, text, layout, and other visual elements on the pages. You can also change the page titles and add indexing information so that search engines correctly reference your page.

The following pages contain visual elements:

- **Wm_genre.asp** or **Wm_nogenre.asp.** These pages display the packaged media files that are available for download. If you choose to organize the site according to genre (see "Organizing the Web site by genre" later in this chapter), the page Wm_genre.asp is used; otherwise, Wm_nogenre.asp is displayed. The downloads page is the first page end users will see, so you might add elements such as a company logo or graphic, or change the layout to match an existing site.

- **Default.asp.** This page is only displayed when you don't have any packaged media files available for download.

- **Download4.asp.** This page displays download instructions for people who use Microsoft Internet Explorer version 4.0.

- **Mainpage.asp** and **Verify.asp.** These are the main pages used for registration. Mainpage.asp contains the registration form requesting an e-mail address, and verify.asp contains the registration form requesting additional information.

- **License.asp.** This page is displayed when a license has been successfully issued. It displays a graphic and a link to play the licensed media file.

- **Nolicense.asp.** This page is displayed when a license is not issued and gives a brief explanation.

Customizing the way the Windows Media Rights Manager Web site works

The functionality of the Windows Media Rights Manager Web site is completely customizable. Even if you don't know anything about scripting, you can customize the way Windows Media Rights Manager works by changing settings in Windows Media Packager or by modifying a few lines in the Web site pages.

If you are familiar with ASP scripting, you can use the Instance Manager and License Server objects to modify the download, registration, and license-acquisition processes. These objects and their interfaces are documented in the Windows Media Rights Manager documentation, which can be installed from the JumpStart CD included with this book.

This section includes information about:

- Organizing the Web site by genre

- Generating new packaged copies of media files on a schedule

- Enabling e-mail address validation

- Identifying returning end users

- Setting up a subscription

- Setting an expiration period for licenses

- Customizing and disabling license recovery

If you are interested in additional customizations to your Windows Media Rights Manager site, more documentation is available in the Windows Media Technologies section of the Web Workshop on MSDN Online, the Microsoft Developer Network (http://msdn.microsoft.com/).

Organizing the Web site by genre

You can organize the media files on your Web site by genre. Then, when end users visit your site, they can find media files they want by selecting a genre such as *Jazz* or *Rock*. This feature is especially useful if your site contains a large number of media files.

Before you organize your site by genre, you need to specify a genre for each media file that you package (see step 6 in the earlier procedure "To package a media file"). Or, for media files you have already packaged, you can edit the media file properties to specify a genre (see the earlier procedure "To edit properties of a media file"). The selection of genres from which you can choose is predefined by Windows Media Rights Manager, but you can modify this list by modifying the Windows Media Rights Manager database.

When you organize your site by genre, Windows Media Rights Manager uses Wm_genre.asp instead of Wm_nogenre.asp as the downloads page. If you want to customize the appearance of your Web site, make sure to customize the correct page.

To organize your site by genre

1. In Windows Media Packager, click the **Site Configuration** tab, and then click the **Web Site** tab.

2. Select **Organize content by genre**.

3. Click **Save**.

To modify the selection of genres

1. On the **Start** menu, point to **Programs**, point to **Microsoft SQL Server 7.0**, and then click **Enterprise Manager**.

2. Expand **SQL Server Group**, expand the name of your SQL Server, expand **Databases**, expand the Windows Media Rights Manager database, and then click **Tables**. (You specified the name of the Windows Media Rights Manager database during installation. This database is named *Music* by default.)

3. In the details pane, right-click **drm_genre**, point to **Open Tables** on the shortcut menu, and then click **Return all rows**.

4. The preset genres are listed, each with a unique identification number:

   - To replace a genre, type over the name in the **genre_name** column.

   - To add a new genre, type a unique identification number in the last row in the **genre_id** column, such as the next sequential number. Then, type a new genre name in the **genre_name** column.

5. On the **Console** menu, click **Exit**.

Any genre names that you replaced are immediately updated throughout Windows Media Rights Manager: the new name is updated in the **Genre** list in Windows Media Packager, in the genre categories displayed on the Web site's downloads page, and in the properties of any media files for which the original genre name was selected. For example, if you select *Blues* as the genre for a media file, then you change *Blues* to *Rhythm & Blues*, the media file's properties will show *Rhythm & Blues* as the genre, plus the downloads page shows *Rhythm & Blues* as a category, and *Rhythm & Blues* is a choice in the **Genre** list in Windows Media Packager.

Any new genre names that you added now appear in the **Genre** list in Windows Media Packager.

Generating new packaged copies of media files on a schedule

When you add media files to Windows Media Packager, the files are encrypted with a key and a packaged copy is generated. However, after creating this initial packaged copy, you may want to regenerate packaged copies on a regular basis so that your media files are periodically re-encrypted with a new key to lessen the risk of piracy. Media files will be regenerated according to a schedule you set (such as every day at 1 a.m.).

If you have provided your media source files in WAV or MP3 format, the files will be compressed each time a packaged copy is regenerated. Compression uses significant system resources, essentially taking the system offline and preventing the Web server from responding to HTTP requests. To prevent your Web server from going offline while files are being compressed, you should provide source files in ASF format (these files are already compressed). To limit the amount of time the Web server is offline, schedule copy generation to occur infrequently.

Windows Media Packager only regenerates copies of those media files for which you have selected the **Regenerate copies on Packager schedule** check box, which is selected by default. The only way to disable copy generation entirely is to clear this option for each media file. If you aren't sure whether this option is selected for a particular media file, view the media file's packaging properties (see the following procedure).

To set the Packager schedule

1. In Windows Media Packager, click the **Site Configuration** tab, and then click the **Packager** tab.

2. To set how frequently you want to regenerate copies, click **Every ____hour(s)**, and then type the interval in hours.

   Or, to set a daily schedule, click **Each day at**, and then type the time at which you want to regenerate copies, using a 24-hour clock format. For example, to regenerate copies daily at 9 p.m., type **21:00**.

3. Click **Save**.

To activate the schedule that you just set, you need to stop and then restart the Windows Media Packager service.

To stop and restart the Windows Media Packager service

1. On the **Start** menu, point to **Settings**, and then click **Control Panel**.

2. Double-click **Services**.

3. In the **Services** list, click **Windows Media Packager**.

4. Click **Stop**, and then click **Yes** to confirm that you want to stop the service.

5. When the service has stopped (the status message disappears), click **Start**.

6. Click **Close**.

To view the packaging properties of a media file

1. In Windows Media Packager, click the **Content** tab.

2. On the **Content** tab, select a media file, and then click **Edit**.

3. Click **Advanced Options**.

4. Now all properties are visible—modify them as needed.

5. Click **Save** to save your changes.

Enabling e-mail address validation

You can enable e-mail address validation, which means that when an end user enters an e-mail address in the registration form, the e-mail address must contain an @ symbol and a dot. Otherwise, an error message is displayed to the end user, and the registration form cannot be submitted. While e-mail address validation does not ensure that a real address is entered, it helps enforce the correct format.

To enable e-mail address validation

1. In a text or HTML editor, open Mainpage.asp, which is located in C:\Inetpub\Wwwroot\Wm by default.

2. Find the following information:

```
//else if (form.email.value.indexOf("@") == -1 ||
form.email.value.indexOf(".") == -1)
//{
//    alert("Email address is invalid. Please check and try again.");
//    return false;
//}
```

3. Remove the comment tags (//) from each line.

4. Save the page.

Identifying returning end users

You can set up Windows Media Rights Manager so that end users who return to your Web site are recognized and are not prompted to re-enter registration information. When this feature is enabled, Windows Media Rights Manager stores a *cookie* (a small piece of data) on each end user's computer to identify him or her. The end user registers one time and does not have to re-register until the cookie expires (the default cookie expiration period is one year).

By default, Windows Media Rights Manager uses this feature because it makes your site more convenient for the end user. However, you can disable this feature if you want, for example for security reasons, and end users must then register each time they acquire a license. If the end user has disabled cookies on her computer, the cookie is not stored on her computer and she will also need to register each time she acquires a license.

To change the cookie settings

1. In Windows Media Packager, click the **Site Configuration** tab, and then click the **License Service** tab.

2. Select **Use cookies to identify consumers who have already registered** if you want to use cookies. Clear this check box to disable the feature.

3. In **Cookies expire after ____ days**, type, in number of days, how long you want cookies to be valid.

4. Click **Save**.

Setting up a subscription

You can set up a *subscription*, which is a set of media items that have the same key and therefore share the same license. This means the end user only needs to acquire one license to play all media files from a subscription. In this scenario, the end user must download and play at least one media file from a subscription to get a license, and then he or she can play the rest of the files in the subscription with that license.

However, another solution would be to issue the license first, and then let the end user download the media files in the subscription (for example, the end user purchases a subscription and receives a license before downloading media files). This solution requires you to be familiar with ASP scripting and to use the License Server object to customize the license acquisition process to issue licenses before a media file is requested. For more information, see "Developing pages for registration and license acquisition" in the Windows Media Rights Manager documentation, which can be installed from the JumpStart CD included with this book.

To achieve the simpler scenario that does not require custom script, create a subscription by setting up a *key group* (a key that is shared by multiple media files) and assigning it to each media file in the subscription.

To create a subscription using a key group

1. Perform the earlier procedure "To package a media file" to package the first media file in the subscription.

   ■ In step 7, select **Create a new key group**, and then type a name for the key group in the box. For example, type **Promotional Special**.

   ■ Clear the **Regenerate copies on Packager schedule** check box.

2. Package the next media file in the subscription (see the earlier procedure "To package a media file").

- In step 7, select **Use an existing key group** (select the key group you just created from the list).

- Clear the **Regenerate copies on Packager schedule** check box.

3. Repeat step 2 for each additional media file in the subscription.

Now each media file in the key group uses the same key; therefore, each file can be played using the same license.

Generally, you should not regenerate packaged copies of media files in key groups because a new key is generated when a media file is repackaged. The result is a subscription for which there may be multiple keys and, therefore, multiple licenses. For example, an end user acquires a license for a subscription and downloads the first song. That night, the media files in the subscription are repackaged. The next day, the end user downloads the rest of the songs. He would then be required to get a new license because the other songs in the subscription now use a different key—a situation you do not want to occur when using subscriptions.

Setting an expiration period for licenses

By default, licenses do not expire. However, you can set an expiration period for licenses, and the expiration date is determined at the time the license is issued. For example, you set licenses to expire after 30 days; therefore, any licenses issued on June 1 will expire on July 1. The license expiration period is a setting in the ASP code that applies to all licenses that you issue—you can't set different expiration periods for each media file without writing additional code in ASP.

To set an expiration period for licenses

1. In a text or HTML editor, open Getlic.asp, which is located in C:\Inetpub\Wwwroot\Wm by default.

2. Find the following line:

```
Days = null
```

3. Change this line in one of the following ways:

- To specify an expiration period in days, replace **null** with the number of days for which you want the license to be valid. For example, type **60** if you want licenses to expire after 60 days.

- To specify an expiration date, replace **null** with **DateDiff("d", Now(), #mm/dd/yyyy#)**, where *mm* is the month, *dd* is the day, and *yyyy* is the four-digit year of the date on which you want the license to expire. For example, type **DateDiff("d", Now(), #12/31/1999#)**.

4. Save the page.

Customizing and disabling license recovery

License recovery is a feature that allows end users to regain all the licenses that have already been issued to them. This feature provides an easy way for you to help an end user who has lost all her licenses (for example, she purchased a new computer) or an end user who has two computers and wants to play media files on both with minimum effort.

By default, the license recovery policy is simply to reissue all licenses for any media file whenever a request for recovery is made. If an end user was issued multiple licenses for one media item, only the most recent license will be reissued. If the media item has an expiration date, the expiration date will be recalculated from the date when the license was first issued.

If you are familiar with ASP scripting, you can create a custom policy (for example, allow license recovery only once per end user). The script for license recovery policy is located in Recpolicy.asp, and the interface and methods you need to use are documented in the Windows Media Rights Manager documentation, which can be installed from the JumpStart CD included with this book.

If you don't want to allow license recovery, you can disable it.

To disable license recovery

1. In a text or HTML editor, open Getlic.asp, which is located by default in C:\Inetpub\Wwwroot\Wm.

2. Find the following line:

   ```
   show_recovery = 1
   ```

3. Change this line to:

   ```
   show_recovery = 0
   ```

4. Save and close the file.

5. Open Recpolicy.asp and find the following line:

   ```
   recover_licenses = 1
   ```

6. Change this line to:

   ```
   recover_licenses = 0
   ```

7. Save and close the file.

8. Open Mainpage.asp and add comment tags (//) before each of the following lines to disable them:

   ```
   <% if Request("recovery") = "ON" then %>
   <input type="hidden" name="recovery" value="ON">
   <% else %>
   <input type="checkbox" name="recovery" value="ON">  Click
   here if you want to recover all your licenses.
   <% end if %>
   ```

9. Save and close the file.

Analyzing site traffic and end user information

After your Web site has been active for a while, you may be interested in knowing how many packaged media files have been downloaded, which media files are the most popular, how many licenses have been issued, and so on. To provide you with this information, Windows Media Packager includes general site statistics, download statistics, license statistics, and registration statistics
pages. For example, the download statistics tell you which five media files are the most requested, and the registration statistics tell you how many end users have registered.

These site statistics display data that has been gathered from the Windows Media Rights Manager database. If you are looking for information that is not included on the statistics pages, you can look in the database tables. For example, the statistics pages do not tell you how many times a particular media file has been downloaded, nor do they tell you the times at which the downloads
occur, but you can locate this information by viewing the contents of the drm_download_statistics table. You can also create an SQL report or query to gather information.

The most important information that is not included in the Windows Media Packager statistics pages is end user registration information. If you want to generate a mailing list, for example, you need to create a list of all the e-mail addresses that you have gathered from registration.

To view statistics

1. On the **Start** menu, point to **Programs**, point to **Windows Media**, point to **Rights Manager**, and then click **Windows Media Packager**.

2. Click the **Statistics** tab, and then click the tab corresponding to the statistics report you want to view.

To view a table from the Windows Media Rights Manager database

1. On the **Start** menu, point to **Programs**, point to **Microsoft SQL Server 7.0**, and then click **Enterprise Manager**.

2. Expand **SQL Server Group**, expand the name of your SQL Server, expand **Databases**, expand the Windows Media Rights Manager database, and then click **Tables**. (You specified the name of the Windows Media Rights Manager database during installation. This database is named *Music* by default.)

3. In the details pane, right-click a table that starts with **drm_**, point to **Open Tables** on the shortcut menu, and then click **Return all rows** to view the information in the table.

For a complete description of the tables in the Windows Media Rights Manager database, see "The database schema" in the Windows Media Rights Manager documentation, which can be installed from the JumpStart CD included with this book.

Summary

You can control how your media files are played by packaging them using Windows Media Rights Manager. A packaged media file is encrypted with graphics and information, such as the artist's name and Web site URL, and can only be played when an end user has a license to do so.

You can use the customizable Web site that is installed with Windows Media Rights Manager to distribute your media files over the Internet. End users visit this site and download the packaged media files. The license acquisition process begins the first time an end user plays a packaged media file. Once the license is issued, the end user can play the media file. In exchange, you have information about the people who download your media. The distribution and registration pages in this Web site are provided as a sample of the functionality of Windows Media Rights Manager; use these pages as a starting point to creating a unique experience for your end users.

Chapter 8, "Streaming PowerPoint Presentations" describes how to stream Microsoft PowerPoint Presentation Broadcasting.

Packaging Media Files Using
Windows Media Rights Manager

Chapter
8

Streaming PowerPoint Presentations

This chapter is about streaming Microsoft PowerPoint presentations using Presentation Broadcasting, a feature of PowerPoint 2000. After reading this chapter, you'll be able to answer the following questions:

- What are the advantages of streaming PowerPoint presentations?

- What configuration does a streaming PowerPoint presentation require, and how do I set it up?

- How do I schedule a presentation?

- How do I inform my audience of presentations?

- How do I make presentations available after the event has occurred?

With Presentation Broadcasting, you can synchronize the audio and video portion of a presentation with slides and stream the event to your company. When the presentation is over, you can archive it so the presentation can be viewed later.

Introducing PowerPoint 2000 Presentation Broadcasting

Slide-show presentations, using PowerPoint, have become an extremely popular way to communicate within an organization. Watching and listening to a presenter standing at the front of a room, using a set of slides to give a presentation on a topic, has become standard practice in today's business environment.

Presentations have been used to communicate information for many years. Recently, however, businesses have started to look at streaming media as a way to improve communications within their organizations. Increasing the capability and reach of a PowerPoint presentation by capturing and streaming it has become the most popular use of streaming media within organizations. Some common requirements for delivering a streaming presentation include:

- Capturing the audio or video of the presenter and streaming this to the audience.

- Synchronizing the slide changes with the presenter's points.

- Archiving presentations so they can be viewed on demand after the presentation ends.

- Allowing the audience to interact with the presenter or with other audience members.

New features in PowerPoint 2000 make all of this possible and much more. To help make streaming presentations something that everyone can do, the Presentation Broadcasting feature of PowerPoint 2000 (included in Microsoft® Office 2000) makes it easy to synchronize the audio and video portion of the presentation with presentation slides. The entire presentation can then be streamed via unicast, transmitted once across a network with multicast, or archived to a file share so it can be viewed after the event has ended. All of this is based on HTML and can be used out of the box or further customized to meet the needs of an organization.

Perhaps the best way to understand what Presentation Broadcasting delivers is to see a previously recorded presentation using this product. To watch this presentation, you need Microsoft Internet Explorer version 4.0 or Internet Explorer 5 installed along with Microsoft Windows Media Player. After you have these installed, watch the pre-recorded presentation about Presentation Broadcasting on the JumpStart CD that is included with this book. When you watch the presentation, you may notice the following features:

- The audio/video of the presenter is played back with Windows Media Player.

- The slides are synchronized with the audio/video from the presenter.

- PowerPoint animations reveal each bullet point when the presenter mentions the topic described by the bullet.

- The slides are rendered using dynamic HTML, so it takes less time to download the slides than it takes to download images of the slides. Dynamic HTML enables transitions between the slides; the slides will resize dynamically when the window is resized.

The menu at the top of the screen displays the following items:

- **View Previous Slides.** Select this to view all of the available slides, so you can read ahead or catch up if you joined a live presentation late.

- **E-mail Feedback.** Select this to launch your preferred mail client and e-mail the presenter.

- **Online Chat.** Select this to launch your preferred chat client. This enables you to join the presentation.

System requirements

To stream a PowerPoint presentation using Presentation Broadcasting, the following five types of computers are required:

1. A presenter workstation. This computer is used to create and broadcast the presentation.

2. An audience workstation. This computer is used to view the presentation.

3. A file server. This computer is used to store the slides. End users can access this computer to view the slides during the presentation.

4. A Windows Media server. This computer is used to stream the audio/video of the presentation.

5. A Chat server. End users can access this computer to participate in online, text-based communication with each other during the presentation.

The minimum requirements for broadcasting a presentation include having a presenter computer and a file server residing on the same system. If you want people to "attend" your live presentation, the audience will need to have their own computers.

Streaming PowerPoint
Presentations

The presenter computer

To broadcast a presentation with PowerPoint 2000 Presentation Broadcasting, you need a system capable of running PowerPoint 2000 and Windows Media Encoder. The system should be powerful enough to capture the audio (and, optionally, the video) in real time and encode it, and have extra processor power available to quickly change the slides. The following sections discuss the typical presenter computer configuration and a possible configuration using two computers to stream Windows Media content.

Typical presenter computer configuration

The following system configuration is recommended for the presenter computer. Although a slower computer with less memory will likely work, the configuration below will yield the best results:

- A computer with an Intel® Pentium II or an Intel® Pentium III processor

- 64 megabytes (MB) of RAM

- 10 MB of free disk space

- A Sound Blaster 16-compatible sound card

- A microphone

- A video camera and a video capture card (optional)

It is recommended that you use a computer with a Pentium II or Pentium III processor as your presenter computer. Your computer has to have adequate processing power to enable audio (and, optionally, video) capture in real-time, compression, streaming, and storage on a hard disk (if you decide to store your content on a hard disk).

It is also recommended that you use a computer with 64 MB of RAM, or more, for the presenter computer. The computer has to have enough RAM to avoid using virtual memory. If sufficient memory is not available, this will impact the quality of the presentation or add a delay of a few seconds when the presenter tries to change slides in PowerPoint.

No specific requirement exists for free disk space for this feature, but it is good practice to have free disk space for temporary files.

Select an audio card and a video card that are compatible with Windows Media Encoder. For audio, a Sound Blaster 16-compatible sound card is sufficient. This includes the sound card capability built into most computers. For video, review the list of supported video cards in Appendix A, "Audio and Video Capture Cards."

Using two computers to stream digital media

Typically, the presenter computer will also be used to capture audio/video and then stream it to the end users or to a Windows Media server. With PowerPoint 2000, you can also choose a separate computer for streaming the digital media. In this scenario, you can use one computer to display and change the slides and another computer to capture the audio/video. You may choose this scenario if the presentation is taking place in a large room and you want to put a video camera at the back of the room. You can put a computer next to the video camera to capture the audio/video and connect both computers to a network. When setting up the broadcast, the presenter specifies the name of the computer, and PowerPoint automatically starts Windows Media Encoder.

If you choose to use two separate computers, make sure that the computer running Windows Media Encoder contains a Pentium II or Pentium III processor and an audio card, a video capture card, and a microphone. In this two-computer scenario, the presenter computer needs only enough processing power to run the PowerPoint presentation.

Finally, the amount of processing power you will need to allocate to the computer running Windows Media Encoder depends on the bit rate you use to encode your audio/video content. By default, PowerPoint will encode video at 100 kilobits per second (Kbps). A computer with a Pentium II processor is capable of encoding video at 100 Kbps. If you encode at a higher data rate, more processing power is required. For example, encoding at 1 megabits per second (Mbps) typically requires a computer with a single high-speed Pentium III processor.

The audience computer

End users who want to view a PowerPoint 2000 presentation need a computer running the Microsoft Windows operating system, Windows Media Player, Internet Explorer 4.0 or later, and a network connection to the presentation. A network connection to the presentation can be the ability to connect to a remote Windows Media server using UDP, TCP or HTTP, or access to a file server where a pre-recorded presentation has been stored. The following sections discuss the typical audience computer configuration and some additional configuration options.

Typical audience computer configuration

The following configuration is recommended for viewing a PowerPoint 2000 presentation:

■ A computer with an Intel Pentium II or an Intel Pentium III processor

■ 32 MB of RAM

- Microsoft Windows 95, Microsoft Windows 98, Microsoft Windows NT 4.0 or Microsoft Windows 2000 operating system

- Windows Media Player

- Internet Explorer 4.0 or later

It is recommended that you use a computer with a Pentium II or Pentium III processor as your audience computer. If you want to broadcast to computers that have a Pentium, Pentium MMX, or Pentium Pro processor, you should stream the video at a low data rate, such as 28.8 Kbps or 56 Kbps, or consider streaming an audio-only presentation.

When determining RAM requirements, make sure enough RAM is available to load the operating system and Internet Explorer while Windows Media Player is streaming audio/video content. Typically, 32 MB of RAM is sufficient to run all of these. If the end user will be doing other things in the background, such as using productivity applications, then additional memory may be required.

The Windows 95, Windows 98, Windows NT 4.0, and Windows 2000 operating systems are all compatible with Presentation Broadcasting. This feature does not currently support Macintosh, UNIX, or Microsoft® Windows® 3.1 clients, although Windows Media Player is available for these platforms.

Windows Media Player is required to stream the audio and/or video of the presentation and to display the presentation to the end user. Any version of Windows Media Player is sufficient; although, if the encoder will make use of intelligent streaming, the latest version of Windows Media Player is required. For more information on intelligent streaming, see the "Selecting the bandwidth" section of Chapter 3.

Additional audience computer configuration options

For Web browsing, PowerPoint 2000 uses Dynamic HTML to implement slide transitions and animations; Internet Explorer 4.0 or later is required. This function is implemented according to the W3C Document Object Model (DOM) standard, which is fully supported in Internet Explorer 4.0 and 5 browsers. Netscape Navigator does not currently implement this standard, but if Netscape adds support for the W3C DOM, then Netscape will be compatible with PowerPoint 2000 presentations.

If the audience will need to interact with the presenter, each audience member will need an e-mail client and/or a chat client.

For e-mail, end users can choose any available e-mail client. Although PowerPoint 2000 works best with Microsoft Outlook 2000, end users can choose any e-mail client that Internet Explorer has been configured to use as the default mail client. If the end user does not have a chat client, they can download Microsoft Outlook Express client. The Outlook Express client is part of Internet Explorer version 4.0 and later. Having an e-mail client is not enough to send e-mail; end users also need to have an e-mail account, server, and the mail client configured properly.

For chatting, the end user can choose any chat client as the default chat client, as long as it is one that Internet Explorer is configured to use. Microsoft provides a free Internet Relay Chat (IRC) compatible client called Microsoft Chat. To download Microsoft Chat, see the Microsoft Personal Online Support Web site (http://support.microsoft.com/support/downloads/DP2578.ASP).

The file server

For PowerPoint 2000, a file server performs two functions. First, PowerPoint 2000 will save the slides in HTML format and direct end users to retrieve the slides using Microsoft file sharing from a file share. The second function is as a Windows Media server, taking the audio/video stream that has been captured by Windows Media Encoder and streaming that to the audience by way of the unicast or multicast network transport.

As a presenter, you may choose not to use a Windows Media server and stream directly from the presenter's computer or Windows Media Encoder. If you do so, you must use a file share to save the presentation, and you must save the presentation in HTML format. For small presentations, you can use your own computer to distribute the slides. For larger presentations, it is recommended that you use a dedicated file server.

Another consideration when determining the system requirements for a file server is whether you will distribute the event via unicast or multicast. Unicast is used to stream one copy of the Windows Media content to each end user, and the slides are accessed from a file server. During a multicast, the digital media content and the slides are transmitted across the network and all end users automatically receive them. For a detailed explanation of the differences between unicast and multicast, see Chapter 1, "Understanding Windows Media Technologies."

If some of your end users will receive the presentation via unicast, they will all access the slides at about the same time. Because the requests will be highly synchronized, typically when the presenter changes a slide, most of the end users will request each slide simultaneously from the same file server. When sizing your file server, consider the peak usage and make sure the file server has sufficient capacity to handle all of the slide requests in a timely manner—in addition to any other file service activities it may be handling.

For more information on determining the proper sizing for your Windows NT file services, see the Microsoft Windows NT Server Web site (http://www.microsoft.com/ntserver/).

The Windows Media server

Windows Media Encoder has the ability to stream the audio/video of the presentation to as many as 15 end users via unicast. While this is a useful feature for small workgroup presentations, be careful. Streaming directly from the encoder takes away valuable resources that could impact the quality of the encoded audio/video. For this reason, it is recommended that you always use a Windows Media server to achieve the best results.

Streaming PowerPoint
Presentations

If you plan to stream the audio/video of the presentation to more than 15 end users or if you want to transmit the stream via multicast, a Windows Media server is required. The Windows Media server provides greater scalability, enables advanced functions such as intelligent streaming, and keeps a detailed log showing who watched the presentation and for how long.

If you want to allow end users to chat with the presenter or with each other while they are watching the presentation, you need to have a chat server available for your end users. In addition to determining which chat client your end users may choose, you should consider which chat server you want to use. In most cases, you'll want to make sure your chat server and clients are compatible with the Internet Relay Chat (IRC) standard. This will give you a wide choice of compatible chat clients and server software.

Microsoft provides a free chat client, called Microsoft Chat, which is distributed as part of Internet Explorer version 4.0 or later. To download Microsoft Chat, see the Microsoft Personal Online Support Web site (http://support.microsoft.com/support/downloads/DP2578.ASP).

When selecting a chat client for PowerPoint 2000, make sure that Internet Explorer can be configured to use it as the default chat client.

Microsoft also has a chat server available for the Windows NT operating system. It is included in Microsoft® and Microsoft BackOffice family of products. If you have purchased either product, you will find an IRC-compatible chat server that runs on the Windows NT operating system. Microsoft Exchange users will benefit from tight integration between the two products.

Installing Presentation Broadcasting

This section contains instructions for installing the Presentation Broadcasting feature of PowerPoint 2000.

The first time you try to use Presentation Broadcasting, Microsoft Office 2000 will automatically install it. This is done using a new feature of Office 2000 called Windows® Installer, which will install features as needed or repair an existing product if required files are missing. Most end users will install Office 2000 with the defaults, and the Presentation Broadcasting feature will be installed the first time they select the feature.

If you are installing Office 2000 for the first time on a PC, you can choose to perform a custom installation in which you can select the options you'd like to install. After you're presented with a list of available options, expand the list of features under **Microsoft PowerPoint for Windows** and you'll see **Presentation Broadcasting** listed. To the left of this feature there is an icon that includes a "**1**"; this means that the first time the feature is used it will be installed dynamically. By clicking this icon, you can choose to install the feature at the same time as Office 2000 or disable the feature altogether. Figure 8.1 shows what installing a custom version of Office 2000 Premium may look like.

Figure 8.1.

*Configuring
a Custom
Installation of
Office 2000.*

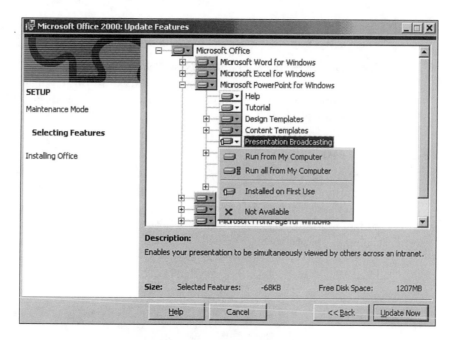

Scheduling a presentation

You begin by creating your slides with PowerPoint just as you would for any other presentation. You're free to include transitions between slides and animations. End users will be able to view large bitmaps you include in your slides. However, for some viewers who are using a modem and a dial-up connection it may take longer to view the slides because the slides are downloaded from a file share or from a Web server.

After your slides are finished, you need to configure and schedule your presentation before you can start presenting. This section describes the process of configuring PowerPoint 2000 to broadcast a presentation.

> **NOTE** The procedure in this section describes the configuration for a presentation without using a Windows Media server. A section later in this chapter discusses what is required to reach a greater number of end users with a Windows Media server and how to multicast the audio/video of the presentation along with the slides.

Setup and scheduling

After you create your slide deck, make sure you save your changes and then open the **Slide Show** menu. Point to **Online Broadcast** and click **Set Up and Schedule**. This will tell PowerPoint you want to configure a Presentation Broadcast for the slide deck you currently have open.

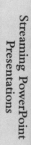

When you set up and schedule a presentation, the Broadcast Schedule Wizard walks you through everything you need to do to set up an online broadcast.

After you click **OK**, the **Schedule a New Broadcast** dialog box will appear. This dialog box has two tabs: **Description** and **Broadcast Settings**. When you click the **Description** tab, you'll be able to enter information that the audience will see before the presentation begins. Based on the information entered here, your audience can understand what the presentation will cover. Figure 8.2 shows the **Description** tab.

Each of the fields listed on the **Schedule a New Broadcast** dialog box is self-descriptive. The **Title** box can display a few words summarizing your presentation. The **Description** box can display a longer, more detailed description of the presentation. The **Speaker** box can display the name of the person giving the presentation, and the **Contact** box can display the presenter's e-mail address or telephone number. If you are planning to stream this on the Internet, or there is a chance that people outside your organization may be able to view it, you should be sure to enter your full Internet e-mail address. When you're done, click the **Broadcast Settings** tab.

Figure 8.2.

The Description tab.

In the **Audio and video** section of the **Broadcast Settings** tab, specify whether you want to include audio/video in your presentation and which computer you'll be transmitting from. To send audio, you need a Sound Blaster-16-compatible sound card with a microphone. Capturing video requires a compatible video camera attached directly to your PC, through a video capture card (for more information, see the system requirements section of this chapter). In most cases, you'll want to connect these devices to the computer you're presenting from, but you also have the option to connect them to another computer. If you plan to use a second computer for audio/video encoding, refer to the system requirements section to learn more about the requirements. You'll also have to configure this computer. The configuration is described in detail in the Office 2000 Resource Kit; for more information, see the Microsoft Office Web site (http://www.microsoft.com/office/ork/).

Figure 8.3 shows the **Broadcast Settings** tab.

Figure 8.3.

The Broadcast Settings tab.

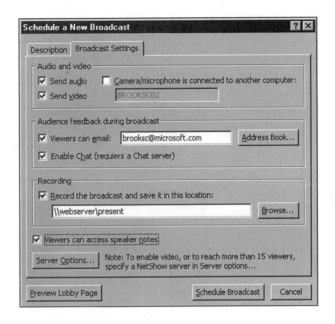

In the **Audience feedback during broadcast** section of the **Broadcast Settings** tab, you can specify a method the audience can use to communicate with you, either during or after the presentation. The most common way to communicate is by e-mail, so if you want to receive questions, check the **Viewers can e-mail** box and type your e-mail address. You can set up a chat server for more elaborate communication. For more information about compatible e-mail and chat client software, refer to the system requirements section of this chapter.

TIP   When specifying your e-mail address, it is a good idea to use a fully qualified e-mail address, such as jdoe@example.microsoft.com rather than just jdoe. This way, if your presentation is shared with people outside of your company (and outside of the e-mail system), they will be able to reach you.

In the **Recording** section of the **Broadcast Settings** tab, you can direct PowerPoint to record the audio/video and slide flips to use for on-demand access later. Specify a directory path where an ASF (Advanced Streaming Format) file should be saved.

> **TIP**   If you do not specify a directory, PowerPoint 2000 will save the slides in the directory containing your slides. This is recommended because it is convenient to have all of the files in one directory.

If you've entered speaker notes into your PowerPoint presentation, you can make these available for viewing by the audience. This is a good place to include the speaking points you'll address during your presentation, as well as reference information such as Web site addresses or additional contact information.

Finally, you will need to make some decisions about how you'll stream the audio/video information across the network. Click **Server Options** to learn more about the requirements. Figure 8.4 shows the **Server Options** dialog box.

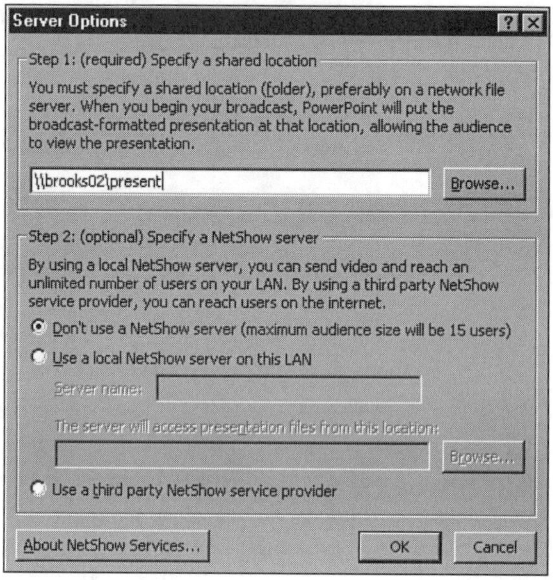

Figure 8.4.

The Server Options dialog box.

In the **Server Options** dialog box, select a destination that PowerPoint should write the files it creates to. If you will be using a Windows Media server, enter the name of the server that will stream the audio/video.

The first step is to specify a shared location, which is a shared directory (either on your own computer or on a server) where PowerPoint will create the Web pages for your presentation. When end users view your presentation they will retrieve all of the pages from this share. Therefore, it's a good idea to put these files on a server with adequate capacity for the files and your audience. Because this path will be written into the data files, it is also a good idea to specify the final location where the presentation will live. If you need to move it to another location, you can edit the files to reflect the new location, but you should avoid doing this if you can.

TIP   It will be easier for your end users to access the files if the end users and file server are members of a Windows NT Domain. If this isn't possible, then you may want to enable the Guest account on the file server so end users without accounts on that computer can still view the presentation. Be aware, however, that enabling the Guest account will allow people to access files without logging in, so do this carefully and with regard to other information on that server.

The second step is to specify a Windows Media server. You have three options:

- You can choose not to use a Windows Media server.

- You can use a Windows Media server.

- You can outsource the hosting entirely to a Windows Media service provider.

NOTE   Windows Media was formerly called Microsoft NetShow, and Office 2000 was released before the streaming audio/video product changed names. The names are used interchangeably, but they refer to the same thing, what is now known as Windows Media.

If you choose not to use a server, end users will connect directly to Windows Media Encoder and stream the audio/video directly. This doesn't require you to configure the server for the broadcast, but it does limit the number of end users who can view the live presentation to 15, and streaming from your presentation computer may slow down slide changes and animation. If you plan to include video in your presentation, it's a good idea to use a Windows Media server to prevent negatively affecting the quality of the video being captured.

If you will have an audience of more than 15 end users, make sure that the audience connects to a Windows Media server from which they'll stream the audio/video of the presentation. Configuring a Windows Media server to accept a PowerPoint 2000 presentation is described in greater detail later in this chapter. Figure 8.5 shows an Outlook 2000 meeting request.

Another option you have with PowerPoint is to use a third-party Windows Media service provider to host the content for you. This is useful if you're broadcasting a presentation out to the Internet and you don't have the bandwidth or servers available to handle the expected load. For more information about outsourcing your presentation, contact a Windows Media service provider listed on the Windows Media Web site (http://www.microsoft.com/windows/windowsmedia/en/partners/).

Streaming PowerPoint
Presentations

Figure 8.5.

*An Outlook
2000 meeting
request.*

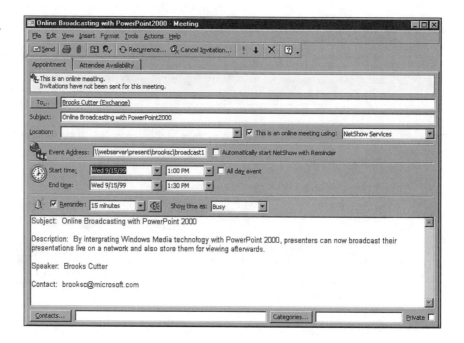

When you're finished with the **Server Options** dialog box, click **OK.** Click **OK** on the **Schedule a New Broadcast** dialog box. PowerPoint will proceed to validate your settings and make sure the appropriate directories exist and everything will work properly. If you've chosen not to use a Windows Media server, PowerPoint will remind you that no more than 15 end users will be able to view your live presentation and a Windows Media server should be used to scale beyond 15 end users.

Creating a meeting request

The last step in scheduling your presentation is to create an Outlook 2000 meeting request with the event information. PowerPoint will create this automatically, and you need to fill in the details, including the time the presentation will begin and end.

If you don't have Outlook 2000 installed, PowerPoint will create an e-mail with your default mail program that includes the details. You'll lose the ability to schedule the time the presentation begins and ends, but you can still send an e-mail message describing the presentation. If you don't use Microsoft Exchange as your messaging system, another option is to install Outlook 2000 and configure it to send e-mail over Simple Mail Transfer Protocol (SMTP). This way you can still schedule the date and time of your presentation and Outlook will send the meeting request to others using the Internet Calendaring standard iCal. Figure 8.5 shows an Outlook 2000 meeting request.

After you've sent the Outlook Meeting request, PowerPoint will confirm that the presentation has been successfully scheduled.

Congratulations! You've now scheduled the presentation and the meeting notice has been distributed to the participants! Before the scheduled time arrives, plan to spend 15 to 30 minutes setting up everything and making sure there won't be any technical problems. Going through the pre-presentation setup will take about five minutes, but it's good to have the extra time to resolve any issues before the scheduled start time.

Giving a presentation

This section walks you through the presenting process. It also discusses the Presenter status window, the Lobby page, and how to best prepare for a presentation.

To give a presentation

1. Set up your computer in the room in which you'll be presenting.

2. On the **Start** menu of your computer, point to **Programs**, and then click **Microsoft PowerPoint.**

3. Select **Online Broadcast** from the **Slide Show** menu.

4. Select **Begin Broadcast** from the **Online Broadcast** menu.

> **TIP** The information configured when you select **Set Up and Schedule** for the presentation is stored in the PowerPoint .ppt file. You can schedule a presentation on one computer and move to another computer to give the presentation, as long as you bring the PowerPoint .ppt file with you.

Selecting **Begin Broadcast** opens the **Broadcast Presentation** dialog box, which will run through a series of quick tests to confirm everything is working before your presentation. Specifically, PowerPoint checks the input from the microphone and adjusts the volume level, it checks for a video signal and shows you what will be broadcast so you can center the camera on the presenter, and it tests connectivity to Windows Media Encoder. Figure 8.6 shows the **Broadcast Presentation** dialog box.

The purpose of the microphone check is to confirm that PowerPoint is able to receive audio from the microphone and allow it to adjust the volume level based on the peaks. Speak normally into the microphone you'll be using during the presentation and make sure the green progress bar changes length while you are speaking. Figure 8.7 shows the **Microphone Check** dialog box.

> **TIP** Another quick way to check the audio level and the quality of the recording is to use Microsoft® Sound Recorder in Windows. To launch Sound recorder, click **Start**, point to **Programs**, point to **Accessories**, point to **Multimedia**, and then click **Sound Recorder.** You can quickly record a clip and play it back to see if the presenter can be heard clearly. If not, check your sound card or try using a better microphone.

Streaming PowerPoint Presentations

Figure 8.6.

The Broadcast Presentation dialog box.

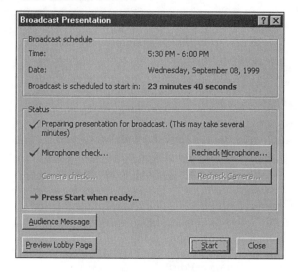

Figure 8.7.

The Microphone Check dialog box.

If you've indicated you'll broadcast video from this computer, the next window you'll see is the **Video Check** dialog box. Use this dialog box to view the video that will be transmitted to the audience as part of your presentation. This is a good time to make sure the video is centered on the presenter.

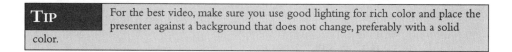

| TIP | For the best video, make sure you use good lighting for rich color and place the presenter against a background that does not change, preferably with a solid color. |

When you're done with the audio/video check, return to the **Broadcast Presentation** dialog box, which is where you wait until it's time for you to begin your presentation. If you are broadcasting the event live, your audience will begin to show up in the "lobby" before the presentation begins. If you'd like to view this page, click **Preview Lobby**

Page. Figure 8.8 shows the Presentation Broadcast Lobby Page. The lobby page describes the presentation; end users wait at this page until the presentation begins.

If you'd like to communicate with the audience, you can type one-line messages to them by selecting **Audience Message**. You may also need to use this if your presentation is delayed.

Figure 8.8.

The Presentation Broadcast Lobby Page.

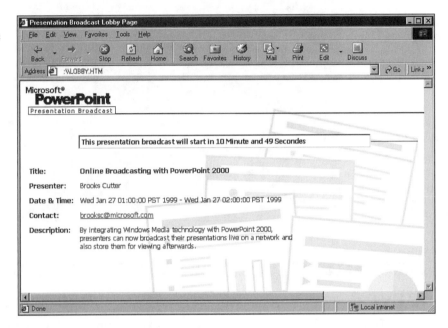

When it's time for your presentation to start, PowerPoint will ask you if you want to begin. PowerPoint will display the slides in full-screen mode, as if you were giving a regular presentation, and the audio/video of your presentation will be broadcast with your slide changes synchronized with your presentation.

Your end users will see an image similar to the picture in Figure 8.9. Based on how you configured PowerPoint in the Schedule a New Broadcast window, your presentation may include the **E-mail Feedback** and **Online Chat** buttons shown in Figure 8.9.

After you've finished your presentation, you can replay it. To learn how to replay a presentation, read "Archiving the presentation" later in this chapter.

Streaming PowerPoint Presentations

Figure 8.9.

An online broadcast.

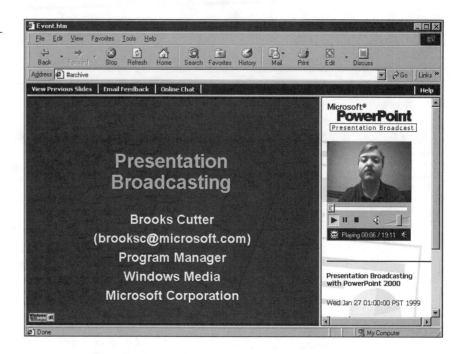

Streaming with a Windows Media server

This section describes the software required to stream through a Windows Media server and lists setup requirements.

The previous two sections discussed configuring PowerPoint 2000 to broadcast a presentation without using a Windows Media server. Using Windows Media Encoder to stream directly to end users is a convenient way to broadcast small workgroup presentations. However, without using a server, you lose a number of benefits including greater scalability, intelligent streaming, and multicast support.

To stream a presentation using a Windows Media server, you first need to have a Windows Media server installed, as described in Chapter 4, "Using Windows Media Services." Next, you need to have the Online Presentation Broadcast service installed. This enables PowerPoint 2000 to automatically configure the Windows Media server. This service is included with Microsoft Windows Media Technologies version 4.0, or you can install it onto an existing Windows Media server from the Office 2000 Resource Kit.

After you install the Online Presentation Broadcast service, you must configure the service before end users will be able to access it. The steps required to configure it are described in detail in the Windows Media Services documentation (Netshow.chm), which can be installed from the Welcome page of the JumpStart CD included with this book; these steps are also in an online broadcasting article on the Microsoft Personal Online Support Web site (http://support.microsoft.com/support/kb/articles/q229/9/51.asp). An overview of the setup requirements follows:

1. Create a Windows NT Domain account, under which the Online Presentation Broadcast service will run. This account must have read privileges on any file server where the slides are stored. This is required so the service can configure the server to support the presentation.

2. On the server where the Online Presentation Broadcast service is installed, configure the service to start using the Windows NT Domain account created in the previous step. If you change the password for this end user account, you must also update the server.

3. On the Windows Media server, add each presenter to the **Administrators** and **NetShow Administrators** group. This is required because it enables the Online Presentation Broadcast service to configure the Windows Media server.

4. Test the configuration by creating a sample presentation and configure it to use the Windows Media server.

If you have questions about the steps outlined above, see the Windows Media Services (Netshow.chm) documentation, which can be installed from the Welcome page of the JumpStart CD included with this book. This documentation discusses each item, step by step.

Archiving the presentation

This section describes how to archive a presentation to a CD-ROM or Web server and explains what changes may be required.

If you've instructed PowerPoint 2000 to record the presentation, it will record an .asf file, which contains the audio, the video (if selected), and the slide synchronizations. If you open the directory you specified, either in the **Record the broadcast and save it in:** dialog box or under Server Options as **Specify a shared location**, several subdirectories will be created under the directory you specify.

Navigate through the directory structure to find a series of files that include the slides saved in HTML format; the frame set used to show the slides, embed the player, display the menu, and so on; and the .asf file (if you chose to save it in this directory).

To watch the previously recorded presentation, open the **default.htm** page. You will first see the Lobby page, which displays some information about the presentation. During a live presentation, you will see a countdown timer. In this case, however, you should see a note that says "The presentation broadcast has ended" and a button to the right labeled **Replay Broadcast**. Click this button and the presentation should begin.

Streaming PowerPoint Presentations

> **NOTE**   If you just finished recording the presentation and do not see the **Replay Broadcast** button, it may be that the presentation was scheduled to end at a time later than the current time. That is, PowerPoint 2000 thinks the presentation is in progress and will not show the **Replay Broadcast** button until the time specified for the presentation to end has passed.

When a presentation is recorded, PowerPoint 2000 stores the paths to the files in a file called global.js. If you open this file in Microsoft Notepad, you will see that it contains a series of key-value pairs that specify settings such as where the slides are stored, where the .asf file is stored, the e-mail address of the presenter, and so on.

To move the presentation to a different computer, make the following changes in the global.js file:

```
BASE_URL = "";
ARCHIVE_URL = "<filename.asf>"
```

This will change the **BASE_URL** to blank and point the **ARCHIVE_URL** directly to the .asf file, not to a fully qualified path.

> **NOTE**   This procedure is based on the assumption that the .asf file is in the same directory. Don't make these changes to the global.js file unless you plan to leave all the files together in the same directory. By leaving the files, you enable end users to retrieve slides from the file share and play Windows Media content from the file share.

The best way to archive a presentation and make it available on the Internet, or on an intranet, is to put the slides on a Web server and make the .asf file available for streaming from a Windows Media server. To do this, change the same values (discussed previously) in global.js, but change them in the following way:

```
BASE_URL = "http://webserver/pp2000/";
ARCHIVE_URL = "mms://windowsmedia/<filename.asf>"
```

In other words, you should:

1. Change BASE_URL to be the base URL of the presentation. For example, if you have a Web server named *webserver*, and you put it in a directory off the root (for Microsoft Internet Information Server the default is C:\Inetpub\Wwwroot) named *pp2000*, the URL to the slides would then be http://*webserver/pp2000/*.

2. Change ARCHIVE_URL to the URL of the .asf file. For example, if you have a Windows Media server named *windowsmedia* and you place the .asf file in the root directory (normally C:\Asfroot), the URL to the clip would then be mms://*windowsmedia/filename*.asf.

Many other fields in the global.js file can be customized after a presentation has ended. After you've made these changes you can move the presentation to another computer.

Customizing Presentation Broadcasting

This section describes how end users can customize Presentation Broadcasting, including changing the audio/video encoding templates and the logos or Web pages used for the presentation.

When end users view a presentation recorded with the Presentation Broadcasting feature, they view the slides, the audio/video of the presenter, and the overall menu structure in their Web browser. If you wish, you can customize much of what the end user sees (from changing the logo to the layout of the entire screen).

To see what you can customize, first open the Broadcast folder in the directory where Office 2000 was installed on your computer. For most computers, this is C:\Program Files\Microsoft Office\Office. In this folder there are about 17 files; these files include Web pages, images, and Windows Media Encoder templates.

The first thing you may want to customize is the audio or video encoding settings. PowerPoint 2000 encodes all video at 100 Kbps, which requires a high-speed network connection, such as a LAN network, or ISDN for remote access. If you would like end users on a dial-up modem to be able to view your presentation, then you'll want to configure the encoder to encode video at 28.8 Kbps or 56 Kbps, depending on what speed modems your audience will use. Double-click the **audio.asd** or **video.asd** templates, which should then start Windows Media Encoder and load the appropriate template. For more information on configuring Windows Media Encoder, see Chapter 3, "Using Windows Media Tools." After you have finished, save the encoder configuration back to disk.

You may want to consider further customizing the presentation in the following ways:

- Brand the presentation by changing the LOGO.GIF and NS_LOGO.GIF images.

- Add a new command to the menu by editing the FEEDBACK.HTM Web page.

- Customize the lobby page by changing the LOBBY.HTM Web page.

- Make further changes to the presentation structure by changing NSFRAME.HTM.

Before making changes, you should make sure that you back up the original files so you can replace them, if needed. After you change these files in your Broadcast folder, you can create a new presentation that will reflect the changes you made or copy these files to a previously archived presentation. In the latter case, you can change the Web pages after a presentation has been recorded, although you cannot change the size or bandwidth of the recorded audio/video.

Streaming PowerPoint Presentations

Deploying Presentation Broadcasting

For companies that want to deploy Presentation Broadcasting widely, as part of Office 2000, this section describes how to pre-configure the product to make deployment easier.

If you are planning to deploy Office 2000 within your organization, you should first read the Office 2000 Resource Kit, which contains information on planning, deploying, managing, and supporting Office 2000 (http://www.microsoft.com/office/ork/2000/).

In Chapter 5 of the Office 2000 Resource Kit, titled "Office 2000 and the Web," you'll find the section, "Broadcasting PowerPoint presentations over the Network." This section walks you through configuring a presentation, configuring a remote encoder or Windows Media server, best practices for maintaining the server, and options for pre-configuring clients to support the Presentation Broadcasting feature.

For more information about Presentation Broadcasting, see the Office 2000 Resource Kit (http://www.microsoft.com/office/ork/2000/), which includes additional details on customizing and administering this feature. The Help files in Office 2000 and in Windows Media Technologies 4.0 also contain valuable information about using this feature.

Summary

Using PowerPoint 2000 Presentation Broadcasting, you can create a streaming PowerPoint presentation across a network. Some features of streaming presentations include adding the presenter's audio and video material, synchronizing the slides with the presenter's speech, saving the presentations as on-demand files, and creating interactive presentations that allow the presenter and members of the audience to communicate online.

When using Presentation Broadcasting, you need to set up computers for the presenter, the audience, the file server, the Windows Media server, and the chat server, depending on your particular situation. Before you deliver a presentation, you need to set it up, schedule it, and then inform your audience of the event. After you have delivered the presentation, you can archive it as an on-demand .asf file.

Chapter 9, "Designing and Developing with Windows Media Technologies," provides information about developing applications and scripts to customize Windows Media Technologies.

Chapter

9

Designing and Developing Using Windows Media Technologies

This chapter provides advanced information about ways you can use and customize components of Microsoft Windows Media Technologies by developing your own applications and scripts. Advanced topics include how to create synchronized multimedia, use Microsoft Windows Media Player in a Web page, use .asx files to do a variety of things, add script commands to an .asf file, program Windows Media Player, and automate Windows Media Encoder. Several code examples are provided to give you a head start; the code listings in this chapter are on the JumpStart CD that is included with this book.

After reading this chapter, you'll be able to answer the following questions:

- What is synchronized multimedia?
- How can I play media files from within a Web page?
- How can I embed Windows Media Player in a Web page?
- What are redirector files, and what are they used for?
- What are playlists, and how can I create them?
- How can I use script commands to control the Web browser?
- How can I control Windows Media Player in a Web page?
- How do I create code to handle events in different Web browsers?
- How do I include URLs and text with a multimedia presentation?
- How can I automate Windows Media Encoder?

Understanding synchronized multimedia

Synchronized multimedia enables you to coordinate the events between Windows Media Player and a Web browser. When you use source content from a traditional medium, such as videotape, it loses some of its original impact and only provides the end user with a passive experience. End users of this media simply sit and view the programming. However, computer users are accustomed to doing more than simply staring at a computer screen for a long time, and computers are capable of providing end users with a more robust, interactive experience.

Synchronized multimedia helps create an environment that engages audiences and enables content authors to communicate their message more effectively.

Synchronized multimedia is a concept, not a technology, so there are several different methods to create it. One method is to use HTML+TIME (timed interactive multimedia extensions)—a standards-based syntax for timing and synchronization in HTML documents. Support for HTML+TIME has been added to Microsoft Internet Explorer 5. In addition, Microsoft has included an HTML+TIME authoring tool called Vizact in Microsoft® Office 2000.

Another method of creating synchronized multimedia is to take advantage of some of the features built into Advanced Streaming Format (ASF) and Microsoft Windows Media Player. Before you can take advantage of features such as the .asx and .wax redirector files, script commands, and playlists, you need to embed Windows Media Player into a Web page.

Using Windows Media Player in a Web page

Windows Media player and a Web browser can be used together to create a fulfilling end-user experience. There are two methods of using Windows Media Player in a Web page: the stand-alone method and the embedded method.

A stand-alone instance of Windows Media Player opens in a window that is separate from the browser window. With this configuration, an end user can continue using the browser while simultaneously receiving a media stream.

The stand-alone method uses standard HTML anchor tags to insert links to content that is played in Windows Media Player. The anchor tags link to the .asx or .wax redirector files that point to the content. The following anchor tag can be added to a Web page to start a stand-alone instance of Windows Media Player.

```
<a href ="/media/filename.asx">Click here</a>
```

If you want to create a more polished, interactive Web page, you can embed Windows Media Player. Use the Windows Media Player ActiveX control to embed the player in Internet Explorer, or use the plug-in to embed the player in Netscape Navigator. Listing 9.1 can be used to embed Windows Media Player in either Internet Explorer or Netscape Navigator. The example script in Listing 9.1 also supports browsers that do not support embedding:

```
<body bgcolor="ff0000">
<br clear=all>
<!— GENERIC ALL BROWSER FRIENDLY HTML FOR WINDOWS MEDIA PLAYER 6.4 —>
<script language="JavaScript">
<!—
    if ( navigator.appName == "Netscape" )
    {
//— This next line ensures that any recently installed plug-ins are
updated in the browser
        //— without quitting the browser.
        navigator.plugins.refresh();
        //— The applet is only needed for event handling. Uncomment it
if needed.
        //document.write("\x3C" + "applet MAYSCRIPT
Code=NPDS.npDSEvtObsProxy.class" )
        //document.writeln(" width=5 height=5 name=appObs\x3E
\x3C/applet\x3E")
    }
//—>
</script>
<OBJECT ID="NSPlay" WIDTH=360 HEIGHT=320 classid="CLSID:22d6f312-b0f6-
11d0-94ab-0080c74c7e95"
 CODEBASE="http://activex.microsoft.com/activex/controls/mplayer/en/
nsmp2inf.cab#Version=6,4,5,715"
```

```
        standby="Loading Microsoft Windows Media Player components..."
type="application/x-oleobject">
<PARAM NAME="FileName" VALUE="http://server/file.asx">
  <Embed type="application/x-mplayer2"
    pluginspage="http://www.microsoft.com/isapi/redir.dll?prd=windows&sbp=
mediaplayer&ar=Media&sba=Plugin&"
      src="http://server/file.asx"
      Name=NSPlay
      ShowControls=1
      ShowDisplay=0
      ShowStatusBar=0
      width=360
      height=320
  >
 </embed>
</OBJECT>
<br>
<a href="http://server/file.asx">Start the presentation in the stand-
alone player.</a>
</body>
```

Using ASF Stream Redirector files

ASX scripting provides you with tools to enhance your end-users' experience and to potentially generate revenue from advertising. Playlists can easily be used to set up jukebox pages, online training material, personalized programming, and corporate information presentations. Events introduce an interactive element to broadcasts.

ASF Stream Redirector (.asx) and Window Media Audio Redirector (.wax) files are powerful tools for controlling Windows Media Player. ASX format files are a text-based collection of custom Extensible Markup Language (XML) tags. The tags specify a sophisticated set of elements that are supported by Windows Media Player. Windows Media Player opens an .asx file and responds to the XML elements.

> **NOTE** Windows Media Audio Redirector files (.asx files given the .wax file name extension) are used to introduce Windows Media Audio .asf files. By using .wax as the extension, Windows Media Player renders the incoming .wma on-demand file as an audio-only stream. The .wax files are an excellent way to create playlists of songs for devices, such as mobile audio players, that can only render audio content.

Windows Media Player supports a number of ASX tags that perform a variety of tasks that include:

■ Providing an alternate URL to use if the transmission from the primary source fails.

■ Arranging a collection of short multimedia titles into a full-featured presentation.

■ Inserting advertisements into a presentation.

- Adding banners and logos to a presentation.

- Playing a brief preview of each track in a presentation.

- Adding descriptive information about the multimedia content.

ASX format files were originally designed to transfer the control of data from Web browsers to Windows Media Player. However, they have evolved into a lot more. They are now called *metafiles* because they perform actions on other files. ASX format files support the XML syntax and can be used to perform a variety of complex tasks.

The history of ASX

In the early days of Windows Media Technologies (when it was called Microsoft NetShow), many browsers did not recognize the protocols used for streaming media. This made it difficult to link directly from a Web page to a Windows Media server. Developers needed a way to prevent browsers from trying to download the presentation and enable the server to stream it instead. The solution was to create ASF Stream Redirector files that contained a reference to the title on the Windows Media server. Several ASX versions have been created; the version of the .asx file determines which features it can support.

ASX version 1 files were extremely small. As a result, the information could be downloaded quickly onto the client computer.

ASX version 2 was built on version 1 and provided support for two new features:

- **Rollover URL.** An alternate URL could be included in the .asx file. If the player had trouble locating and playing the primary URL, it could attempt to play the rollover URL.

- **Direct link to an .nsc file.** The URL of a NetShow station descriptor file containing stream format information about a multicast could be included in an .asx file.

The latest version, ASX version 3, is used in Windows Media Technologies version 4.0 and provides support for the following features:

- **Playlists.** Media files are contained in a list; the files are played in order, one after the other.

- **Overriding metadata in the .asf file.** Display properties, such as title and author, that are contained in an .asf file are overridden by the same information included in an .asx file.

- **Advertising.** Scripting that can be added to an .asx file that displays an advertising banner in Windows Media Player. A URL can be associated with the banner and other areas of the player; an end user can click the URL to browse to a site for more information or to send e-mail.

- **Event syntax.** A method of switching between a live broadcast stream and media files specified in a playlist. During a broadcast, script commands are sent that instruct all instances of Windows Media Player to seamlessly switch from playing the broadcast to playing the files. When the player reaches the end of the playlist, it can switch back to the broadcast.

The following examples show what you can do with .asx files. For a description of all of the ASX-supported tags, see "Using ASX metafiles" in the Windows Media Player Control Software Development Kit (SDK) and the section called "ASX Metafile Reference" in the Windows Media Services documentation (Newshow.chm); both can be installed from the Welcome page of the JumpStart CD included with this book.

Announcing a presentation

The simplest form of an .asx file contains an entry specifying one .asf file. This type of .asx file is commonly called an *announcement*. The .asx file can be sent in an e-mail message or posted on a Web site. A client that runs the .asx file is directed to the specified .asf file.

Listing 9.2 shows a simple announcement file:

```
<ASX>
        <ENTRY> <REF href = "http://MediaServer1/SampleVideo.ASF"
        /></ENTRY>
</ASX>
```

The <REF> tag specifies the location of the presentation being announced.

Building a playlist

One compelling feature of .asx files is the ability to arrange a collection of multimedia clips into a show or playlist. When dealing with playlists, Windows Media Player uses the concept of clips and shows. A *clip* refers to the track currently being rendered, and a *show* refers to all of the tracks specified in the .asx file.

Listing 9.3 shows an ASX playlist with four different clips arranged into a show:

```
<ASX>
        <ENTRY> <REF href = "http://MediaServer1/Clip1.ASF" /> </ENTRY>
        <ENTRY> <REF href = "http://MediaServer1/Clip2.ASF" /> </ENTRY>
        <ENTRY> <REF href = "http://MediaServer1/Clip3.ASF" /> </ENTRY>
        <ENTRY> <REF href = "http://MediaServer1/Clip4.ASF" /> </ENTRY>
</ASX>
```

Each <ENTRY> element contains information about one clip. The <REF> element specifies the location of the multimedia clip. Windows Media Player opens the .asx file and renders each of the specified .asf files in the order listed.

Adding clip and show descriptions

With .asx files, you can add information describing the clip and the show. This information includes, among other things, the title, author, copyright, and rating of each clip and of the entire show. The information is presented to the end user on the display panel of Windows Media Player. It can also be accessed from the Windows Media Player property pages. You can also access this information programmatically, using the **GetMediaInfoString** method of the Windows Media Player ActiveX control.

Figure 9.1 shows Windows Media Player with show and clip information from an .asx file in the display panel:

Figure 9.1.

*Show and clip
information.*

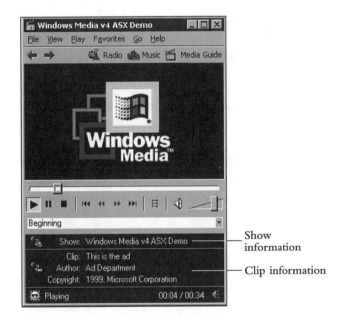

Listing 9.4 shows ASX code that demonstrates how clip and show information can be added to a presentation:

```
<ASX Version="3.0">

<TITLE>"Sample Show"</TITLE>

<AUTHOR>"Windows Media Team"</AUTHOR>
<COPYRIGHT>"© 1999, Microsoft Corporation"</COPYRIGHT>
```

```
<ENTRY>
        <TITLE>"Sample Clip Number 1"</TITLE>
        <AUTHOR>"Kim Abercrombie"</AUTHOR>
        <COPYRIGHT>"© 1999, Microsoft Corporation"</COPYRIGHT>
        <REF href = "http://MediaServer1/Sample1.ASF" />
        </ENTRY>
        <ENTRY>
        <TITLE>"Sample Clip Number 2"</TITLE>
        <AUTHOR>"Ketan Dalal"</AUTHOR>
        <COPYRIGHT>"© 1999, Microsoft Corporation"</COPYRIGHT>
        <REF href = "http://MediaServer1/Sample2.ASF" />
</ENTRY>
</ASX>
```

The first <Title>, <Author>, and <Copyright> tags provide global information for the entire show. Subsequent <Title>, <Author>, and <Copyright> tags are enclosed in the <Entry> tags, and describe their respective clips.

You can also define your own parameters for clip and show information. The ASX <PARAM> tag includes name/value pairs that specify more information for Windows Media Player. For example, Listing 9.5 could be used to add producer and director information to a presentation:

```
<PARAM Name="Director" Value="Katan Dalal" />
<PARAM Name="Producer" Value="Kim Abercrombie" />
```

Creating playlists with ad insertions

Playing a sequential list of ASF clips is the simplest form of a playlist. However, with ASX, you can do a lot more.

Listing 9.6 shows the XML code that could be used to insert advertisements periodically into a live stream. It plays the live radio feed for 30 minutes, and then an advertisement is played. After playing the advertisement, playback returns to the live feed for another 30 minutes:

```
<ASX Version = "3.0">
<REPEAT>
        <ENTRY>
        <TITLE>"Live Feed From Radio Station"</TITLE>
        <DURATION Value = "30:00" />
        <REF href = "mms://MediaServer1/RadioStation" />
        </ENTRY>

        <ENTRY>
        <TITLE>"Advertisement 2"</TITLE>
        <REF href = "http://MediaServer1/Ad2.ASF" />
        </ENTRY>
</REPEAT>

</ASX>
```

The previous example shows how easy it is to use ASX to introduce your content and insert advertisements. It also demonstrates how powerful ASX can be for creating a compelling show and generating a revenue stream.

Processing script commands with ASX

Advanced Streaming Format files can send script commands to Windows Media Player at specific times in the presentation. These script commands consist of two strings. The first string specifies the *type* of command and the second string specifies a command parameter. *Events* are one type of script command processed by Windows Media Player. The command parameter of an event script contains the name of the event. When Windows Media Player receives an event script command, it searches the .asx file for an <EVENT> element with a matching name. If a match is found, control of Windows Media Player switches to the commands contained in the <EVENT> element.

The ASX script in Listing 9.6 plays a live stream in 30-minute intervals. This can be useful, but in most cases the timing of live events is not so predictable. By using script commands in conjunction with event scripting, timing is controlled manually at the point where the stream is being encoded. Instead of playing the advertisement at consistent intervals, the content author can determine when the advertisement is streamed.

In Listing 9.7, Windows Media Player opens the .asx file and starts streaming the radio station content. The radio station plays until Windows Media Player receives an event type script command with "Advertisement" as the command parameter. Windows Media Player stops playing the radio station content, and plays the advertisement. With the WHENDONE tag set to RESUME, Windows Media Player returns to playing the live radio content when the advertisement finishes:

```
<ASX Version="3.0">
<ENTRY>
        <TITLE>"Live Feed From Radio Station"</TITLE>
        <REF href = "mms://MediaServer1/RadioStation" />
</ENTRY>

<EVENT Name="Advertisement" Whendone="RESUME">
        <ENTRY ClientSkip="No">
        <TITLE>"Advertisement"</TITLE>
        <REF href = "http://MediaServer1/Advertisement.ASF" />
        </ENTRY>
</EVENT>
</ASX>
```

Switching media streams

By preceding an EVENT type script command with an OPENEVENT command, the switch between the live stream and on-demand event can be seamless. Normally when a switch is made between streams, a pause occurs while Windows Media Player stops the current stream and buffers incoming data. However, if an OPENEVENT command is sent five to 10 seconds prior to when a switch should take place, Windows Media Player prebuffers a portion of the incoming content. When it receives the EVENT command, Windows Media Player is able to cut to the new content seamlessly by playing the prebuffered data. The amount that a player buffers is determined by the **Buffer** value in the player **Advanced playback settings** dialog box.

Ten seconds before a switch from a live stream to an on-demand event is to take place, send a script command with type OPENEVENT and command "Advertisement". Ten seconds later send a script command with type EVENT and command "Advertisement," and Windows Media Player will switch seamlessly to the event.

Adding script commands to an .asf file

The power of ASF is its ability to send script commands that are timed within an ASF stream. These commands are not handled intrinsically by Windows Media Player but are instead handled by the underlying JavaScript environment in both Netscape Navigator and Internet Explorer. You can use these commands to create rich, dynamic, multimedia content.

By using script commands in an ASF stream, you can command the browser to do anything that the browser supports. You can enable the Windows Media Player control to interact with dynamic HTML, Java applets, plug-ins, and more.

The most powerful event in Windows Media Player is the *ScriptCommand* event. Normally, events happen at predetermined times, such as when a file begins or ends. With the *ScriptCommand* event, you can create custom interaction between the player and the browser. A script command is just like any other Windows Media Player event, except that, with it, you can send whatever kind of data you want to the browser.

Script commands can be added to an .asf file using Windows Media ASF In-dexer. Script commands can also be added to live streams from within Windows Media Encoder or during encoding with Windows Media On-Demand Producer. For more information about adding script commands to .asf files using these tools, see Chapter 3, "Using Windows Media Tools."

Creating URL script commands

The most common type of script command is the **URL** command. This script command is very easy to include, because Windows Media Player handles it intrinsically, with no programming involved. Unlike other events, neither the plug-in nor the player needs a callback method, because the player will launch the specified URL in the specified window automatically. The script command type is **URL** in all capital letters. The parameter data is the URL, followed by a double ampersand delimiter, and then the name of the frame into which the player will put the URL. With the double ampersand, Windows Media Player can determine where the URL ends and where the frame name begins.

For example, if you want to place the file myFile.htm into a frame named bullseye, the parameter syntax looks like the following example:

```
http://myserver/path/myFile.htm&&bullseye
```

The preceding script command works well in the stand-alone instance of Windows Media Player, the Windows Media Player ActiveX control, and the Windows Media Player plug-in.

Creating TEXT script commands

Another script command that Windows Media Player handles intrinsically is the **TEXT** script command. With this command, you can put data into the Windows Media Player closed-captioned text display panel with no programming. The closed-captioned text display panel is below the video screen on Windows Media Player. It can be accessed in the stand-alone version of Windows Media Player, the Windows Media Player ActiveX control, and the Windows Media Player plug-in.

The closed-captioned text display panel itself is a base HTML-rendering engine that you can use to include HTML and images. For example, it is simple to include not only captioning text but hyperlinks, stock quotes, or just about anything else, though the area is limited to the width and height of the captioning window.

For example, if you want to create a hyperlink in the closed-captioned text display panel, create a script command of type **TEXT**, with a parameter of:

```
<A HREF="http://myServer/path/myFile.htm" TARGET="_blank"><FONT
➥COLOR="#ffffff">Link</FONT></LINK>
```

If the client is embedded, the *ShowCaptioning* parameter of Windows Media Player must be set to **True**. This enables the player to display the text. In the stand-alone player, the end user must turn on captions by clicking the **View** menu and then clicking **Captions**.

> **NOTE** Do not put too much data into a script command. The maximum length of any script command, including the type, parameter, and time, is 255 characters. If you exceed 255 characters, the script command is truncated to fit within this limitation.

Creating custom script commands

Handling custom script commands is a lot like handling any other event in Windows Media Player. The browser receives the *ScriptCommand* event, along with two parameters. The first parameter is used to determine the type of script command that is being sent. Then your JavaScript code can perform whatever functionality you specify using the second parameter of the script command as data.

For example, you might create a script command event called *swapImage*. Through code handled by the *ScriptCommand* event, you could change the **SRC** attribute of an <IMG> tag based on the data held in the second parameter of the script command.

Listing 9.8 shows some simple Internet Explorer code to handle a custom script command:

```
<SCRIPT FOR="MediaPlayer1" EVENT="ScriptCommand(bstrType, bstrParam)"
➥LANGUAGE="Jscript">
if (bstrType.toLowerCase() == "caption") {
        document.all.contentIE.innerHTML = bstrParam;
} else if (bstrType.toLowerCase() == "swapimage") {
document.dynImage.src = imgArr[bstrParam].src;
}
</SCRIPT>
```

For the Windows Media Player plug-in, you first must register the *ScriptCommand* event handler during the onload event. This is carried out like any other event, as shown in Listing 9.9:

```
function loader(){
        if ((navigator.userAgent.indexOf('IE') > -1) &&
➥(navigator.platform == "Win32")) {
        bControl = true;
        } else {
        var plugIn = document.MediaPlayer1;
        bControl = false;
            // listen for ScriptCommand event
        document.appObs.setByProxyDSScriptCommandObserver(plugIn,true);
        }
        document.MediaPlayer1.Play();
        }
```

When the event is registered, it will attempt to call **OnDSScriptCommandEvt** whenever a script command is detected. The code in Listing 9.10 is an example of **OnDSScriptCommandEvt**:

```
function OnDSScriptCommandEvt (bstrType, bstrParam){
        if (bstrType.toLowerCase() == "caption") {
        var sCommand;
        sCommand = "document.contentNav.document.writeln(\"";
        sCommand = sCommand + bstrParam;
        sCommand = sCommand + "\");document.contentNav.document.close();
```

```
                    ";
            timerID = setTimeout(sCommand,0);
            } else if (bstrType.toLowerCase() == "swapimage") {
            timerID = setTimeout("document.dynImage.src = imgArr[" + bstrParam
➥+ "].src",0);
            }
            }
```

Programming and Windows Media Player

One of the strengths of Windows Media Player is that it's programmable. It features more than 100 properties, 20 methods, and 20 events, all of which are available to the content author. Many of the properties of Windows Media Player are *available read/write properties*. This means that they can be updated in the Web page as content plays. For example, based on end user input, the content author can change the file name property of Windows Media Player in the middle of a stream, causing a new file to load into the player.

Using the 20 methods of Windows Media Player, the content author can perform a myriad of tasks, from starting and stopping the player, to seeing how much of the file has been buffered before playback.

Windows Media Player events, sometimes called callback methods, enable dynamic, synchronized multimedia presentations. When something happens in Windows Media Player, such as when the stream finishes playing, the player sends an event that is exposed to the content author.

For more information about the properties, methods, and events that can be programmed, see the Windows Media Player Control SDK, which can be installed from the Welcome page of the JumpStart CD included with this book.

Controlling Windows Media Player with scripts

Writing script for Windows Media Player (after the Windows Media Player control has been embedded in a page) can be as easy as clicking **Play** in Windows Media Player. The following line of code makes a call through the scripting Document Object Model (DOM) to the player, invoking the **Play** method:

```
document.MediaPlayer1.Play();
```

NOTE	DOM describes the way elements on a Web page are addressed.

Methods are handled similarly in both the Windows Media Player ActiveX control and the Netscape Navigator plug-in.

Pausing and stopping Windows Media Player are handled in the same way:

```
document.MediaPlayer1.Pause();
document.MediaPlayer1.Stop();
```

If Windows Media Player resides in another frame in the Web page, the code might look like this:

```
parent.frames[0].document.MediaPlayer1.Pause();
```

Using Windows Media Player methods makes it easier to create script to customize the player. Listing 9.11 shows an example of creating custom buttons in Windows Media Player.

```
<FORM NAME="myButtons">
   <INPUT NAME="btnPlay" TYPE="Button" VALUE="Play" onclick=
➥"document.MediaPlayer1.Play();">
   <INPUT NAME="btnPause" TYPE="Button" VALUE="Pause" onclick=
➥"document.MediaPlayer1.Pause();">
   <INPUT NAME="btnStop" TYPE="Button" VALUE="Stop" onclick=
➥"document.MediaPlayer1.Stop();">
</FORM>
```

Using Windows Media Player properties

Because Internet Explorer uses the ActiveX model for incorporating components into HTML pages, and Netscape Navigator uses its own plug-in architecture, you must write your code in a way that will work in both environments. Through the ActiveX model, properties, methods, and events can be accessed directly through DOM. Through the plug-in model, only methods can be passed directly to the browser. For code to work in both browsers, it has to perform a *browser check* (sometimes called a *browser sniff*) and run browser-specific code.

The Windows Media Player methods (**Play**, **Pause**, **Stop**, and so on) work with both the ActiveX control and the Netscape Navigator plug-in without modification. However, modifying Windows Media Player properties requires different scripting syntax for the ActiveX control and the plug-in. For a given property, such as the read/write **FileName** property, plug-in code must access the property using the **SetPropertyName** and **GetPropertyName** methods.

The following statement for ActiveX browsers:

```
MediaPlayer1.FileName = "demo.asf";
```

is analogous to the following statement for the plug-in:

```
MediaPlayer1.SetFileName("demo.asf");
```

This code would set the **FileName** property of Windows Media Player to Demo.asf, interrupting play by assigning a new file for Windows Media Player to play.

To get information about a property of the Windows Media Player plug-in, the property must be retrieved by invoking a **GetPropertyName** method. For example, the following statement for ActiveX browsers:

```
var sFileLoc = document.MediaPlayer1.FileName;
```

is analogous to the following statement for the plug-in:

```
var sFileLoc = document.MediaPlayer1.GetFileName();
```

All that remains is to place both pieces of code into the same script. First, do a browser check. To perform a simple check, determine whether the end user is running a platform that supports the Windows Media Player ActiveX control. ActiveX controls run in Microsoft® Internet Explorer version 3.0 or later on 32-bit Windows platforms. The easiest way to check for this is to look at the **navigator** object. One of the most important properties of this object is the "navigator.userAgent" string.

Using the intrinsic Microsoft® JScript® **indexOf()** function, it is easy to determine whether the end user is running Internet Explorer or some other browser. The following line of code returns the position in the "userAgent" string of the letters "MSIE". If these letters are not found, **indexOf()** returns –1:

```
navigator.userAgent.indexOf("MSIE")
```

Because Internet Explorer is available on a wide variety of platforms that do not support ActiveX controls (including UNIX and Macintosh), you must also check for the platform on which the end user's computer is running. Microsoft® Internet Explorer version 4.0 added a property of the navigator object (called the navigator platform) that helps you do this.

Now put it all together and perform both checks simultaneously, as shown in Listing 9.12. Check to see whether **navigator.userAgent** contains a string with the consecutive letters "MSIE". Also, make sure the platform is "Win32". Win32 is the value contained in the navigator platform property when the computer is running on Microsoft Windows 95, Microsoft Windows 98, Microsoft Windows NT Server version 4.0, and Microsoft Windows NT Workstation 4.0:

```
if ((navigator.userAgent.indexOf("MSIE") > -1) && (navigator.platform ==
➥"Win32")) { // This is Internet Explorer.
var test = document.MediaPlayer1.FileName;
} else {  // This is not Internet Explorer.
var test = document.MediaPlayer1.GetFileName();
}
```

Windows Media Player event handling in Internet Explorer

Normally, Web pages are built to be event-driven, so in most interactions with Web pages, the end user must take some action. Windows Media Player events enable a greater level of interactivity between Windows Media Player and the Web page in which it is embedded. By listening for and trapping events, errors can be handled more gracefully and synchronized data can be presented to the end user in a more automated way.

Event handling in Internet Explorer is simple, using the Internet Explorer FOR=*"Object"* EVENT=*"Event"* syntax shown in Listing 9.13:

```
<SCRIPT FOR="MediaPlayer1" EVENT="EventName()" LANGUAGE="JScript">
// Perform operations here.
</SCRIPT>
```

The **EVENT** attribute of this <SCRIPT> element defines the type of event that the code will handle. Examples of events include the *PlayStateChange* event, the *NewStream* event, and the *EndOfStream* event. Each event has its own functionality. For more information, see the Windows Media Player Control SDK, which can be installed from the Welcome page of the JumpStart CD included with this book.

You'll notice that the **LANGUAGE** attribute of the <SCRIPT> tag is set to "JScript." This is a kind of built-in browser checker. Internet Explorer sees "JScript" as a derivative of JavaScript and uses the code appropriately. Netscape Navigator 4.0 does not recognize the language version and ignores all of the code inside.

Windows Media Player event handling in Netscape Navigator

With the Netscape Navigator plug-in model, events are not handled as smoothly as with the ActiveX model that Internet Explorer uses. Creating code to work with both Netscape Navigator and Internet Explorer is often difficult. The most important aspect of handling events within Netscape Navigator is that it does not support a true connection with the browser. Therefore, use the appObs proxy applet to send callback methods to the Windows Media Player plug-in. This Java applet resides on the page and listens to all of the events that Windows Media Player sends out. The applet itself can be installed on a page with the code in Listing 9.14:

```
<script language="JavaScript">
<!—
    if ( navigator.appName == "Netscape" )
    {
        // This next line ensures that any plug-ins just installed are
        // updated in the browser without quitting the browser.
    navigator.plugins.refresh();
```

```
        // The applet is not needed within Internet Explorer, and is
➥treated
        // as an implied end to the OBJECT tag by the IE HTML parser.
        // ***If you do not need to script events,
        // you can safely remove the next four lines***
    document.write("\x3C" + "applet MAYSCRIPT ");
    document.write("Code=NPDS.npDSEvtObsProxy.class ");
    document.write("width=5 height=5 name=appObs ");
    document.writeln("\x3E \x3C/applet\x3E");
    }
//-->
</script>
```

Before an event is triggered, an event observer must be enabled to trap the event. The
following code example shows how to enable event observers:

```
document.appObs.setByProxyDSEventNameObserver(plugin, true);
```

Each registered event observer requires a corresponding event handler. In JavaScript for
Netscape Navigator, an event handler is declared, using the syntax in Listing 9.15:

```
function OnDSEventNameEvt (paramter, ...)
{
        // code goes from here ...
}
```

In the previous code examples, *EventName* is the Windows Media Player event that is
being handled. Replace this with the name of the Windows Media Player event to which
you want to listen.

After an instance of the appObs applet is enabled, set it to listen to browser events. This
sample only uses the *PlayStateChange* event when the page loads. First, call the
appropriate function when the browser sends the *onload* event:

```
<BODY BGCOLOR="#ffffff" onload="loader()">
```

Listing 9.16, which goes inside the main <SCRIPT> block, actually sets the appObs
applet to use appropriate callback events and shows a browser check:

```
var bControl; // This Boolean variable holds True if an
              // ActiveX platform is being used, and False otherwise.

function loader(){
        if ((navigator.userAgent.indexOf('MSIE') > -1) &&
            (navigator.platform == "Win32"))
        {
                bControl = true;
        } else {
                var plugIn = document.MediaPlayer1;
```

```
                    bControl = false;
                     // The following line of code registers the
                     // PlayStateChange event in the appObs applet, so
                     // that when a PlayStateChange event occurs,
                     // appObs sends the appropriate callback
                     // method.
          document.appObs.setByProxyDSPlayStateChangeObserver(plugIn,true);
            }
          document.MediaPlayer1.Play();
}
```

The callback method shown in Listing 9.17 also resides in the main <SCRIPT> block:

```
function OnDSPlayStateChangeEvt (oldState, newState){
      doPlayStateChanges(oldState,newState);
}
```

Because you're handling events in both Netscape Navigator and Internet Explorer, the **OnDSPlayStateChangeEvt** callback method passes its information on to the **doPlayStateChanges** function. The Internet Explorer event handler does the same. This way, both browsers use the same piece of code to handle events, as shown in Listing 9.18:

```
<SCRIPT FOR="MediaPlayer1"
      EVENT="PlayStateChange(oldState,newState)"
      LANGUAGE="Jscript">
          doPlayStateChanges(oldState, newState);
</SCRIPT>
```

The **doPlayStateChanges** function is defined in the main <SCRIPT> block and can contain any code you want to use with JScript or DHTML. Listing 9.19 is an example of swapping custom player images based on the current *PlayState* of Windows Media Player:

```
function doPlayStateChanges(oldState,newState){
      timerID = setTimeout("document.i1.src = \"pllow.gif\"",0);
      timerID = setTimeout("document.i2.src = \"palow.gif\"",0);
      timerID = setTimeout("document.i3.src = \"stlow.gif\"",0);

      switch(newState) {
      case 0:
            timerID = setTimeout("document.i3.src = \"sth.gif\"",0);
            break;
      case 1:
            timerID = setTimeout("document.i2.src = \"pah.gif\"",0);
            break;
      case 2:
            timerID = setTimeout("document.i1.src = \"plh.gif\"",0);
            break;
      }
}
```

> **NOTE**   A **setTimeout** function is being used for the DHTML script. This is necessary because Netscape Navigator requires a new thread for DHTML called from the appObs proxy applet.

> **NOTE**   The AutoStart feature of Windows Media Player is not being used because Netscape Navigator will not run the *onload* event until after Windows Media Player has loaded and started playing its file. The *PlayStateChange* events would be missing if Windows Media Player didn't start until after the page had been loaded.

Automating Windows Media Encoder

Windows Media Encoder is an OLE automation server and can be automated using the interfaces described in the Windows Media Technologies SDK, which can be installed from the Welcome page of the JumpStart CD included with this book. Windows Media Encoder also supports a simple command-line interface. You can start Windows Media Encoder and load an .asf description file, for example, *MyEncoding.asd*, by typing this command on the command line:

```
Nsrex.exe MyEncoding.asd /START
```

This will start the encoding process. The .asd file was created in Windows Media Encoder and saved previously.

Windows Media Encoder can also be controlled programmatically using its Automation interface. The following C++ code demonstrates how to programmatically connect to a running Windows Media Encoder, or start a new instance of Windows Media Encoder and load its configuration. To see examples of Microsoft® Visual Basic® code or to learn more about Windows Media Encoder Automation, see the Windows Media Technologies SDK, which can be installed from the Welcome page of the JumpStart CD included with this book.

Listing 9.20 is fully functional and can be run by copying it into a simple console mode project as created by Microsoft® Developer Studio®:

```
#include "windows.h"
#include "stdio.h"
#include "tchar.h"
#include "oaidl.h"


///////////////////////////////////////////////////////////////////
static const GUID CLSID_IAsfRTEncoder =
    { 0x7DEBA670, 0x68AB, 0x11D0, { 0x98, 0xEB, 0x00, 0xaa, 0x00, 0xbb,
0xb5, 0x2c } };
```

```
#define HYPHEN      '-'              // Hyphen character
#define SLASH       '/'              // Forward slash character

#define SETDISPPARAMS(dp, numArgs, pvArgs, numNamed, pNamed) \
    {\
    (dp).cArgs=numArgs;\
    (dp).rgvarg=pvArgs;\
    (dp).cNamedArgs=numNamed;\
    (dp).rgdispidNamedArgs=pNamed;\
    }

#define SETNOPARAMS(dp) SETDISPPARAMS(dp, 0, NULL, 0, NULL)

#define DISPID_LOADASD   31

//////////////////////////////////////////////////////////////////////
class CEncoderSample
{
public:
    CEncoderSample( INT nArgc, LPSTR *prgArg );
    ~CEncoderSample( VOID );

    HRESULT Init( VOID );
    HRESULT Connect( VOID );
    HRESULT LoadConfig( VOID );

protected:

    HRESULT ParseArgs( VOID );

    HRESULT ConnectToEnc( VOID );
    HRESULT StartNewEnc( VOID );

    HRESULT InvokeMethod( DISPID dispID, ULONG cVar, LPVARIANT prgVar );
    VOID FreeExcepInfo( EXCEPINFO *pei );

protected:

    INT         m_nArgc;
    LPSTR       *m_prgArgs;

    WCHAR       m_wszFile[ _MAX_PATH ];
    BOOL        m_fCurrent;
    IDispatch   *m_pDispEncoder;
};


//////////////////////////////////////////////////////////////////////
// main - sample code main entry point
//////////////////////////////////////////////////////////////////////
extern "C" int __cdecl main( int argc, char **argv )
{
```

```
    CEncoderSample    *pes;
    HRESULT           hr;

    pes = new CEncoderSample( argc, argv );

    if( NULL != pes )
    {
        hr = pes->Init();

        if( S_OK == hr )
        {
            hr = pes->Connect();

            if( SUCCEEDED( hr ) )
            {
                hr = pes->LoadConfig();
            }
        }

        delete pes;
    }

    return( FALSE );
}


//////////////////////////////////////////////////////////////////////
// CEncoderSample - class constructor
//////////////////////////////////////////////////////////////////////
CEncoderSample:: CEncoderSample( INT nArgc, LPSTR *prgArg ) :
    m_nArgc( nArgc ),
    m_prgArgs( prgArg ),
    m_fCurrent( FALSE ),
    m_pDispEncoder( NULL )
{
}


//////////////////////////////////////////////////////////////////////
// ~CEncoderSample - class destructor
//////////////////////////////////////////////////////////////////////
CEncoderSample::~CEncoderSample( VOID )
{
    if( m_pDispEncoder )
    {
        //
        // Release our reference to Windows Media Encoder. The instance
        // of the encoder may have been
        // running already, in which case this will release our
        // reference to it. If we started the encoder, this release
        // will cause the encoder to be unloaded from memory.
```

```
        //
        m_pDispEncoder->Release( );
        m_pDispEncoder = NULL;
    }

    CoUninitialize();
}



/////////////////////////////////////////////////////////////////////
// Init - Class initializer. Portion of class construction prone to
//        failure.
/////////////////////////////////////////////////////////////////////
HRESULT CEncoderSample::Init( VOID )
{
    HRESULT

    hr = CoInitialize(NULL);

    if( SUCCEEDED( hr ) )
    {
        hr = ParseArgs();
    }

    return( hr );
}



/////////////////////////////////////////////////////////////////////
// ConnectToEnc - Method to connect to an already running instance
//                 of Windows Media Encoder
/////////////////////////////////////////////////////////////////////
HRESULT CEncoderSample::ConnectToEnc( VOID )
{
    HRESULT hr;
    IUnknown *pIEncoderUnknown = NULL;

    //
    // Windows Media Encoder registers itself in the active object
    //table; call
    // GetActiveObject to find the registered instance.
    //
    hr = GetActiveObject(CLSID_IAsfRTEncoder, NULL, &pIEncoderUnknown);

    if( pIEncoderUnknown )
    {
        if( SUCCEEDED( hr ) )
        {
            hr = pIEncoderUnknown->QueryInterface(IID_IDispatch,
                                        (LPVOID *)&m_pDispEncoder );
        }
```

```
        pIEncoderUnknown->Release();
    }

    return( hr );
}


//////////////////////////////////////////////////////////////////////
// StartNewEncoder - Method to create a new instance of the encoder
//////////////////////////////////////////////////////////////////////
HRESULT CEncoderSample::StartNewEnc( VOID )
{
    HRESULT hr;

    hr = CoCreateInstance(CLSID_IAsfRTEncoder,
                          NULL,
                          CLSCTX_SERVER,
                          IID_IDispatch,
                          (LPVOID *)&m_pDispEncoder);

    return( hr );
}


//////////////////////////////////////////////////////////////////////
// Connect - Method that initiates a connection to an encoder instance
//           either by
//           connecting to an instance of Windows Media Encoder that is
//           running or by starting
//           a new encoder instance. By default, this code starts
//           a new instance.
//////////////////////////////////////////////////////////////////////
HRESULT CEncoderSample::Connect( VOID )
{
    HRESULT hr;

    if( m_fCurrent )
    {
        hr = ConnectToEnc();
    }
    else
    {
        hr = StartNewEnc();
    }

    return( hr );
}
```

```
//////////////////////////////////////////////////////////////////////
// LoadConfig - Method to invoke the loading of an .asd file into the
                encoder
//////////////////////////////////////////////////////////////////////
HRESULT CEncoderSample::LoadConfig( VOID )
{
    VARIANT     var;
    HRESULT     hr = S_OK;

    ::VariantInit( &var );

    //
    // Load the variant into the param structure. This param contains
    // the name of the .asd file to load as the encoder configuration.
    //
    V_VT(&var) = VT_BSTR;
    V_BSTR(&var) = ::SysAllocString( m_wszFile );

    if( NULL == var.bstrVal )
    {
        hr = E_OUTOFMEMORY;
    }

    if (SUCCEEDED(hr))
    {
        //
        // Invoke the LoadASD method on Windows Media Encoder
        //
        hr = InvokeMethod( DISPID_LOADASD, 1, &var );
    }

    ::VariantClear(&var);

    return( hr );
}


//////////////////////////////////////////////////////////////////////
// InvokeMethod - Helper function to simplify the user's access to
//                Idispatch::Invoke
//////////////////////////////////////////////////////////////////////
HRESULT CEncoderSample::InvokeMethod
(
    DISPID dispID,              // Method to invoke
    ULONG cVar,                 // Count of params to method
    LPVARIANT prgVar            // Array of variant parameters to method
)
{
    DISPPARAMS  dispparams;
    UINT        uArgErr;
    HRESULT     hr;
```

```cpp
    EXCEPINFO    ei;
    VARIANT      retVar;


    //
    // Set disp params to be passed to the method
    //
    SETDISPPARAMS(dispparams, cVar, prgVar, 0, NULL);


    ::VariantInit(&retVar);


    //
    // Call the method requested on the dispatch entry
    //
    hr = m_pDispEncoder->Invoke(dispID,                    // Method ID to invoke
                            IID_NULL,                      // Reserved
                            LOCALE_SYSTEM_DEFAULT,         // Locale context
                            DISPATCH_METHOD,               // Method
                            &dispparams,                   // Supplied disp params
                            &retVar,                       // Results
                            &ei,                           // Exception information
                            &uArgErr);

    if( DISP_E_EXCEPTION == hr )
    {
        hr = ei.scode ? ei.scode : DISP_E_EXCEPTION;
        FreeExcepInfo(&ei);
    }
    else
    {
        if( SUCCEEDED( hr ) )
        {
            hr = retVar.scode;
        }
    }

    return( hr );
}


////////////////////////////////////////////////////////////////////////
// FreeExcepInfo - Helper function for properly releasing all resources
//                 associated with the returned EXCEPTINFO as returned
//                 by Idispatch::Invoke calls.
////////////////////////////////////////////////////////////////////////
VOID CEncoderSample::FreeExcepInfo( EXCEPINFO *pei )
{
    if( NULL != pei )
    {
        if( pei->bstrSource )
        {
            ::SysFreeString(pei->bstrSource);
```

```
        }

        if( pei->bstrDescription )
        {
            ::SysFreeString(pei->bstrDescription);
        }

        ZeroMemory( pei, sizeof(EXCEPINFO) );
    }
}


/////////////////////////////////////////////////////////////////////
// ParseArgs - Parse the command-line arguments as supplied by the user
/////////////////////////////////////////////////////////////////////
HRESULT CEncoderSample::ParseArgs( VOID )
{
    INT     i;
    HRESULT     hr;
    TCHAR       *pszParam;

    hr = (m_nArgc > 1) ? S_OK : E_INVALIDARG;

    m_wszFile[ 0 ] = NULL;

    for( i = 1; ( i < m_nArgc ) && ( S_OK == hr ); i++ )
    {
        pszParam = m_prgArgs[i];


        if( ( pszParam[0] == HYPHEN ) ¦¦ ( pszParam[0] == SLASH ))
        {
            switch( _toupper( pszParam[1] ) )
            {
            case L'F':
                //
                // The user is supplying the name .asd file
                // to load as the encoder configuration.
                //
                if( ( ++i == m_nArgc ) ¦¦ ( !_tcslen( m_prgArgs[i] ) ) )
                {
                    hr = E_INVALIDARG;
                }
                else
                {
                    MultiByteToWideChar( CP_ACP, 0, m_prgArgs[i],
                                          -1, m_wszFile, _MAX_PATH );
                }
                break;

            case L'C':
```

```
                    //
                    // The user is indicating to connect to an
                    // encoder instance that is already running. By
                    // default, a new
                    // instance of the encoder will be started.
                    //
                    m_fCurrent = TRUE;
                    break;

                default:
                case '?':
                    hr = S_FALSE;
                    break;
                }
            }
            else
            {
                hr = E_INVALIDARG;
            }
    }

    if( NULL == m_wszFile[ 0 ] )
    {
        hr = E_INVALIDARG;
    }

    if( S_OK != hr )
    {
        _tprintf( TEXT("EncoderSample -f <filename> [-c]\n") );
        _tprintf( TEXT("  -f : ASD configuration file\n") );
        _tprintf( TEXT("  -c : Connect to current running encoder\n") );
    }

    return( hr );

}
```

Summary

Windows Media Technologies can be controlled in different ways using scripts and applications, giving you greater freedom in creating and delivering multimedia. Windows Media Player is completely programmable, enabling you to control your media presentations through ASF script commands and Windows Media Player events. You can embed Windows Media Player in a Web browser to create a media presentation that is dynamic and interactive.

Additional features, such as Windows Media Audio Redirector files, offer you more flexibility in your presentations. Redirector files are text-based files that contain tags that you can use to create playlists (multiple media files in one presentation), insert advertisements, add banners and logos, play previews, and add descriptive information to presentations. You can also automate Windows Media Encoder, enabling you to encode live content or existing files into an ASF stream using your own applications.

Chapter 10, "Principles of Digital Compression and Encoding," describes the underlying principles of creating and compressing audio and video content.

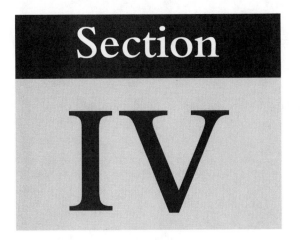

Section

IV

Underlying Concepts

This section contains detailed information about digital compression, the codecs included with Microsoft Windows Media Technologies, Advanced Streaming Format (ASF), networking concepts and protocols, network capacity, and firewall considerations. Chapters in this section include:

Chapter 10—Principles of Digital Compression and Encoding. This chapter presents the basic concepts of audio and video and describes how audio/video content is compressed and encoded to produce a stream or file in ASF.

Chapter 11—Principles of Networking. This chapter describes the basic concepts of networking technologies to help you design your streaming media system.

Chapter

10

Principles of Digital Compression and Encoding

This chapter presents the basic concepts of audio and video and describes how audio/video content is compressed and encoded to produce a stream or file in Advanced Streaming Format (ASF). After reading this chapter, you'll be able to answer the following questions:

- How does analog media compare to digital media?

- How do I determine the resolution to use for my video media?

- What sampling rate do I need to use for my audio media?

- What are the most common file formats for digital audio, and how do they differ?

- What are the most common forms of compression, and how do they work?

- Why does the ASF format work well with streaming media?

- What are the benefits of using .asf files?

- What information does an .asf file contain?

Traditionally, you experience audio and video media in analog form, such as when listening to the radio, watching television, and recording with your video camera. However, because computers communicate using digital data, media must be captured and converted to a digital format. Then, the media must be prepared for transmission over a computer network by compressing and encoding it into a streaming file format. ASF is the optimal format for streaming high quality multimedia at a variety of bit rates.

Capturing audio and video

The first step in producing Windows Media streaming content is capturing or *digitizing* the source content. Source content can be in the form of a live broadcast that you digitize with a capture card directly to Windows Media format, or it can be an existing piece of audio or video content. The following section provides an overview of audio and video technology, and describes how it is converted to a digital form.

Video basics

Most types of content are in analog form. When we view a video or movie that has been stored on magnetic tape, for example, we are experiencing the playback of an analog signal. An analog signal is a complex wave that is produced by rapid variations in voltage. Everything in the wave is relative to everything else in the wave. You can vary the overall voltage of an analog signal and amplify or reduce the level of the audio or video that is produced by the wave.

In contrast, a computer interprets its environment in the form of binary digits. Every piece of data is made up of ones and zeros. The way these ones and zeros are combined defines the data. In digitized video, the picture is defined by a collection of pixels. Each pixel is a piece of data, a precise value that represents a color by blending the luminance values of red, green, and blue. The greater the number of pixels used to create the picture, the higher the resolution of the picture. When a picture has been digitized, its pixel value is set. If you zoom in to a digitized picture, you will not necessarily see more detail because the number of pixels does not increase. Each pixel just gets larger. If a digitized picture is over-enlarged, you see the individual pixels as blocks.

Early computer video cards and monitors could display only a limited number of colors and resolutions. When pictures were digitized, the quality degradation was noticeable. Programmers at that time turned to animations and drawings because they could control the colors and tonal variations within the limitations of the available hardware. Video cards, monitors, and CPUs have progressed to the point where they can now produce digital quality that is comparable to the original analog signal. As a result, digital cameras and other video devices have emerged. However, because most producers are still using analog cameras, most video sources are still analog.

Video content is a collection of images rendered so quickly that the images appear to be in motion. One way to think of this is to remember the flip-page animations that many of us experimented with as children. By making a series of drawings on separate pages and flipping them quickly with your thumb, you could make a car or a stick figure move across a page. If you flipped the pages too quickly, you couldn't see the pictures, and if you flipped them too slowly, you would see each picture too clearly. You had to flip the pages at just the right speed to produce the illusion of motion.

The same factors apply to video. In video, the images are called frames, and the speed at which they are flipped is measured in frames per second. Each frame is made up of more than 500 horizontal lines. Broadcast television in the United States uses a permutation called interlaced frames, shown in Figure 10.1, in which each frame is composed of two fields, each of which contains every other line of the television frame—half of the image. One field contains the odd lines, the other the even lines.

The television signal is rendered at 30 frames per second, 60 fields per second. When video is converted to a digital format, using a capture card, the two interlaced fields are combined into a complete frame (deinterlaced) and rendered at 30 frames per second.

Video formats

Another important aspect of video rendering is color composition of the video. Color information is transmitted using luminance and chrominance values. The standards that define how broadcasters transmit these values differ depending on the country of origin.

The United States developed the *National Television System Committee* (NTSC) standard in 1957. This is the broadcast system standard accepted by and used in North America, Japan, most of Central America, and portions of Southeast Asia. The NTSC system is based on a black and white component with two additional color difference signals. By using this system, black and white television sets and color television sets can receive the same signal. The black and white component is called *luminance* and is normally represented by the letter Y. The color difference signals are called *chrominance* and are normally represented by I and Q or U and V. The luminance value plus the color difference signals are called the color space. NTSC can use either the YIQ or YUV color space. The NTSC format specifies that video must contain 525 lines per frame, at an update rate of 30 frames per second.

Figure 10.1.

Interlaced video.

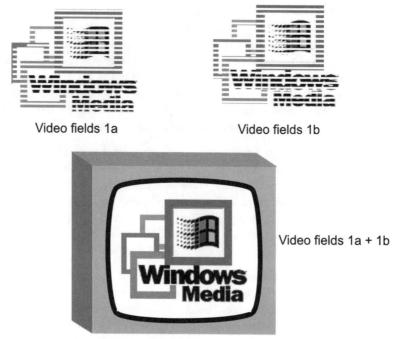

Video fields 1a   Video fields 1b

Video fields 1a + 1b

Television

Phase Alternation Line (PAL) is the broadcast standard for most of Europe, Africa, China, South America, and the Middle East. PAL uses the YUV color space. It was adopted by Germany and the United Kingdom in 1967 and has been accepted by many countries since then. The PAL format specifies that video must contain 625 lines per frame at an update rate of 25 frames per second. PAL video has higher resolution than NTSC, but it also displays more flicker in the image.

Sequential Couleur Avec Memoire (SECAM), or Sequential Color with Memory, was developed in France in 1967. SECAM specifies that each frame must contain 819 lines per frame at an update rate of 25 frames per second. However, unlike NTSC and PAL, SECAM transmits its chrominance signals on alternating lines using frequency modulation (FM). SECAM also uses a different color space: YDrDb. France and many Eastern European, African, Middle Eastern, and Asian countries have adopted SECAM.

Many different versions of the PAL and SECAM standards are used in the countries that have adopted one or the other of these overall standards. When acquiring video source from a different country, be sure to verify the standard used so that you can ensure that you have the proper hardware or can obtain conversion assistance locally.

Digitizing video

After you have determined the video source and format, use a video capture card to convert the analog video to digital video. There are many different capture cards available. When choosing a capture card, consider the following questions:

- Are you going to use it for live encoding to Windows Media format?

- What kind of input sources do you plan to use with the card?

- What output formats does the card support?

Microsoft maintains a list of capture cards that can be used with Windows Media Encoder; this list is on the Windows Media Web site (http://www.microsoft.com/windows/windowsmedia/). The list changes as new cards are continually tested and approved by the Windows Media test team. If your capture card isn't listed, it may still work with Windows Media Encoder. The most current list is included in Appendix A, "Audio and Video Capture Cards."

Before capturing video, determine the resolution. Higher resolution video equals higher image quality, but a higher resolution image also requires more system resources to render. If you want to find out the data rate requirements for a piece of uncompressed content, use the following formulas:

Video resolution × video frame rate = Total number of pixels per second

Total number of pixels per second × Number of bytes = Number of bytes per second

> **NOTE** Number of bytes is the number per pixel that is produced by the capture card. If the card uses the YUY2 format, the number of bytes is 2.

Number of bytes per second × 8 = Number of bits per second

The resolution of a frame and the number of frames per second are the two factors that determine the bit rate. The only way to reduce the bit rate, then, without resorting to compression is to reduce either of the two. There are two common implementations of this in digital video: Common Interchange Format (CIF) and Quarter Common Interchange Format (QCIF). CIF provides the video signal on half of the available screen size. QCIF provides the video signal on one-quarter of the available screen size. Table 10.1 provides an overview of video resolution versus perceived quality and bit rate requirements.

Table 10.1. Video resolution versus perceived quality.

Resolution	Frame rate	Name	Quality	Bit rate (megabits per second [Mbps])
720 × 480	30	Digital Original	DVD	160
640 × 480	30	Full Screen	Broadcast	128
320 × 240	30	CIF	VHS	32
160 × 120	15	QCIF	Video conferencing	4

As you can see in Table 10.1, the bit rate of even the lowest quality uncompressed video exceeds the bandwidth available to most Internet users. Therefore, if you are going to provide video data from a Web site, you must compress the video data.

To this point, we've only been dealing with the image portion of the data. However, video data normally has audio information associated with it. Before you can decide on the best compression techniques for your content, you must understand the nature of audio data and its manipulation.

Digitizing audio

Audio often starts out in analog form, and, like video, must be converted to a digital format before it can be manipulated on a computer. To digitize an audio signal, the audio waveform is sampled a given number of times per second, and each sample is assigned a value. The sampling method used to digitize audio is defined by the Nyquist theorem, which states that the sampling rate must be equal to, or greater than, twice the highest frequency component in the analog signal. The human ear can hear sound up to a frequency of approximately 20 kilohertz (kHz). Therefore, to accurately capture all the sound a human can hear, an analog audio waveform must be sampled at a rate of at least 40,000 times per second or 40 kHz. Table 10.2 shows the relationship between digital audio quality and sample rate.

Table 10.2. Digital audio quality and sample rate.

Quality	Expectation	Highest frequency (in kHz)	Sampling rate (in kHz)
Excellent	Compact disc recording	22	44 to 48
Good	FM radio	15	30 to 32

Quality	Expectation	Highest frequency (in kHz)	Sampling rate (in kHz)
Acceptable	AM radio	4	8 to 10
Poor	Telephone	2.5	5 to 6

At a high enough sampling rate, it is difficult for the average person to tell the difference between digital and analog sound. The *Red Book* standard that defines CD audio has become the benchmark for high-end realistic digital audio. CD audio includes three basic standards: two discrete audio tracks to provide stereo, a sampling rate of 44.1 kHz, and a bit depth of 16 (the number of bits in one sample).

Though CD audio is the standard of quality, achieving this level of quality requires a great deal of storage space and a system capable of rendering a high bit rate. The bit rate of audio can be calculated by multiplying the number of tracks (2 for stereo) by the number of samples per second (44,100 for CD) by the bit depth (16). Using these values, you see that CD audio plays back at 1,411 kilobits per second (Kbps), which is quite a bit higher than the average modem speed of 28.8 Kbps. To convert audio so that it renders at a lower bit rate, you can start by converting the audio to mono (one track), resampling the audio for a lower rate, or cutting the bit depth in half:

- **Convert to mono.** Summing the audio tracks does not remove any sound. The only element missing after conversion to mono is the stereo effect. Converting your content to mono cuts your uncompressed file size in half.

- **Lower the sampling rate.** The sampling rate has a considerable effect on the sound quality of a digital file. If you apply the Nyquist theorem, you see that audio sampled at 11 kHz, for example, cannot accurately digitize frequency components above 5.5 kHz. To reproduce every sound a human can hear, you need a 44-kHz sampling rate; but voice sampled at an 11-kHz rate can be an acceptable compromise when file size or bit rate is an issue.

- **Reduce bit depth.** A CD audio sample is composed of 16 bits. Though this provides a very clean sound, cutting the bit depth in half is an option used by many computer sound designers. The unpleasant ringing and buzzing sound is often masked by the audio signal, and reducing the bit depth to 8 bits does cut file size and bit rate in half.

When capturing audio, make sure the input level is as high as possible without distorting. If your capturing program has a sound meter, adjust the line or microphone input sliders so that the level is well into the green area but only rarely goes into the red.

Principles of Digital
Compression and Encoding

When audio is digitized, it becomes, in effect, a very long list of numbers, which are the sample values. The red area of the vu meter represents the highest number—the absolute upper limit. A player cannot render audio that has been recorded continuously in the red because all audio waveform detail is missing—all the sample values are the same maximum value. The result is a highly distorted, unpleasant sound. Aside from sounding bad, digital distortion cannot be repaired. When digitizing audio, avoid distortion by maintaining a record level well below the red area.

Digital audio file formats

Microsoft Windows Media Technologies can directly encode sounds that are stored as a .wav or .mp3 file. If your source sound is in another format, it must be converted before you use it. If a converter is not available, you can use Windows Media Encoder to encode the sound directly from the capture card. Some of the most common sound formats you may encounter include .wav, .mp3, AIFF (used primarily on Macintosh® computers), and AU or Mu-law (the NeXT/Sun AU format).

Compressing audio and video

The bit-rate requirements for audio and video content are enormous. This is why effective, high-quality compression techniques are necessary for streaming content over a computer network.

Compression techniques are usually referred to as either *lossy* or *lossless*. In determining which technique to use, consider that:

- Lossless compression methods preserve all of the data of the original content and can be reversed if necessary.

- Lossy compression methods change enough of the original data so that the process is irreversible.

Lossless compression methods reproduce the highest quality sound, but only lossy methods are capable of compressing audio enough to achieve the low bit rates necessary for streaming on the Internet. This section discusses different lossy and lossless compression methods. Each method has been applied in various ways to create compressor/decompressor algorithms (codecs) that can be applied to your content.

Lossless compression

There are a number of lossless compression methods. In this section, one method called entropy encoding is described. In entropy encoding, each piece of data is analyzed based on its distinct characteristics. No assumptions are made based on the data source or its inherent characteristics. The amount of compression available using this method is limited. The following compression techniques are examples of entropy encoding.

Repetitive sequence suppression

Areas of redundancy within the data are replaced with a code that identifies the data characteristics and the number of repetitions. Two methods of compression that use repetitive sequence suppression are *Zero or blank suppression*, and *Run length encoding*.

Zero or blank suppression

Zero or blank suppression is used to replace repetitive zeroes in a data stream. Figure 10.2 shows the effect of applying zero suppression to a data stream.

Principles of Digital Compression and Encoding

Figure 10.2.
Zero or blank suppression.

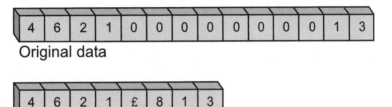

Original data

After applying zero suppression

As you can see in the illustration, this method assumes that the zero is the character to be replaced. The character is replaced by a code symbol, which is then followed by a number representing the number of zeroes removed from the data sequence.

Run length encoding

Run length encoding (RLE) is commonly used in fax machines. Run length encoding replaces any character that is repeated several times with a code that represents the character and the number of repetitions. Figure 10.3 shows the result of applying run length encoding on a data stream.

Figure 10.3.
Run length encoding.

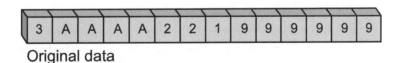

Original data

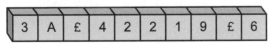

After applying run length encoding

This method differs from zero suppression encoding in that any character in the data can be replaced. In this method, the code must first identify the character, then insert the code that signifies that it was removed and the number of characters.

Neither of these techniques is especially useful as a stand-alone method of encoding multimedia content. However, understanding how they work is the basis of understanding more complex compression methods. Compression techniques are composed of various formulas and methods that all have, at their core, the same goal. That goal is to reduce the total amount of data while still having the means to restore that data, when requested, so that the data can still be used as if it were in the original format. All methods use some sort of code and must have a means of reading the code. More complex compression methods can contain the decoding information in a separate file referred to as a *codebook*.

Statistical encoding

A more sophisticated form of entropy encoding is called statistical encoding. Statistical encoding uses a codebook to encode the data. The codebook is a table that identifies various symbols as having specific meanings when decoding. Codebooks can be either generated in advance or generated dynamically during the encoding process. Two common forms of statistical encoding are *pattern substitution* and *Huffman encoding*.

Pattern substitution

This method is most useful for encoding text. Frequently used words are replaced with a shorter code word. The codebook for this method can either be generated dynamically or pre-written using established standards.

Huffman encoding

This lossless compression method is used for encoding images, videos, and movies. The codebook must be generated dynamically. In the case of video content, the codebook can be calculated either per frame or per movie.

Although Huffman encoding can be used to compress video, it cannot compress the video enough to be useful for encoding video that is to be streamed over a network. To create streaming content, a more efficient compression method is required.

Lossy compression

Lossy encoding methods use a different paradigm than the lossless entropy encoding methods to reduce the size of the data. When lossy encoding methods are used, the data is compressed based on the known characteristics of the source material. Two common examples of lossy encoding are the removal of silent portions of an audio sequence, and the identification of redundant blocks in two video frames.

Source characteristics are identified by the processes of psycho-acoustic and psycho-visual modeling. Where lossless methods focus on the data, lossy methods focus on analyzing the audio and visual characteristics of the uncompressed content that relate to human perception. Researchers have determined the threshold levels of perceptual acuity for human subjects when exposed to various types of audio and visual data. The human ear has been shown to be very sensitive to even slight distortions in sound, so lossy audio codecs must be very resistant to the degradation of sound from the original content.

Fortunately, the range of frequencies that the human ear can perceive is limited. Removing those frequencies from the source media that are above and below the range of human hearing is the first step in compressing an audio sample. If this step does not sufficiently compress the sample to your target bandwidth, further compression methods can be included in your model. For example, if a loud sound at a particular frequency dominates a weaker sound at a different frequency to a great enough degree, the weaker sound can be safely removed from the sample without a loss in perceptive quality. This is called *audio masking*. In addition, sounds at some frequencies are less significant to the audio signal and can be encoded less precisely. These compression techniques are capable of maintaining a high perceptive quality. However, if removal or less precise encoding methods are used on frequencies that are highly significant to the sound sample, then perceptive quality decreases.

Psycho-visual modeling is used to create the formulas for compressing images. The eye is much less sensitive to change than the ear. Video compression techniques can be much more aggressive than audio compression techniques. Video codecs use either intraframe or interframe compression methods. Intraframe methods compress each video frame separately and are not as efficient as interframe methods. However, intraframe compression usually produces much higher quality content.

Lossy encoding techniques can be used with both audio and video content. The following sections describe four of the techniques.

Transform encoding

Certain data types can be more easily compressed if they are first transformed into another data type. When we watch a video or listen to music, we are experiencing the content in the spatial or temporal domain. Our minds interpret the change in the content as either space or time differential. However, that is not always the most efficient way of interpreting content for compression. Rather, it is more efficient for a computer to receive the content in the frequency domain. By measuring the frequency variation and depth of the content, the same information can be stored in much less space. An example of transform encoding that is commonly used with multimedia content is the Moving Picture Expert Group codecs (MPEG-1 through MPEG-4). These codecs are used for compressing audio and video. The .mp3 music files are compressed using the MPEG Audio Layer-3 codec.

Sub-band encoding

Sub-band coding (SBC) is designed for encoding audio at low bit rates. It is a form of lossy audio compression that saves signal bandwidth by discarding information about frequencies that have been masked. This results in a smaller compressed file that will sound the same as the original file when played back.

Differential encoding

This method encodes content based on the degree of change from one piece of content to the next. Instead of storing the complete value, the difference from the preceding value (*prediction difference* or *error term*) is stored. This type of encoding is effective when the information contains small amounts of variation. However, if your content contains large amounts of variation, by using this schema you can use the same number of bits as by directly encoding the content.

There are several different types of differential encoding. Figures 10.4, 10.5, and 10.6 show how differential encoding reduces the number of bits necessary to reproduce an audio waveform, using three commonly used differential compression techniques. The source contains the complete waveform. The differentially coded signal contains only the differences in the source signal, which can be represented by fewer bits. The three techniques include:

- **Differential pulse code modulation.** DPCM is the simplest method of differential encoding. A piece of content is encoded by recording only the difference between the base content and the following data. The base content sample is updated on a set schedule (for example, every 8 frames).

Figure 10.4.

Differential pulse code modulation.

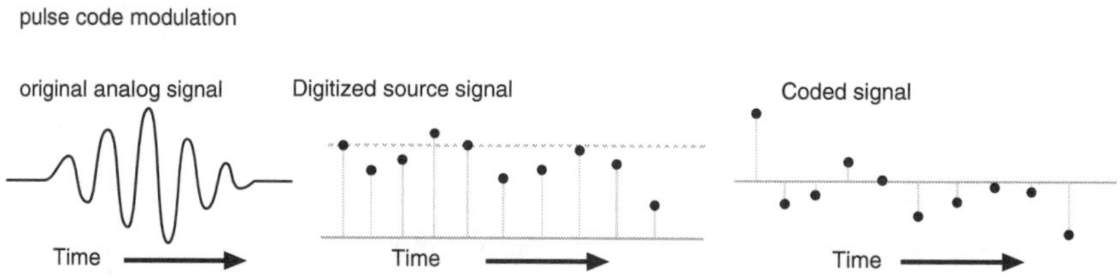

- **Delta modulation.** Accomplishes a greater degree of compression by encoding just one bit of information that represents the amount of change from the baseline content.

Figure 10.5.

Delta modulation.

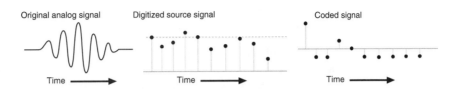
Delta modulation

Original analog signal   Digitized source signal   Coded signal

Time   Time   Time

■ **Adaptive differential pulse code modulation.** ADPCM is the most aggressive type of differential encoding. The baseline is dynamic and predictive over the time sample, so the amount of compression that is achieved is greater. However, it requires much greater computing power due to the use of the predictive algorithm.

Figure 10.6.

Adaptive differential pulse code modulation.

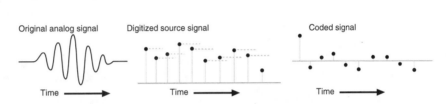
Adaptive differential pulse code modulation

Original analog signal   Digitized source signal   Coded signal

Time   Time   Time

Vector quantization

Vector quantization (VQ) is a special case of pattern substitution in which a data sample is divided into vectors. A vector of information is replaced with a single value (normally represented by the symbol K) that indicates a clustering of vectors that are similar in nature. For example, a vector may consist of a block of accumulated digital samples that have the same frequency range or consist of a subset of frames that have similar parameters.

When a set of vectors is determined, K clusters can be defined so that each vector in the sample is a member of a cluster. Each cluster is then represented in a codebook by one of its members or by some symbol or vector. The codebook contains K entries for each cluster in the sample. The clusters and codebook are chosen to best represent the original collections of vectors.

When source content is encoded, each vector is compressed separately. The VQ compressor determines which cluster the vector belongs to and substitutes for the incoming vector the appropriate symbol or value. The codebook for this compressor can be constructed before or during this process.

Applying compression technology

The following terms are often used to describe compression methods that have been derived from the basic concepts just presented:

- **Simultaneous auditory masking.** Auditory masking is a technique for reducing data when storing compressed audio. When a strong audio signal is present at one frequency, you cannot hear a weaker audio signal at a frequency that is close to the stronger signal. The stronger signal masks the weaker signal. Auditory masking discards the weaker, inaudible audio signal. This is called simultaneous masking because it takes place when a weak signal is rendered inaudible by a simultaneously occurring stronger signal. The stronger signal is called a *masker*. Each masker has a masking threshold based on its frequency, intensity, and tonality. A masking threshold can be measured below which any signal will be inaudible.

- **Perceptual encoding.** Perceptual encoding is a form of lossy compression based on the concept that a portion of the source data cannot be perceived, and is, therefore, irrelevant and can be removed. The removal of this imperceptible data is called masking. If an adequate bit rate for the complete masking of irrelevant data is available, the decoded signal will be perceptually indistinguishable from the source.

- **Lateral inhibition.** Lateral inhibition filters out slowly varying changes in intensity that might be due to gradual changes in illumination. Lightness algorithms have used this assumption to extract edges that are more likely due to material reflectivity changes than to illumination changes. In addition, lateral inhibition formulas can be used to improve the perceptual quality of encoded images by adding resolution to the edges of objects. This effect is part of the normal functioning of the human eye, and thus the lack of resolution is not perceived until the person looks at an encoded image that does not seem to have the sharpness of the original.

Frame encoding

A concept that is fundamental to encoding primarily video is *frame encoding*. The encoding methods we have described can be either *interframe* or *intraframe*, most are a combination of both. An intraframe compression method compresses each video frame as a separate independent unit—each frame is a complete image. Interframe compression uses a system of key and delta frames to eliminate redundant information—a key frame is a complete image, but a delta frame includes only the parts of the image that are different from the frame before it. Interframe methods can achieve far greater compression than intraframe methods, while producing a higher quality presentation.

Key frames, also known as I-frames, are generated at set intervals during the data stream, such as every five seconds. A key frame is also generated whenever the level of change between frames reaches a certain threshold, such as if 30 percent or more of the image is different. *Delta frames*, also known as P-frames, are generated between key frames. If a key frame is generated every five seconds and the frame rate of a video is 15 frames per second, 10 seconds of video contains two key frames and 148 delta frames. The key frame interval can be configured before encoding a stream with Windows Media Encoder by changing the Seconds/I-frame setting. For more information about this setting, see Chapter 3, "Using Windows Media Tools."

Motion estimation can be added to interframe compression methods to further increase the amount of compression achieved. In video content, motion estimation algorithms attempt to predict movement in the video frame. By using motion estimation, delta frames do not have to contain portions of an image. They only have to relay vector information to the decompressor—tell the player that one part of the image has moved there.

By using interframe, video can be highly compressed and still render a good quality presentation at Internet bit rates. However, the key to creating a high quality stream using interframe, is low motion video. High motion video requires more key frames and larger delta frames, which reduce the compression power that can be gained from an interframe compressor. If a compressor is not able to reduce the bit rate of a video enough, the quality of the image suffers and the presentation appears jerky because frames must be discarded.

Because lossy compression involves analyzing psycho-acoustic and psycho-visual characteristics of content, its affects should be factored into the process when creating content. Just as a video camera produces better pictures with the right light and film must be developed with just the right mix of chemicals, codecs used for streaming media create better sound and pictures if certain guidelines are followed when the source content is created and captured. For more information, see Chapter 2, "Creating and Improving Multimedia Content."

Windows Media Technologies compression applications

The Windows Media Technologies group has done extensive research into compression techniques that produce the best live and stored content. The goal of the research is to offer codecs that produce the highest quality, while still compressing content sufficiently to stream it within common Internet bandwidths. This section discusses the codecs that we have found to work best for creating Windows Media content.

Microsoft MPEG-4 video codec

MPEG-4 is the latest of the Moving Picture Experts Group standards to be approved by the International Standards Organization (ISO). Microsoft has created the first implementation of this standard in the United States in Windows Media Technologies with the release of the Microsoft MPEG-4 version 3 video codec. This standard was developed specifically for encoding multimedia content efficiently in a variety of bit rates—from low Internet rates to rates that reproduce a full-frame, television-quality presentation.

The Microsoft MPEG-4 video codec intrinsically supports streaming multimedia by allowing for multiple streams within one encoded data stream. It also has an advanced motion estimation algorithm, which allows for greater compression.

Windows Media Audio codec

Windows Media Audio is a new audio codec created by Microsoft. The codec is designed to handle all types of audio content. Windows Media Audio is very resistant to signal degradation caused by loss of data. This loss tolerance makes it excellent for use with streaming content. In addition, by using an improved encoding algorithm, this codec processes audio quickly. The improved compression algorithm also creates smaller audio files than those created with other codecs compressing the same content. This smaller file size means that content created using the Windows Media Audio codec can be downloaded more quickly. If you are creating audio files for download, the Windows Media Audio codec is a great choice because it provides CD-quality sound at half the bandwidth required by most codecs.

During tests against comparable codecs, the Windows Media Audio codec provided much clearer sound with greater tonal distinction than the others did. The combination of superb clarity and tonal depth produces better-sounding music content across all supported bandwidths. The Windows Media Audio codec is highly scalable, meaning that it provides high-quality mono and stereo audio content over a wide range of bandwidths.

Sipro Labs ACELP.net codec

Sipro Labs ACELP®.net audio codec is a version of the ACELP (Algebraic-Code-Excited Linear Prediction) compression methodologies that has been optimized for use on Internet Protocol (IP) networks and the Intel Pentium platform. Using the ACELP net-adapted packetization method, it is able to minimize the impact of errors and significantly improve the error correction possibilities in case of data-packet loss. This codec uses frame concatenation and interlacing to more efficiently encode data. In Windows Media Encoder, ACELP.net can be used to compress audio to bandwidths ranging from 5 Kbps to 16 Kbps. This codec is most useful for encoding low bit rate voice content.

After content has been sufficiently compressed, the data must be formatted so that it can be easily streamed over a network. To create Windows Media content for streaming, or downloading as a .wma file, the content is encoded in the Advanced Streaming Format (ASF).

Encoding Windows Media content

Tools like Windows Media Encoder and Windows Media On-Demand Producer produce a live stream or file in two basic steps. In the first step, source content is compressed down to a bit rate that is compatible with the selected bandwidth. In the second basic step, the compressed audio and video are combined and encoded in ASF. This section describes the structure of the format and how the structure relates to the streaming of media over a network.

Developed by Microsoft in 1996, ASF is one of the first file formats designed specifically for streaming multimedia. ASF is a highly flexible format that contains a description and a compressed digital representation of audio, video, images, captions, and events that are synchronized to a shared timeline, as shown in Figure 10.7.

ASF is an open format. A number of software companies outside Microsoft have developed exceptional products that encode and play ASF content. While most often referred to as a file format, ASF can also describe the data structure of a live stream. Each ASF stream contains one or more media streams, most commonly an audio stream and one or more video streams, the delivery and presentation of which are synchronized to a common timeline.

Figure 10.7.

Stream delivery and presentation.

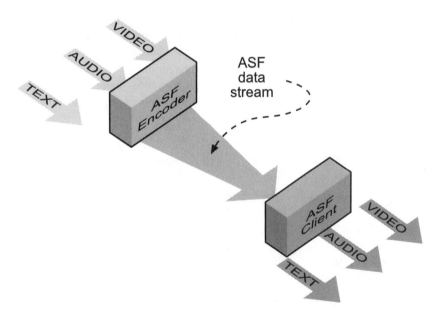

ASF is loaded with features that make it the ideal format for streaming multimedia over networks. However, ASF is also more than adequate for local playback. Using ASF, compelling content can be created, streamed, and rendered; it's also possible to tap the unlimited potential of multimedia streamed over the Internet.

ASF background

When Microsoft developers set out to create a streaming media solution, it became apparent that existing multimedia file formats (WAV and AVI) were not adequate. WAV and AVI work well for local playback, but they are not optimized for streaming. The following list describes several of the technical inadequacies of these formats that ASF addresses:

- **Common timeline.** Streaming multimedia often requires the synchronization of streams to a common timeline. WAV and AVI format files don't contain time stamps on the multimedia data. ASF data is time-stamped, allowing audio, video, and script command streams to be synchronized.

- **File size.** WAV and AVI format files conform to the Resource Interchange File Format (RIFF) specifications. RIFF files are made up of data units called *chunks*. The header for each chunk contains a 32-bit *length field* that specifies the size in bytes of the chunk. Using a 32-bit field limits the length of a chunk to 4 gigabytes. In ASF, chunks are replaced by objects. ASF objects use a 64-bit length field that specifies the size of the object. By increasing the length field from 32 to 64 bits, the size of an ASF object can be substantially larger than a RIFF chunk. An ASF object can potentially contain many hours of video or audio.

- **Bit rate.** WAV and AVI format files assume a fixed sampling rate or constant bit rate (CBR). ASF is designed to support variable bit rate (VBR) audio and video compression. RIFF formats specify a header followed by unstructured chunks of multimedia data. The only way to find a precise time in a RIFF file is to use an estimate of the average number of bytes being consumed. ASF allows for VBR compression schemes with an index for locating a specific time in the presentation.

- **Media support.** WAV and AVI format files are not considered robust enough for the next generation of multimedia. WAV format files are limited to audio content, and AVI format files are limited to audio and video content. The next wave of digital media requires a file format that will also support captions, still images, script commands, and slide shows. ASF is specifically designed to be extensible, which ensures that ASF will support new types of multimedia data as they evolve.

ASF features

ASF is an exceptional format for transporting multimedia data over networks efficiently, and adapting to variable bandwidths and changing network conditions. ASF does *not* require any special codecs, network protocols, or media composition frameworks. It also provides many benefits for rendering content. Some of the key features of ASF include:

- **Synchronization.** One important aspect of streaming is the ability to synchronize multiple media streams along a common timeline. ASF makes it easy to synchronize different types of media to precise times in a presentation. A simple example is the synchronization of audio and video. Each stream has its own data structure, but both streams must be synchronized for proper playback. ASF provides a common timeline for all of the streams in a presentation and individual time stamps for objects in each stream.

- **Codec independence.** ASF is codec independent. It does not replace existing media compression-decompression algorithms; instead, the data contained in an ASF presentation can be compressed by using any codec. Information stored in the ASF header object specifies the codec that was used to compress the data. This enables the player to recognize which codec to use to decompress the data. Microsoft Windows Media Player supports component download. If a client does not have the codec necessary to play some content, Windows Media Player automatically locates the codec on a Microsoft Web site, and then downloads and installs it. The codec that is needed to render the content is always available to the client computer.

- **Network protocol independence.** ASF defines a file-level interchange format that is network protocol independent. It does not specify how the data is broken into packets. ASF can be transported over any underlying data communication transport protocol. ASF is an efficient format for streaming data over unicast- or multicast-enabled networks, using a variety of protocols, including UDP, TCP, and HTTP.

- **Scalability.** ASF is scalable to any bandwidth. Each media type is stored as an individual stream. The size of each stream is variable, and the number of streams is variable. ASF can contain mutually exclusive instances of the same content that has been encoded for delivery at different bandwidths. This enables the server to improve stream quality during a presentation if network congestion eases and data can be transferred faster.

- **Extensibility.** ASF is an open, extensible format. ASF already supports a wide variety of existing media types, such as audio, video, slide shows, and still images. ASF also supports many innovative new media types, such as text, URLs, and script commands. As new types of media evolve, for example, three-dimensional animation, ASF can be extended tosupport them.

ASF architecture

Building on the lessons learned from earlier media formats, ASF was designed so that it could be optimized for streaming and rendering multimedia. By basing ASF on *objects,* the format is flexible and powerful. This section provides a general overview of the structure of ASF objects and shows how they are arranged in a multimedia presentation.

Principles of Digital
Compression and Encoding

ASF objects

An *ASF object* is the basic unit of organization for an ASF presentation. There are three types of ASF objects:

- **Header objects**, which contain information about the multimedia presentation and the content in each stream in the presentation.

- **Data objects**, which contain a linear stream of multimedia data packets.

- **Index objects**, which contain an index of entries to the packets in the data stream.

ASF objects, regardless of their type, adhere to the format depicted in Figure 10.8.

Figure 10.8.

Parts of an ASF object.

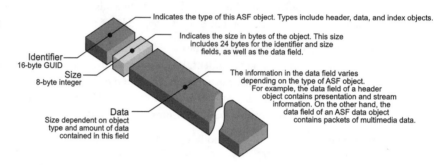

Indicates the type of this ASF object. Types include header, data, and index objects.

Indicates the size in bytes of the object. This size includes 24 bytes for the identifier and size fields, as well as the data field.

Identifier
16-byte GUID

Size
8-byte integer

Data
Size dependent on object type and amount of data contained in this field

The information in the data field varies depending on the type of ASF object. For example, the data field of a header object contains presentation and stream information. On the other hand, the data field of an ASF data object contains packets of multimedia data.

ASF objects can contain other ASF objects. For example, ASF header objects contain a properties object that contains information about the multimedia presentation.

The size field of an ASF object includes the length of all ASF objects contained in that object. The ability to read the first 24 bytes of an object to determine its type and size, provides the foundation for applications to quickly and easily navigate through ASF files.

Header objects

ASF header objects contain information needed by Windows Media Player to correctly render the presentation. ASF multimedia presentations must have one (and only one) header object.

Various objects contained in the header object specify properties of the entire presentation, as well as properties that are specific to each stream. Objects that are contained by the header object include:

- **The properties object.** This object contains information about the multimedia presentation, such as length of the file, playback duration, and transmission duration. One properties object is required for each ASF presentation.

- **The stream properties object.** This object contains information about each stream in the presentation. A stream properties object is required for each media stream in an ASF multimedia presentation. For example, the audio and video streams have an associated stream properties object in the header object. Information contained in stream properties objects include the type of stream, error concealment strategy, and information about locating and acquiring the appropriate rendering engine.

- **The content description object.** This object contains metadata describing the contents of the presentation. Content information includes the title, the author's name, copyright information, and a rating. The content description object is optional.

- **The error correction object.** This object contains a description of the algorithm used for error correction. The error correction object is optional.

- **The script command object.** This object contains a list of script commands to be executed at specified times in the presentation. Script command objects are optional.

- **The marker object.** This object contains a list of points in the timeline. Adding markers to a presentation enables the end user to seek specific points in the presentation. For example, a music compilation might contain markers at the beginning of each song. Marker objects are optional.

Data objects

An ASF data object contains all of the digitized media streams for the multimedia presentation. The streams are organized into *data units* (or data packets) that are ready to be streamed and/or rendered.

ASF is network protocol independent; therefore, data units can be optimized for delivery over a variety of networks. ASF data units are transport independent and support transmission over reliable or unreliable protocols. Some of the features that make ASF data units so flexible and efficient for streaming include:

- The multimedia data is packaged into uniformly sized data units that are inserted into network packets for digital transmission. The data units can be sized to optimize transmission over any network.

- ASF data units can contain data from one stream or data interleaved from several streams. Interleaving multiple streams allows data units to be densely packed with data. This feature enables efficient transmission over any network.

ASF data units are arranged in the data object according to when they are scheduled to be transmitted by the media server. This is called the *send time*. In addition to the send time, each piece of data carried in a data unit carries a time stamp that specifies when that data should be rendered by Windows Media Player. This is called the *presentation time*. Knowing the send and presentation times enables the server and Windows Media Player to work together to send and receive a presentation at a constant bit rate. This is ideal for transmission over networks.

Index objects

An ASF presentation can contain an index object for each video stream. The index object is a list of time-based entries of data units in the data object. Index entries generally point to *video key frames* (also called *index frames*). The ability to find key frames enables the player to seek to specific times in the presentation and fast-forward and rewind at varying speeds.

ASF file organization

In addition to defining objects optimized for streaming media, ASF specifies how the objects are organized into a multimedia file. All .asf files have a header object at the beginning of the file, followed by a data object. The header object provides the player with the information it needs to process the data units that are contained in the data object as they arrive.

Each .asf file must contain one header object and one data object. In addition, one index object can be present for each video stream in the ASF presentation. Figure 10.9 depicts the layout of a typical ASF file.

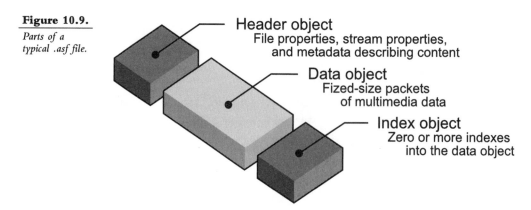

Figure 10.9.

Parts of a typical .asf file.

Header object
File properties, stream properties, and metadata describing content

Data object
Fized-size packets of multimedia data

Index object
Zero or more indexes into the data object

ASF header objects are transmitted to the client independently of the data and index objects. Header objects are sent to the client to be processed in their entirety. However, the data object is never sent whole. It is sent one data unit at a time. Rendering is based on arriving packets, not on the data object as a whole. In this way, the player can inspect the contents of the header object and acquire the information it needs to render the presentation before it receives any data units.

Sending the header and data independently also means that the header object can be sent using a reliable protocol that may not be suitable for streaming multimedia. This ensures that the player has all of the information necessary to render the stream. Packets from the data object can then be sent using a faster, less reliable protocol. This enables the rendering application (the player) to determine how to deal with lost packets. In most cases, a few lost packets will not detract from the presentation. However, waiting for the retransmission of lost packets can.

Using ASF

Aside from its utility for streaming audio, video, images, text, and other data over a network, ASF is being used in other creative ways. The following examples describe some of them.

Multiple bit rate video streams

One useful way of using the ability of ASF to encapsulate multiple media streams is to simultaneously encode multiple video streams that are designed for delivery over different network speeds. In this way, the server and the player can negotiate the optimal stream quality for the available bandwidth.

Local playback

Although ASF was designed primarily as a streaming format, sometimes it is desirable to have the multimedia file stored locally on the computer running Windows Media Player. For example, local storage is a requirement for portable compact audio players. There are several mobile audio players currently available that play music stored in ASF and WMA format. These players can download titles from a personal computer or a server. However, most do not maintain a network connection. Therefore, streaming media from a server is not the best method for distributing media to these clients. This makes it necessary for Windows Media content to support the downloading of content for later playback.

Windows Media Audio files

The explosion of digital music available on the Internet spurred the development of new audio compression routines. With Windows Media Technologies version 4.0, Microsoft introduced a new codec for high quality audio, the Windows Media Audio codec. This codec provides CD-quality music, while compressing audio files to about half the size of those created with conventional codecs (like MP3). ASF audio files that have been compressed using this new codec are called Windows Media Audio (.wma) files.

Many mobile audio players that are currently available are designed to exclusively support the playback of .asf files containing an audio stream encoded with the Windows Media Audio codec. By giving these special .asf files the .wma file extension, music-playing applications can recognize them.

It's very likely that the next version of Windows Media Technologies will support streaming files conforming to the ASF version 2 specification. Look for new file extensions that specifically state the type of media contained in the ASF presentation. This should eliminate confusion about the type of media contained in a presentation.

Using descriptor files

Two files are used by Windows Media Technologies to exchange and save header and stream format information. This section describes ASF Stream Descriptor (.asd) and Windows Media Station (.nsc) files and how they are used.

ASF Stream Descriptor files

ASF Stream Descriptor (.asd) files are configuration files used by Windows Media Encoder. They identify the amount of bandwidth used by the stream, the number of streams encoded, the audio and video codecs used, and the source of the content. You create .asd files with Windows Media Encoder by choosing the **File** menu and clicking **Save**. The next time you start the encoder, you can re-configure it by opening the .asd file. The file can also be used to configure other encoders and to add stream formats to a Windows Media Services multicast station.

In Windows Media Technologies version 4.0, *template stream formats* can be used to configure Windows Media Encoder. Template stream formats are a set of standard configurations that are included with both Windows Media Encoder and Windows Media Services. They provide an easy, quick way to configure Windows Media Encoder. In addition, if you encode a live stream using one of the templates, you can stream from a multicast station immediately without having to add a stream format. For more information about configuring a multicast station, see Chapter 4, "Using Windows Media Services."

Windows Media Station files

Windows Media Services uses the concept of *stations* to enable multicasting. With Windows Media Administrator, part of Windows Media Services, you can create two different kinds of stations:

- *Multicast stations* that define a location from which clients can receive a multicast.

- *Distribution stations* that can be used to stream content past firewalls and distribute streams between network segments that are not multicast-enabled.

Windows Media Station files (.nsc), contain all of the information needed to deliver ASF presentations. The .nsc extension was derived from earlier brand names and concepts used by Windows Media Technologies.

Windows Media Station (.nsc) files store information about the streams contained in a station (for example, which bandwidth they are using and which codec they were encoded with). They also contain information that is specific to the station configuration (for example, which ports the station uses on the server, the URL for the multicast, and the scope of the multicast).

Supplemental reading

Bhaskaran, V. and Konstantinides, K. 1995. *Image and Video Compression Standards: Algorithms and Architectures.* Boston: Kluwer Academic Publishers.

Gersho, A. and R.M. Gray. 1992. *Vector Quantization and Signal Compression.* Boston: Kluwer Academic Publishers.

Jack, K. 1993. *Video Demystified, A Handbook for the Digital Engineer.* Brooktree Corporation. (Solana Beach, CA: HighText Publications Inc.)

Ozer, J. 1994. *Video Compression for Multimedia.* Boston: AP Professional.

Sayood, K. 1996. *Introduction to Data Compression.* San Francisco: Morgan Kaufmann Publishers.

Solari, S.J. 1997. *Digital Video and Audio Compression.* New York: McGraw-Hill.

Principles of Digital
Compression and Encoding

Summary

Analog audio and video is converted to digital form with capture cards. Because of the great bandwidth required by video, you can lessen the size of the video file by decreasing the resolution and/or the frame rate. To reduce the amount of information required in an audio file, you can collapse it into a mono track, use a lower sampling rate, and/or reduce the bit depth.

To handle the bandwidth required by streaming media, compression codecs are used to reduce the size of a file and the bit rate. Windows Media Technologies offers the Windows Media Audio codec, which provides CD-quality sound at half the bandwidth required by most other codecs, and the Microsoft MPEG-4 video codec, which offers scalability and high-quality video.

To deliver synchronized media streams over a network, Windows Media Technologies encodes files in Advanced Streaming Format (ASF). This format is especially suited to streaming because ASF can synchronize different types of media; ASF is independent of any particular codec or protocol; ASF can be scaled to any bandwidth; and ASF is an extensible format.

Chapter 11, "Principles of Networking," describes the basic concepts of networking technologies to help you set up a streaming media system.

Chapter

11

Principles of Networking

This chapter describes the basic concepts of networking technologies to help you design
your streaming media system. After reading this chapter, you'll be able to answer the
following questions:

- What are the basic types of LANs and WANs, and what are the
  limitations of each?

- What are the basic Internet protocols, and how do they differ?

- What are the client/server protocols used by Microsoft Windows Media Technologies,
  and how are they used?

- What is intelligent streaming, and how does it work?

- What are the considerations when streaming through a firewall?

- How do network traffic and bandwidth resources affect the performance of a
  streaming media system?

By understanding the basic concepts of networks, protocols, and capacity planning, you will be able to design a better and more reliable streaming media system. Knowing the impact of each component of your network can help you anticipate problems that might otherwise consume countless hours of troubleshooting when the system is placed into production.

Understanding network topologies

Most networks today are composed of heterogeneous technologies that are combined to achieve the common goal of efficient data transfer between computers. Generally, local area network (LAN) protocol requirements differ from wide area network (WAN) protocol requirements. As a result, the network administrator must understand how to make both LAN and WAN topologies interoperate to build a streaming media system. In addition, the limitations of each technology must be understood to design a system to handle the network traffic caused by streaming media.

LAN topologies

This section describes the following LAN topologies: Ethernet, Fast Ethernet, Gigabit Ethernet, Token Ring, Asynchronous Transfer Mode, and Fiber Distributed Data Interface.

Ethernet

Ethernet (also called IEEE 802.3, one of the standards set by the Institute of Electrical and Electronics Engineers, Inc.) is a widely used base-band network-ing technology. The technology is designed to allow dissimilar computers to communicate over a standard network interface. Ethernet arbitrates for the right to transmit by using the Carrier Sense Multiple Access with Collision Detect (CSMA/CD) algorithm. Ethernet typically operates at a transmission rate of 10 megabits per second (Mbps).

Fast Ethernet

Fast Ethernet is technically composed of two separate competing standards. The 100BaseT standard is an enhancement to the original IEEE 802.3 specification that sped up the data transfer rate to 100 Mbps over the original 10 Mbps transfer rate. The CSMA/CD algorithm is still used in 100BaseT to arbitrate for the right of each node to transmit data on a network segment. The 100BaseT standard is covered under the updated IEEE 802.3 specification. Today, most Fast Ethernet networks are composed of the 100BaseT standard.

100VG-AnyLan is the other standard categorized as Fast Ethernet. This standard employs a new method to negotiate the transmission of data on a segment. Instead of CSMA/CD, 100VG-AnyLan uses a *demand priority* mechanism that is largely controlled by the network switch or hub. The 100VG-AnyLan implementation is documented under the IEEE 802.12 standard.

Gigabit Ethernet

Gigabit Ethernet is a further progression of the IEEE 802.3 standard. Gigabit Ethernet operates at a data transfer rate of 1,000 Mbps. It is used typically for server connections and also for backbone connections. Gigabit Ethernet still uses the CSMA/CD algorithm for arbitrating data transmissions on a given segment.

Token Ring

Token Ring is a base-band network topology that employs a *token* passing mechanism to enable computers to arbitrate for the ability to transmit on the physical network segment. The original Token Ring standard operated at 4 Mbps. The data rate was updated to 16 Mbps.

Asynchronous Transfer Mode

Asynchronous Transfer Mode (ATM) is a broadband network topology designed for advanced networking applications in both LAN and WAN environments. ATM is based on small 53-byte cells to simplify switch design and minimize switching latency. ATM is a multipurpose protocol intended for voice, data, and even digital video traffic. The ATM standard includes provisions to handle increases in data rates automatically as technology progresses. Common data connection rates for ATM in use today include OC-3 (155 Mbps) and OC-12 (625 Mbps).

Unlike Ethernet or Token Ring, ATM offers the inherent ability to dedicate resources to individual connections called *virtual circuits* (VC). A VC can be used to carry a phone conversation or stream video data between two major cities. Multiple VCs can be carried over the same physical cabling. Because the VC can be initialized to require dedicated bandwidth, other applications using the same physical network segments will not adversely affect the dedicated VC. This results in ATM being able to claim that it provides a guaranteed quality of service (QoS).

Although ATM is perhaps the most technically superior networking topology (especially for streaming media), it is not widely used today for connectivity to the desktop. ATM equipment costs remain higher than other competing networking topologies, such as Fast Ethernet. In addition, ATM often requires specialized configuration that adds to the total cost of deployment to the desktop. Instead, it is used for WAN applications and backbone links in corporate LANs.

Fiber Distributed Data Interface

The ANSI X3T9.5 committee developed the network topology Fiber Distri-buted Data Interface (FDDI) as an enhanced networking alternative to other existing network topologies. FDDI operates with a data transmission rate of 100 Mbps. It employs dual ring architecture to allow for redundancy in case the ring is accidentally severed. FDDI is also used for backbone links in corporate LANs.

Principles of Networking

WAN topologies

This section describes the following WAN topologies: digital subscriber line services, ATM, Integrated Services Digital Network, X.25, frame relay, cable modems, analog modems, and T1 digital circuits.

Digital subscriber line services

Digital subscriber line (DSL) is a relatively new WAN topology designed to take advantage of the existing copper-pair phone wires commonly used to connect homes to the local telephone company throughout the world. By replacing existing legacy phone modulation equipment on both sides of the copper-pair phone wires (sometimes called the local loop) with DSL equipment, total data transfer bandwidth can be increased from 56 kilobits per second (Kbps), common with today's analog phone modems, to rates as high as 14 Mbps.

DSL is available in several different versions, one of which is asymmetrical digital subscriber line (ADSL). ADSL has a much smaller upstream bandwidth from the home. Since most Internet client traffic results in a vast majority of the data flow downstream, ADSL is becoming popular for end user usage. However, the fact that DSL is available in several different versions must be considered when choosing a WAN topology to connect a server or encoder to the Internet. Certain versions of DSL may not be good network topologies for both servers and encoders because they require a significant amount of bandwidth to stream data. DSL does generally perform well for streaming media clients, although the bit error rates are often higher than typical LAN connections.

Some versions of DSL support concurrent voice and data traffic. This enables end users to use a standard analog phone while accessing the Internet over the same copper-wire pairs. DSL has some technical limitations. The distance between the home and the local telephone company switching office must be reasonably close for the technology to work. As the distance grows, the data transmission rates that can be achieved with DSL generally drop. Eventually, a distance is reached where DSL is not feasible. Therefore, DSL may never be available to customers that are significantly distant from their local phone switching station.

One attractive aspect of DSL is that the connection between the end user and the phone company is dedicated. Therefore, traffic from other end users will not affect the link. This is in contrast to other home networking connectivity options such as cable modems. Cable modems share bandwidth and can provide varying network throughput performance, depending on the number of end users on the local segment.

ATM

In addition to being a robust LAN topology, Asynchronous Transfer Mode (ATM) is also used as a WAN topology. Many of the new core backbone segments that are being added to the Internet are ATM. This cell-based topology is designed to handle a variety of transmission rates and physical media. This makes it capable of seamlessly handling both LAN and WAN environments.

Integrated Services Digital Network

Integrated Services Digital Network (ISDN) is an established all-digital technology designed to take advantage of the existing copper-pair phone wires commonly used to connect homes to local phone companies throughout the world. ISDN is composed of three separate channels. The first two channels, called *B channels*, are generally 64-Kbps channels that can be used for voice or data traffic. The third channel, called the *D channel*, is used to provide signaling to control the two B channels.

X.25

X.25 is a Consultative Committee for International Telegraph and Telephone (CCITT) standard developed for point-to-point transmission of data. The technology has been used for connecting terminals to mainframe computer systems. With X.25, it is assumed the analog line carrying the data is very lossy. As a result, X.25 is designed to perform considerable error checking along each link. This adds significant overhead to the transmission. Because modern data lines are not nearly as lossy as they were when X.25 was designed, robust error checking is not needed. Therefore, X.25 is not widely used anymore. There are more appropriate WAN networking topologies available, such as frame relay, that provide better efficiency and are more cost effective for streaming media.

Frame relay

Frame relay is a packet-switching architecture similar to X.25, but it does not perform as much error checking. As a result, it has much lower overhead and is considerably faster. The technology was developed as an improvement to X.25 and ISDN. Various data rates can be purchased from a service provider, depending on the needs of the organization. This data rate is often called the *Committed Information Rate* (CIR). This is the minimum sustainable guaranteed transmission rate that will be available. Additional transmission rates may occasionally become available, but the CIR determines the minimum amount that will always be
present. This is important for streaming media, because it is generally desirable to control the minimum amount of available bandwidth.

Many organizations use frame relay to connect encoders at remote sites to the distribution server at another location. Frame relay is often considered very affordable for point-to-point WAN links.

Principles of Networking

Cable modems

The cable modem is a relatively new technology that offers high-speed network access. Cable modems are generally used for Internet connectivity. They are theoretically capable of speeds up to 30 Mbps, although the actual rates achieved depend greatly on a variety of factors.

Cable modems use shared bandwidth with other customers on the same cable segment. As more end users create traffic on the cable network segment, the bandwidth available to each customer declines. The network connection can become noticeably slower under busy conditions. This characteristic should be considered when using cable modems for streaming.

Various types of cable modems are available. Many cable modem designs are asymmetrical. This means the downstream bandwidth is generally much greater than the upstream bandwidth. This factor must be taken into account when considering cable modems for both server and encoder connectivity.

Analog modems

Most modems used today are designed to operate on the standard analog phone lines installed in most homes in the world. These phone lines are often called *plain old telephone service* (POTS) lines. Analog modems use analog signals to send data across the 3,000-hertz (Hz) spectrum supplied by the POTS lines. Newer analog modems have throughput rates that vary depending on the phone line conditions. Generally, native transmission rates range from 28 Kbps to 56 Kbps.

T1 digital circuits

T1 digital circuits are a network topology service that is offered by many communications companies. It is a standard digital line service that can carry both voice and data communications simultaneously, using multiplexing equipment on both ends of the link. The T1 digital circuit has a transmission rate of 1.544 Mbps. T3 services are similar in concept but provide a total transmission rate of 45 Mbps. T1 and T3 services are widely used by corporations for various networking needs. T1 and T3 services still comprise a significant number of links on the Internet.

Understanding network protocols

Microsoft Windows Media Services relies on the Transmission Control Protocol/Internet Protocol (TCP/IP) architecture. TCP/IP is an industry-standard suite of protocols designed for large internetworks spanning both LAN and WAN links. TCP/IP was developed by the U.S. Department of Defense Advanced Research Projects Agency (DARPA). It was the result of a resource-sharing experiment called Advanced Research Projects Agency Network (ARPANET). The purpose of TCP/IP was to provide high-speed communication network links. Since 1969, ARPANET has grown into a worldwide community of networks known as the Internet. Today, TCP/IP is the most widely used and supported computer networking protocol architecture.

Standard Internet protocols

This section describes the following standard Internet protocols: Internet Protocol, Transmission Control Protocol, User Datagram Protocol, and Hypertext Transfer Protocol.

Internet Protocol

Internet Protocol (IP) is a routable network layer protocol responsible for host addressing and the fragmentation and reassembly of packets. All data and control network traffic generated by Windows Media Services are carried by IP packets.

Transmission Control Protocol

Transmission Control Protocol (TCP) is a transport layer protocol. TCP provides a one-to-one, connection-oriented, reliable communications service. TCP is responsible for the establishment of the connection, the sequencing and acknowledgment of packets sent, and the recovery of packets lost during transmission. TCP transmission specifies that the destination computer will occasionally send an acknowledgement for reliably received data packets. If an acknowledgement is not received from the destination computer for a set of consecutive packets, the specification calls for the retransmission of those packets.

User Datagram Protocol

User Datagram Protocol (UDP) is a transport layer protocol that provides a one-to-one or one-to-many, connectionless, unreliable communications service. The UDP protocol is ideal for streaming media. UDP is used in the following situations:

- When the amount of data to be transferred is small (such as the data that would fit into a single packet).

- When the overhead of establishing a TCP connection is not desired.

- When reliable delivery is not needed.

- When certain packets should be delivered to multiple destinations (during a multicast).

- When the applications or upper-layer protocols provide reliable delivery.

Principles of Networking

Hypertext Transfer Protocol

Hypertext Transfer Protocol (HTTP) is an application layer communications protocol initially designed to transfer hypertext documents between computers over the World Wide Web. HTTP defines what actions Web servers and browsers should take in response to various commands.

Windows Media Services client/server protocols

Windows Media Services uses the following client/server protocols: Microsoft Media Server protocol, Microsoft Media Server protocol/UDP, Microsoft Media Server protocol/TCP, and Hypertext Transfer Protocol.

Microsoft Media Server protocol

Microsoft Media Server (MMS) protocol is an application protocol used to access unicast content from a Windows Media publishing point. MMS is the default method of connecting to the Windows Media Unicast service. If end users are going to type a URL in Microsoft Windows Media Player to connect to content rather than access the content through a hyperlink, they must use the MMS protocol and have a reference for the stream.

The MMS protocol contains both a control mechanism to handle client requests, such as Play or Stop, and a data delivery mechanism to ensure media packets arrive in a format that the client recognizes. The control requests are always carried over TCP. The data packets are carried over either TCP or UDP.

When connecting to a URL using the MMS protocol, the *protocol rollover* procedure is used to get the best connection. Protocol rollover starts when a Windows Media server tries to connect the client to the server by using the *MMSU* protocol. MMSU is the MMS protocol that employs the UDP data transport. If the MMSU connection is unsuccessful, the server attempts to use *MMST*. MMST is the MMS protocol that employs the TCP data transport.

When you connect to a publishing point from a stand-alone instance of Windows Media Player, you must specify the URL to the unicast content. If your content is being published on demand over the home publishing point, the URL is composed of the server name and .asf file name. For example:

```
mms://Windows_media_server/Samples.asf
```

Where *Windows_media_server* is the name of the Windows Media server, and *Samples.asf* is the name of the .asf file you want to stream.

If you have live content to publish with a broadcast unicast, the URL is composed of the server name and publishing point alias. For example:

```
mms://Windows_media_server/LiveEvents
```

Where *Windows_media_server* is the name of the Windows Media server, and *LiveEvents* is the name of the publishing point.

Microsoft Media Server protocol/UDP

Microsoft Media Server protocol/UDP (MMSU) is a subset of the MMS protocol. MMSU is used to explicitly request the file to be streamed using the UDP protocol. When MMSU is specified in the URL, protocol rollover to other data protocols such as TCP or HTTP will not occur. This can be useful for testing purposes.

Microsoft Media Server protocol/TCP

Microsoft Media Server protocol/TCP (MMST) is a subset of the MMS protocol. MMST is used to explicitly request the file to be streamed using the TCP protocol. When MMST is specified in the URL, protocol rollover to other data protocols, such as UDP or HTTP, does not occur. This can be useful for testing purposes.

Hypertext Transfer Protocol

You can configure your Windows Media server to use the Hypertext Transfer Protocol (HTTP) to stream content to clients. Using HTTP streaming helps to overcome firewalls as obstacles because most firewalls allow HTTP to pass through. By default, HTTP streaming is not enabled on Windows Media Services. Before enabling HTTP in either the Windows Media Unicast service or the Windows Media Station service, you should be aware of the issues that result. You cannot enable HTTP streaming in both services on the same computer. Figure 11.1 shows a typical configuration that benefits from HTTP streaming.

To use HTTP streaming from the desired Windows Media component service, ensure that HTTP streaming is enabled. Invoke the stream request in the same way you would use MMS in a Web page reference, but instead, use HTTP. For example:

```
http://Windows_media_server/Samples.asf
```

Where *Windows_media_server* is the name of the Windows Media server, and *Samples.asf* is the name of the .asf file you want to stream.

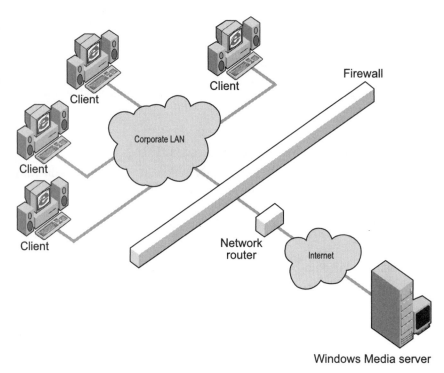

Figure 11.1.

Streaming to clients through a firewall using Hypertext Transfer Protocol (HTTP).

Windows Media Encoder and Windows Media Services protocols

Windows Media Encoder and Windows Media Services use the following protocols: Media Stream Broadcast Distribution protocol and Hypertext Transfer Protocol.

Media Stream Broadcast Distribution protocol

Media Stream Broadcast Distribution (MSBD) protocol is used to distribute streams between Windows Media Encoder and the Windows Media server components and to transfer streams between servers. MSBD is a connection-oriented protocol optimized for use with streaming media. MSBD is useful in testing client/server connectivity and ASF content quality. However, MSBD should not be used as the main method for the client to receive ASF content. Windows Media Encoder can support a maximum of 15 MSBD clients. A Windows Media server can support a maximum of five MSBD clients.

Hypertext Transfer Protocol

HTTP can also be used as a distribution protocol to penetrate firewalls. Encoders or distribution servers often reside on opposite sides of a firewall. Using HTTP, Windows Media Services may be able to penetrate the firewall without having to make configuration changes to the firewall. For example, Figure 11.2 shows an intranet scenario where all the computers reside on the corporate LAN except the encoder. This can be done because the remote encoding site does not have a direct connection to the corporate LAN. In this case, HTTP distribution can be used to provide a way to feed the distribution server.

There are many different scenarios that can greatly benefit from the use of HTTP streaming. By creatively using all the available technologies in Windows Media Services, you can minimize the changes to the existing network infrastructures and maintain the level of Internet security for the corporate LAN.

If you are running Windows Media Services on the same computer as a Web server, such as Microsoft Internet Information Server (IIS), be sure there is not a conflict on port 80. For more information, see "Running Windows Media Services and IIS on the same server" in Chapter 4.

Figure 11.2.

An encoder feeding a distribution server through a firewall.

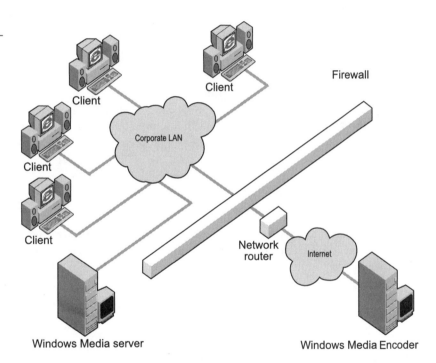

Principles of Networking

Understanding basic client streaming

Client streaming is the ultimate goal of Windows Media Services. It is important to understand the issues surrounding client streaming to effectively design the entire system and also to troubleshoot problems as they occur. This section describes many of the issues that affect client streaming, including protocol rollover, changing client proxy settings, proxy auto-detection, and measuring reception quality.

Protocol rollover

When Windows Media Player attempts to open a URL containing a reference to the MMS protocol, the final protocol used to actually stream the data is not necessarily known. When you use the MMS protocol to publish your .asf file, protocol rollover is automatic from the MMS data protocol over UDP (MMSU), to the MMS data protocol over TCP (MMST), and finally to HTTP. When attempting to connect to the stream source, Windows Media Player tries each protocol in turn until a successful connection to the source is made. This ensures that Windows Media Player can reach the data.

> **NOTE** In certain situations protocol rollover may hide a potential problem. If the configuration of the Windows Media Services system ensures that no one will be able to successfully stream over MMS, then use of the MMS protocol is not optimal even with protocol rollover. In such cases, a URL explicitly referencing HTTP may be the most appropriate. This is because protocol rollover adds delay as each protocol is attempted.

Protocol rollover can also be controlled using a <REF> tag in an .asx file. The <REF> tag can be used to specify different protocols to reach the same source. For example, if the first <REF> tag specifies the MMSU protocol and the second <REF> tag specifies the HTTP link, clients that cannot connect by using MMSU (because they are behind a firewall) can automatically try to connect using HTTP. Windows Media Player performs this type of rollover automatically when you specify the MMS protocol as you create a unicast publishing point, but the .asx file allows the end user to come up with alternative ways to implement protocol rollover.

URL rollover can also be used to specify different Windows Media servers that contain the same content. For example, if the first <REF> tag specifies an .asf file on a server called *hound1* and the second <REF> tag specifies a copy of the file on *hound2*, Windows Media Player can reach the file using either server. If *hound1* is too busy or fails, Windows Media Player automatically connects to *hound2*. This is a simple but effective way to provide both load distribution and fault tolerance.

Changing client proxy settings

Windows Media Player can be configured with three basic HTTP proxy settings. This can be accomplished using the **Advanced playback settings** tab shown in Figure 11.3.

Figure 11.3.

The Advanced playback settings tab in Windows Media Player.

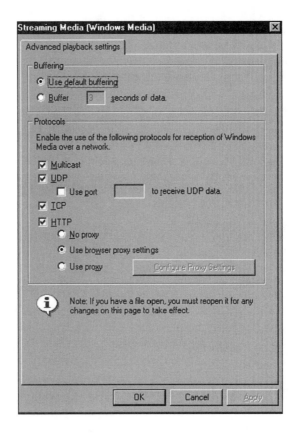

The **No Proxy** option should not be used for most installations. It means that the player will not use any proxy settings at all. The **Use browser proxy settings** option is the default value when the player is installed. Even if a proxy is not used, this value is generally desirable because it implies that only the browser settings need to be changed if a configuration change to the network is performed. The **Use proxy** option is appropriate if no browser is installed on the system, but a proxy is required to stream HTTP from the Internet. The **Use proxy** option is also appropriate if you want to use a different proxy for streaming media. The **Use proxy** option is also useful for troubleshooting proxy settings directly without having to alter your browser settings.

Proxy auto-detection

Web Proxy Auto-Discovery (WPAD) Protocol is an Internet Engineering Task Force (IETF) draft proposed to ease the use of network proxies. Proxies are typically used in corporations as a single gateway to the outside world. It enables security via firewall support as well as efficiency via caching. The problem with using proxies is that, typically, every client machine must manually configure the name of the proxy in its browser or other software. WPAD alleviates some of this work by providing a mechanism to automatically discover the proxy name.

WPAD became available in Microsoft Internet Explorer 5. By using the WPAD feature in Internet Explorer 5 and ensuring that the Windows Media Player client is configured to use browser proxy settings, network administrators can update proxy settings for both browsers and Windows Media Player from a central location. It is no longer necessary for end users to manually change these values on each client computer.

The first HTTP streaming request should result in an auto-detection attempt if:

- Windows Media Player has been installed or upgraded from version 3.

- Internet Explorer 5 is installed and configured to use WPAD, and **Use browser proxy settings** is selected in the player.

If auto-detection succeeds, the proxy information is stored in the registry. If the attempt fails, the time of the failure is recorded and stored in the registry, and a new attempt to detect the proxy settings is performed one week later.

If the end user applies any change to the HTTP proxy settings in Windows Media Player, the auto-detection information in the end user's registry is cleared, and auto-detection logic is invoked. This behavior can be useful to force a new auto-detection attempt on demand for testing purposes.

Measuring reception quality

Measuring reception quality is important to determine overall end user satisfaction. Measuring reception quality is also an excellent data point for troubleshooting problems. It is highly recommended that you pay attention to these statistics because poor reception quality generally indicates serious problems somewhere in the overall system. This section describes how to gather that information and what you can interpret from it.

Windows Media Player statistics

The Windows Media Player **Statistics** dialog box can be displayed while the end user watches or listens to a program. The **Statistics** dialog box provides information critical to understanding the quality of the reception and determining where problems may lie. Figure 11.4 shows the Windows Media Player **Statistics** dialog box.

The **Statistics** dialog box displays useful information about reception rate and quality. A large number of lost or recovered packets suggest a problem in the system. On reliable LAN networks, the reception quality is generally 100 percent with only occasional packet loss. On the Internet, depending on the data protocol, it is more common to lose packets. Excessive packet loss can sometimes indicate the networking infrastructure between the client and the server is not sufficient to handle sustained bandwidth.

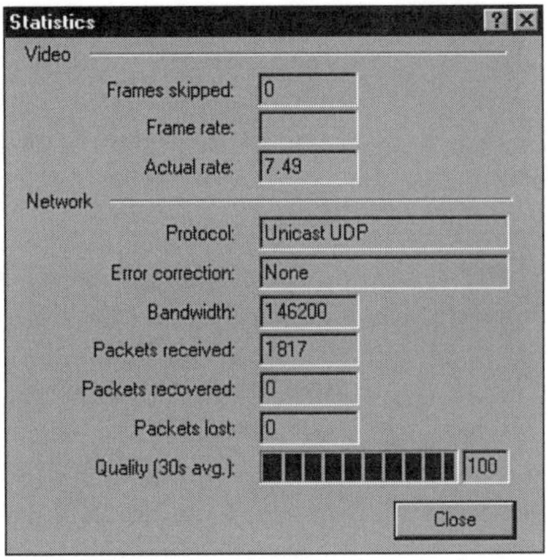

Figure 11.4.

*The Statistics
dialog box.*

It is often valuable to use Windows Media Player at various points along the network to determine where possible bottlenecks exist. If Windows Media Player is connected on the same corporate LAN segment as the server streaming the data and reception quality is still poor, the server or local switch configuration may be to blame. By strategically measuring reception quality at points along all possible network segments, the problem can be isolated.

Intelligent streaming

Intelligent streaming helps compensate for router queue build-up, network congestion, and packet loss to ensure stream delivery to the end user.

Routers on the Internet receive and deliver data on network segments that are often very busy. At times, the router can become congested due to an overburdened downstream link. When this happens, some routers buffer the data until the transient congestion on the downstream segment eases or until the router runs out of memory space to buffer additional packets. This temporary buffering can sometimes add enough jitter to the packet arrival times at the client to cause problems.

Limitations of TCP for real-time traffic

TCP is inherently limited for use in streaming multimedia in a real-time environment. When there is network congestion, a TCP connection will reduce the data transfer rate without notifying the server. The server, therefore, doesn't have an opportunity to reduce the video bit rate. This is especially true if any of the network links used to deliver the streaming data is approaching saturation. TCP employs an acknowledgement (ACK) mechanism for each packet sent. If an ACK is not received from the destination computer for each packet after a certain amount of time has elapsed, the transmitting computer resends the packet. This is a problem for streaming media because the ACK messages add more traffic to the overall network. In addition, because of the general-purpose nature of the TCP implementation, it continues to retry sending the packet if an ACK is not received. When streaming real-time live data over a link that is nearly saturated, a point is reached when retransmission of the same packet must be stopped and new packets must be sent.

Imagine this scenario: a real-time transmission of a live show. If the data being streamed is transmitted at a rate approaching the modem speed of the client, and TCP resends a packet because an ACK is not received the first time, a problem will develop. New packets will also be sent with the retransmitted packets. Because the modem link is not capable of receiving this additional traffic burden simultaneously, new packets will not arrive at the client. The server will then resend more and more packets until the modem link is hopelessly overburdened and the client has fallen considerably behind in receiving the live data. Noticeable gaps and pauses in the audio and video will result.

UDP unicast with retransmissions

UDP is much better suited to the needs of real-time multimedia streaming. Loss of any one packet of streaming data is not considered catastrophic, but efforts are made to minimize packet loss. UDP unicast with retransmission is an excellent method to achieve minimal packet delivery overhead while still maintaining a reasonable amount of delivery quality.

With MMS, ACKs are not delivered from the client back to the server. Instead, the client sends negative acknowledgments (NAKs) whenever a packet is not received, or if the packet received is corrupted. The server then attempts a single retransmission of the packet. If that retransmission also fails, the packet is simply lost and the client will observe a momentary glitch in the multimedia program.

IP multicast with forward error correction

Implementing UDP retransmissions is not feasible when using a multicast scenario. This is because when a packet is lost in a multicast scenario, it is generally lost simultaneously by many clients. This will cause all these clients to submit a retransmission request at the same time. This could also result in a severe spike in the processing load of the server as well as huge additional demands on the network.

Instead of using UDP retransmissions, Windows Media Services uses an error correction technology called *forward error correction* (FEC). FEC is a technology that adds parity information to the data packets sent by multicast to the client. When packets are occasionally lost, the client can use the parity information in the surrounding packets to reconstruct the lost packet. Windows Media Services uses a FEC pattern that allows the client to reconstruct about one packet for every 10 sent. If more packets are lost in a sequence of 10 multicast packets, data loss still occurs.

Multiple bit rate video

With Windows Media Technologies version 4.0, content providers can offer as many as five different bit rates for both on-demand and live video streams in a single Advanced Streaming Format (.asf) file. When Windows Media Services and Windows Media Player connect, they automatically determine the available bandwidth between the client and the server. The server then selects and serves the appropriate video stream. If the available bandwidth changes during a transmission, the server will automatically detect this and switch to a stream with a higher or lower bit rate.

Network gateways

This section provides information on firewalls, proxy servers, and network address translation (NAT). Many corporations are connected to the Internet with a device commonly called a *firewall*. A firewall filters the traffic between the corporate LAN and the Internet, mainly for security purposes. The firewall is generally configured to allow only certain types of traffic to flow between the Internet and the corporation. Corporations often use different policies for traffic. Many corporations allow HTTP traffic to cross through the firewall (or proxy server) as long as the request originated within the corporate LAN. However, they may use a policy that denies other TCP or UDP traffic. Because of this, HTTP is often a convenient way for streaming media to penetrate corporate firewalls.

Firewalls and proxy servers

The firewall receives formatted network requests from clients inside the corporation and marshals them out onto the Internet. It also marshals traffic from the Internet that is destined within the corporation. This work is generally done at the network layer and/or the transport layer of the Open Systems Interconnection (OSI) model.

A *proxy server* is generally considered to be a firewall with additional capabilities such as caching. Proxy servers can act as application gateways, meaning they are capable of operating on the higher OSI model layers, such as the application layer.

Network address translation

A network address translation (NAT) is a device used to translate IP addresses from an internal network to IP addresses that are valid on the Internet. This is done for a variety of reasons. The number of available valid Internet IP addresses is dwindling. NATs allow the network administrator to assign IP addresses to an internal network that are not reserved for use on the Internet. The NAT then translates the internal IP address (which isn't necessarily valid on the Internet) to an official Internet IP address.

The assignment is usually done dynamically. This means that only computers that are currently active on the Internet require a valid Internet IP address. This greatly reduces the number of IP addresses that a company must obtain to allow all computers access to the Internet.

Another benefit of using a NAT is security. When the IP translation occurs dynamically, it is nearly impossible to determine the identity of the end user inside the internal network, based solely on the IP address. This helps with maintaining the confidentiality of the end user.

Network capacity planning

Streaming media places demands on the network infrastructure that should be understood before a deployment. Unless care is taken, the additional traffic caused by streaming media could affect the performance of other network applications.

Multicast versus unicast transmission

Windows Media Services uses the terms *unicast* and *multicast* to describe how clients receive data packets from a Windows Media server. A unicast is a point-to-point connection between the client and the server. *Point-to-point* means that each client receives a distinct stream from the server. Unicast streams are sent only to the client that requested it. Unicast streams can be distributed to a client using either an on-demand stream or a broadcast stream.

A *multicast* is a content stream delivered over a multicast-enabled network. All clients on the network share the same stream. The biggest advantage of streaming ASF content this way is that it saves network bandwidth. Consider a scenario in which 1,000 clients are watching a 28.8-Kbps program. If all clients are streaming by way of the unicast method, the total bandwidth transmitted by the server is 28.8 Mbps (1,000 Kbps). However, if all the clients are streaming via multicast, the server will only be transmitting a total of 28.8 Kbps.

Not all networking equipment supports multicasting. In addition, not all network administrators have the multicast functionality of their networking equipment enabled. Consult your network administrator for information about this. In general, multicast support is not yet available on the Internet. Therefore, use of multicast to deliver content is limited to intranet-style deployments.

You can extend a multicast through areas of the network that are not multicast-enabled by setting up Windows Media servers on each segment of your network—this is called server distribution. As part of a multicast from a server, you can distribute a single stream (of that multicast) to other Windows Media servers on other segments of the network. The servers subsequently provide the stream to their network segment by way of unicast or multicast, depending on the availability of multicast; this is known as *re-distribution*. By chaining one server to another, you can overcome routers that are not multicast-enabled. This model also works for getting through a firewall or through a segment of the Internet.

The Windows Media Services administrator must create three items to support a multicast:

- A station serves as the reference point for clients who want to connect to the stream.

- A program organizes content items that are going to be broadcast over the station.

- A stream is the actual content.

After all of these are created, Windows Media Administrator creates an .asx file that links clients to the correct IP address for the station; this file is also called an *announcement*. You can link to the announcement file from a Web page, place it in a public share point on the network, or send it to clients by e-mail.

Using multiple servers

Use of multiple servers can increase scalability considerably. Consider the scenario of a large corporation with several remote sites inter-networked with a T1 network link. Each remote site may employ thousands of workers. Now consider a company meeting being shown by unicast with Windows Media Services. If only one server is used in this configuration, the T1 links connecting the remote sites will become overloaded. In this scenario, a distribution server makes good sense. By using a distribution server in each remote site, only a single media stream will pass over each of the T1 links. The clients at each remote site can then attach directly to the distribution server located at their site.

Another way multiple servers can enhance scalability is by duplicating servers. This can provide fault tolerance as well as increased scalability. However, duplication implies some technical challenges that must be overcome.

Load balancing of new requests across servers

If multiple servers are used to stream the same unicast data, clients must somehow be directed to attach to the least loaded server. This concept of load balancing across computers can be accomplished in a few different (although imperfect) ways.

The Domain Name Server (DNS) round-robin technique is frequently used on the Internet to balance the load across servers. When a client requests a name-to-IP address resolution from the DNS server and the name has multiple IP addresses associated with

Principles of Networking

it, the DNS server reorders the list of IP addresses each time it answers a client name resolution request. The client takes this list and attempts to connect to the first server IP address in the list. If the client cannot contact the first IP address in the list, the second IP address is attempted. This continues until the client successfully contacts a valid IP address or until there are no more addresses left to contact.

This method does have shortcomings. First, there is no way to ensure that clients do not attempt to stream from the busiest server in the group. In addition, if the server is connected to the network, but Windows Media Services is not running on that particular server because of some failure or configuration error, the client will not attempt to contact the other servers in the DNS list.

Another way to provide load balancing across servers is to use Microsoft® Windows NT® Load Balancing Service (WLBS). For more information, see "Windows NT Load Balancing Service" later in this chapter.

Load balancing can even be accomplished indirectly using dynamically generated Web pages to point the client to the least busy media server when they browse the Web page containing the title URLs. For example, the Windows Media Services administration control can be used to monitor the status of the individual server. When a client requests the Web page that contains the titles that are available on the server cluster, a process can query the status of each server through the administration control and then build the URL for each title accordingly. This method provides the most robust design, but it also requires considerable software development.

Data replication

Multiple servers that provide load balancing generally must be configured with the same data. This places a burden on the administrator to ensure that the data files on each of the servers are synchronized. Various tools exist to help make sure this happens. For instance, Microsoft Windows NT Server has a service called Directory Replication. Software vendors offer more sophisticated tools to accomplish this task.

Enabling HTTP streaming

By default, HTTP streaming from Windows Media Services is disabled. Enabling HTTP streaming can greatly increase the number of clients who can access your server. Many corporations have firewalls that prevent non-HTTP traffic from passing through to internal clients. By enabling HTTP streaming on Windows Media Services, these corporate clients are able to successfully stream data from the Internet to their computer located on the internal LAN.

Web servers generally receive HTTP requests on TCP port 80. Therefore, many firewalls typically pass through port 80 HTTP requests destined for machines on the Internet. Windows Media Services uses this feature of firewalls by allowing the end user to stream

HTTP through port 80. However, there is a problem with this. Because both Windows Media Services and most common Web servers, such as Microsoft IIS, attempt to bind to port 80 to service client HTTP requests, a conflict may occur if both services are run on the same computer
and care is not taken. For further details about how to handle this issue, see "Running Windows Media Services and IIS on the same server" in Chapter 4.

To enable HTTP streaming for either the Windows Media Unicast service or Windows Media Station service, use Windows Media Administrator to connect to the specific server you want to enable. Select the **Server Properties** menu to access the **Configure Server – Server Properties** page in Windows Media Administrator.

Select the service for which you want to enable HTTP, click **Apply**, close the Web Administrator, and restart the server. The change will be in effect after the server is restarted.

HTTP streaming can be used to stream content from Windows Media Encoder through a firewall to a Windows Media server. It can also be used to connect Windows Media servers that are separated by a firewall.

Windows NT Load Balancing Service

Windows NT Load Balancing Service (WLBS) works by using a single IP address that is shared between the servers in the cluster. WLBS is installed as a standard Windows NT networking driver and runs on an existing LAN. After it's installed, it basically operates in a manner that is transparent to both the server applications and to the TCP/IP clients. TCP/IP clients can access the cluster as if it is a single computer by using one IP address. Under normal operations, WLBS automatically balances the networking traffic between the clustered servers, scaling the performance of one server to the level required across the servers in the cluster. When a server fails or goes offline, WLBS automatically reconfigures the cluster to direct the client connections to the remaining servers. The offline server can transparently rejoin the cluster and regain its share of the workload.

Windows Media Services version 4.0 is not specifically integrated with WLBS. Therefore, WLBS measures server loading mainly by raw connection requests. For Windows Media Services to work properly, WLBS should be configured with a single client affinity.

Using multiple network cards

One method to achieve higher throughput from a single server is to use multiple network cards. This method requires careful examination to ensure no other problems are encountered. For example, even though additional network bandwidth may be available, when using multiple network cards, it is important to ensure that other adequate resources such as CPU power, available RAM, and disk throughput are also available. Load balancing among each network card also must be handled. For example, the system may not behave well if 90 percent of the clients attach through one network card and only 10 percent of the clients connect to the other network card. Load balancing approaches, such as round-robin DNS or the use of multiple publishing points, should be considered.

On systems with heavy loads, it is sometimes advisable to use multiple network cards for reasons other than the additional aggregate bandwidth. Ethernet and Fast Ethernet are essentially *base-band technologies*. This means that only one computer can transmit data at any given time on a particular network segment. If a server is configured to receive data from an encoder and also simultaneously transmit the data out to a hundred or even thousands of client computers, network segment contention issues can result in delays in video reception. As the system becomes more loaded, these delays can become noticeable to the end user. An effective workaround to this problem is to receive encoder data on one network card and service client connections on the other network card. This ensures that additional client connection traffic will not affect the reception of the encoder data.

Effective versus rated network card bandwidth

The sustained effective throughput of a network card is generally lower than the rated line speed. For example, the Fast Ethernet network card is rated to transmit data at 100 Mbps, but the sustained throughput is often much lower. The discrepancy between effective and rated throughput can vary between network card manufacturers, driver versions, operating systems, reception traffic patterns, and transmission traffic patterns.

Laboratory tests with Windows Media Services have shown that the effective sustained throughput of various Fast Ethernet network cards can vary between 60 Mbps, for some of the lower-quality network cards, to around 80 Mbps, for some of the higher-quality network cards. These rates can also vary depending on your particular traffic patterns and the type of content that is being streamed.

Laboratory tests with Windows Media Services have also shown that the effective sustained throughput of various Gigabit Ethernet network cards have a much higher throughput discrepancy. It is important to consider these discrepancies when designing the overall system. The throughput of each individual link must be sustainable over the various transient conditions for the end user to be assured reliable delivery of streaming content. Consult the manufacturer for details on the effective sustained throughput rates of the network card when used in a Windows NT environment.

Client connection rates

A server running Windows Media Services processes client connection requests at a rate of 25 per second. Processing client connection requests uses system resources (CPU cycles and memory) and, depending on your computer hardware configuration, may adversely affect server performance and the quality of the media streams to clients connected to your server.

The value for the number of client connection requests processed per second is set to 25 because a computer that meets the minimum system requirements for a Windows Media server can process 25 connection requests per second without impacting the quality of streams being delivered to connected clients. If you are using a computer with multiple processors and a large amount of memory, your computer may be able to process a greater number of connections per second. However, before deciding to increase this value, it is recommended that you carefully evaluate the use of your computer's CPU and memory. When a server is delivering content to many end users, the number of connection requests it can handle may decrease due to resource constraints.

To set the server connection rate to a custom value, you must edit the system registry for each Windows Media server you want changed. The registry key HKEY_LOCAL_MACHINE\SYSTEM\CurrentControlSet\Services\nsunicast\Parameters\MaxConnectionsPerSecond can be set to a custom value if the connection rate is too high or too low for a particular hardware configuration. The default value for this key is 25.

When a connection request is sent from a client to a Windows Media server, the request is placed in a connection queue. After connection requests are received by the server and placed in a queue, they are processed. If the rate of clients attempting to connect to the server exceeds the client connection rate for processing these connection requests, the queue becomes full. The value for the number of client connection requests placed in the queue is equal to 20 times the value of client connections per second, or 500 by default. This value is set to 20 times the connection rate because Windows Media Player is set to wait 20 seconds before attempting to connect using a failover URL. All requests in the queue get processed within the 20-second wait period.

The server keeps a count of clients placed in the queue. When the maximum allowed number of requests has been placed in the queue, the server stops listening for connection requests. Any client that attempts to connect is immediately sent a message that the server is unavailable. The end user making the request does not wait in a queue before being informed that the connection request was unsuccessful. Each time this occurs, a Windows Media log entry is made with the error code 503. A Microsoft Windows NT Server Application Event Log entry is also made with the message "Windows Media Services has reached its maximum pending connections value of %1." However, this entry is only made when the server stops listening and a log entry has not been made in the preceding minute. Here, %1 is a variable, and the number displayed is the size of the queue. The server then checks every 2.5 seconds to see if the queue is full. If clients have been processed out of the queue, the server again begins to listen for connection requests.

Principles of Networking

Network configuration and design issues

Some larger Windows Media Services configurations require significant system bandwidth resources. These requirements must be considered when selecting all network devices used to connect the clients, servers, and encoders. Line speeds of individual network ports on a switch are one of the many considerations that are important.

Network duplex settings

Many network switches allow for half duplex, full duplex, or auto-negotiate configurations. *Full duplex* is a term used to describe the ability to simultaneously transmit and receive data. Equipment that operates in half duplex cannot transmit and receive data simultaneously. Instead, *half-duplex* operation means that if a transmission is occurring, no data can be received until the transmission is complete.

For Windows Media Services, it is very important that servers and encoders are placed on network segments that operate in full duplex. This helps prevent data jitter or loss caused by any handshaking or flow control from the underlying protocols during the streaming process.

Some networking devices attempt to auto-negotiate the duplex setting. While this is convenient from a configuration perspective, the auto-negotiation often results in a non-optimal duplex setting. It is strongly suggested that you explicitly configure all capable network devices to full duplex whenever possible to prevent inadvertent half-duplex operation. Network congestion caused by inappropriate equipment configuration can often be time consuming to troubleshoot. Using full duplex whenever possible can help minimize the problems encountered—especially when the system is used under heavy load.

Network switch throughput capabilities

Some switches are known as *blocking*. This means that the switch fabric (used to interconnect the switch ports) is not capable of supporting the maximum speed of each individual port simultaneously. In other words, if a blocking switch is under heavy load, a port that normally can handle 100 Mbps worth of data traffic may only be able to process a smaller amount of data. Problems caused by blocking network switches are extremely difficult to diagnose. Therefore, it is important for the network designer to understand all of the issues when designing a solution. This is especially true when the overall throughput of the Windows Media Services system approaches many megabits per second. Consult your network device technical specifications to ensure the device is capable of the sustained aggregate throughput you require for your system.

Network router throughput capabilities

Router throughput is typically less than switch throughput. Therefore, when streaming large data rates through a router, it is important to ensure the router is designed to handle the required sustained aggregate data throughput.

Network link segment saturation and effective throughput

Consider link segment saturation and effective throughput when designing a Windows Media Services system or when you are troubleshooting problems. Bandwidth between any two points is always restricted by the least capable segment. In addition, some network segments (such as WAN segments) are shared between various applications. The aggregate traffic must be considered.

Summary

The infrastructure of your network is the key to the performance and reliability of your streaming media system. To prevent the additional traffic of streaming media from adversely affecting the performance of other network applications, you should understand and anticipate the unique demands placed on your network by streaming media.

By understanding how LAN and WAN topologies work together and the limitations of each, you can configure your system to handle network traffic. Windows Media Technologies uses protocols in addition to TCP/IP to handle streaming media; by understanding how these protocols work together, you can ensure that your system can reliably deliver streaming media over a network, as well as stream through a firewall. Finally, you should take into consideration the different ways you can compensate for network limitations; for example, use intelligent streaming, multiple servers, or load balancing.

Principles of Networking

Audio and Video Capture Cards

This section lists the video capture cards that have been tested with Windows Media Encoder and are known to be reliable for encoding Windows Media content. Any sound card compatible with Creative Labs Sound Blaster 16 is recommended for capturing audio.

NOTE For an updated list of supported audio and video capture cards, see the Windows Media Web site (http://www.microsoft.com/windows/windowsmedia/).

Multimedia Access Corporation

http://www.osprey.mmac.com/
Osprey 100
Compatible with Microsoft Windows 98 and Microsoft Windows NT 4.0
(x86 and Alpha)

ATI Technologies Inc.

http://www.atitech.ca/
All-In-Wonder
Compatible with Windows 98

Hauppauge Computer Works

http://www.hauppauge.com/
WinCast/TV
Compatible with Windows 98 and Windows NT 4.0 (x86)

Winnov

http://www.winnov.com/
Videum
Compatible with Windows 98 and Windows NT 4.0 (x86)

VideumCam PCMCIA
Compatible with Windows 98

Philips

http://www.pcstuff.philips.com/
PCA645VC USB Camera
Compatible with Windows 98

Appendix

B

Getting Help

Both the novice and the expert have a number of ways to get help with
Microsoft Windows Media Technologies.

Microsoft Windows Media Technologies

The Windows Media Technologies Web site contains numerous troubleshooting
guides, answers to Frequently Asked Questions, product documentation, and the
latest product news.

http://www.microsoft.com/windows/windowsmedia/

Windows Media Technologies Online Special Interest Group

The Windows Media Technologies Online Special Interest Group (OSIG) is a
developer community that offers free online technical support, code samples,

downloads, discounts on software and hardware from partners, and interaction with other Windows Media Technologies developers.

http://msdn.microsoft.com/osig/wm/default.asp

MSDN Online Windows Media Technologies Workshop

The Microsoft Developer Network (MSDN) Online Windows Media Technologies Workshop contains guides for beginning and intermediate streaming media content authors and Web developers.

http://msdn.microsoft.com/workshop/imedia/windowsmedia/default.asp

WindowsMedia.com

WindowsMedia.com is part of the Microsoft Network (MSN), and provides an audio and video guide to Windows Media content that is available on the Internet.

http://www.windowsmedia.com/

Windows Media Technologies Discussion Group

The Windows Media Technologies Discussion Group focuses on topics concerning developing products for Windows Media Technologies.

To subscribe, send an e-mail message to WMTALK@discuss.microsoft.com. Leave the subject blank, and in the message, type **subscribe Windows Media** *your name.*

To unsubscribe, send an e-mail message to WMTALK@discuss.microsoft.com. Leave the subject blank, and in the message, type **signoff Windows Media**.

Windows Media Technologies Newsgroups

The following newsgroups for Windows Media Technologies and the beta releases of Windows Media Technologies version 4.0 and Microsoft Windows Media Rights Manager are also available:

microsoft.public.windowsmedia.technologies

microsoft.public.windowsmedia.technologies.beta

microsoft.public.windowsmedia.technologies.rightsmanager.beta

Appendix

C

Using Content Leally

In creating and compiling content, you must be sure you are using it legally. The following information discusses how to do so, but is only intended as a starting point; consult an attorney for answers to specific questions.

After it is created, all video, audio, text, and graphics are automatically owned by their creator and/or the company employing the creator. The owner of copyrighted material is entitled to receive compensation when another person or company uses his or her work. Even if you only incorporate a portion of someone else's work into your own work, that person still owns the rights to his or her work. When you use someone else's creation without permission, you may be infringing on his or her copyright, and there can be severe penalties for doing so—up to $100,000 plus compensation for the copyright holder's lost revenues. For this reason alone, obtaining permission is a *very* good idea.

Obtaining permission

To obtain permission to use copyrighted material, contact the copyright holder listed in the copyright notice attached to the work. In some cases, you will be referred to an agent or attorney who will tell you what the royalty fees are and will send you the appropriate paperwork. Royalties are generally charged on a per-use basis[md]the more often you broadcast a work, the more you will pay. You will usually be required to display the copyright notice with a "used by permission" statement attached, and there may be restrictions on whether you must use the entire work.

Some copyright holders will not give permission to use their material until a certain amount of time has passed after the original release of the material. In the case of a film, it is usually a set amount of time after the movie has finished playing in movie theaters. For a theatrical production, it is usually after the first touring company has completed its performances. Songs, photographs, and graphic art may be available immediately.

Educational institutions are exempt from obtaining permission when the work is being used for legitimate educational purposes. Always check with your institution's attorney to make sure you are covered under the fair use clause of the copyright law. Pieces of copyrighted work can be used without permission as part of a review or critique, also under the fair use clause.

Public domain

Content that is not copyrighted is in the public domain. Material usually comes into the public domain in one of three ways:

- The copyright expires. Most content that is more than 100 years old is out of copyright.

> **NOTE** While a work, such as a Gilbert and Sullivan operetta, may be in the public domain, individual performances of that work are not. For example, though *"H.M.S. Pinafore"* is in the public domain, you would be violating the copyright of the Acme Gilbert and Sullivan Society if you used a video of their 1995 production of that work without their permission.

- The artist (or the artist's estate) releases the rights to the public.
- The material is owned by the U.S. government and is available to the public. Most United States government items are in the public domain, for example, NASA video content (see http://www.nasa.gov/gallery/photo/guideline.html).

The Berne Convention

The United States of America, along with 96 other countries, subscribes to the Berne Convention for copyright rules and regulations. This is a relatively recent development (1989) and extends copyrights far beyond the 1976 U.S. copyright laws. Under the old U.S. laws, a copyright was only good for 28 years from the time the copyright was secured, and could be renewed for an additional 47 years. Under Berne, an artist owns the copyright for life, and the artist's estate retains the rights for another 75 years after the artist's death, not to exceed a total of 100 years.

In addition to the longer copyright period, an artist is no longer required to put a copyright © mark on a work or to register the work. Under older U.S. laws, a work was not considered copyrighted until two copies were filed, with a registration fee, at the Library of Congress.

The full text of the Berne Convention is available on the Web at http://www.law.cornell.edu/treaties/berne/overview.html.

For details on copyright rules, go to the U.S. Copyright Office Web site at http://lcweb.loc.gov/copyright/. The site includes information on both United States and international copyright issues.

If you have any doubt about the copyright status of a work, consult an attorney.

Stock footage

There is one other way to obtain rights to audio and video clips. You can purchase the rights from companies that sell stock footage. These clips are always generic, so they can be used for many purposes; for example, a shot of a Paris monument at sunset may end up in a number of movies as well as a travel film. Stock music is called production or needle-drop music, and is usually written and performed as background music for commercials, corporate videos, and films. Sound effects are usually purchased as libraries. You can find more information about companies that sell stock footage, production music, and sound effect libraries in the backs of professional audio and video trade magazines and on the Internet.

Windows Media Technologies

Glossary

Advanced Streaming Format (ASF) The data structure that defines Windows Media content. The structure of the Advanced Streaming Format is particularly suited for streaming audio, video, images, and text over a network. The ASF specification calls for data to be organized into small packets, which can be streamed or saved as a file.

alias An alternative name for an object, such as a URL or live stream. For Microsoft Windows Media Services, aliases are names that are assigned to broadcast and on-demand unicast publishing points.

announcement An ASF Stream Redirector (.asx) file that can be generated automatically by Windows Media Administrator when a multicast station is created. It is called an announcement file because it can be attached to an e-mail message or linked from a Web page to announce an upcoming broadcast event.

ASF Stream Descriptor (.asd) file A configuration file created and read by Windows Media Encoder. The file contains encoder settings that describe the characteristics of a stream. In addition, .asd files are used by the Windows Media Station service to add stream formats to multicast stations.

ASF Stream Redirector (.asx) file A metafile that, when opened, provides Microsoft Windows Media Player with the following types of information:

- Content URLs. The location of Windows Media on-demand and live streaming media and other audio and video media.

- Playback control. Scripting that instructs Windows Media Player in how to play media.

- Display properties. Scripting that defines text, images, and other elements that appear on the Windows Media Player interface.

authentication The process of validating logon information from a client. A Windows Media server can be set to limit access to certain .asf files and publishing points, and require authentication before the content can be played.

authorization A process that works with Windows Media Services authentication for granting or denying access to protected ASF content. Authorization is implemented as a service or through plug-in components.

bandwidth The data transfer capacity of a digital communications system, such as the Internet or a local area network (LAN). Bandwidth is usually expressed in the number of bits transferred in a second: bits per second (bps). High bandwidth refers to a network capable of a fast data transfer rate.

banner image A small image that appears in Windows Media Player when a media file is played. When clicked, the banner image opens the Web browser to a banner image URL.

batch For Microsoft Windows Media Technologies, a group of source files that are processed and encoded as a unit.

batch file For Microsoft Windows Media Rights Manager, a file that runs the commands that encode, protect, and sign media files. The default batch file is Generate.cmd. The default file can be modified or a custom file can be created using Microsoft Windows NT shell scripting.

bit rate The speed at which binary content is streamed on a network. Bit rate is usually measured in kilobits per second (Kbps), for example, 28.8 Kbps. The bit rate of an .asf file or live stream is determined during the encoding process, when the streaming content is created. Bandwidth is the bit rate capacity of a network.

broadcast One method of streaming in which playback of a stream is controlled at the point where the stream originates. The other method is on-demand streaming. The two methods differ in how control of the stream occurs. A client receives a broadcast stream, but cannot, for example, pause and fast-forward the stream.

broadcast multicast One method of broadcasting in which a single stream provides Windows Media content to many clients over a network. The other method is unicast. A client receives a multicast stream by monitoring a specific IP address. Because only one stream is broadcast on the network, multicast has the advantage over unicast when network bandwidth is low or restricted.

broadcast unicast One method of broadcasting in which a single stream delivers Windows Media content to one client over a network: a one-to-one connection. For each additional client that requests the content, another stream is established. The other method of broadcasting is multicast.

buffer To store data in a temporary memory repository. Windows Media Player continuously buffers a certain amount of streaming content before the content is presented to help correct for the unevenness of data transfer on a network. If network conditions deteriorate, the buffer can empty. When there is no data left in the repository, the presentation stops so that the player can refill the buffer. This is called buffering.

caption Text that appears in the captioning area of Windows Media Player. *See also* script command.

capture To convert live analog video or audio content to a stream of digital data, which can be stored as a file on a computer or encoded and broadcast; digitize. A capture card is an add-on board for providing digitized images on a computer. With a video capture card, you can provide live camera or VCR input to Windows Media Encoder.

certificate For Windows Media Rights Manager, a piece of data that is used to sign a media file. A certificate contains information about the content owner, who the certificate was issued to, the public key to verify the signed media file, and identification numbers. When the media file is played in Windows Media Player, a legitimacy icon appears if the file has been signed and has not been tampered with.

client On a local area network or the Internet, a computer that accesses shared network resources provided by another computer (called a server). A computer playing content with Windows Media Player is often called the client.

closed captioning An accessibility feature of Windows Media Player that provides a method for displaying text in synchronization with the playback of media. Text and timing information is contained in a Synchronized Accessible Media Interchange (SAMI) file.

codec Short for compressor/decompressor. Hardware or software that can compress and uncompress audio or video data. For Windows Media Technologies, codecs are used to decrease the bit rate of media so that it can be streamed over a network. Windows Media Encoder compresses the content for streaming, and Windows Media Player decompresses it for playback.

compression The coding of data to reduce file size or the bit rate of a stream. Content that has been compressed must be decompressed for playback. A codec contains the algorithms for compressing and decompressing audio and video. With a lossless compression scheme, no data is lost in the compression/decompression process. With a lossy compression scheme, data may be lost or in some way changed. Most codecs used for streaming media use lossy compression.

content A general term that refers to audio and video media, images, text, and any other information that is seen or heard as part of a media presentation. Data is said to contain content if it can be converted to an analog form and produce images or sound.

copy generation For Windows Media Rights Manager, the process of creating new packaged copies of media files.

delta frame *See* interframe compression.

destination The location to which a file is copied or a live stream is sent. The destination is where the output goes. The source, on the other hand, is the input file or live stream. The destination of one program is the source of another.

destination address An IP address and port from which a listening client can receive a multicast.

distribution A feature of Windows Media Services that enables the delivery of an ASF stream from one server to another.

distribution mode A setting that is made when a multicast station is configured. Distribution mode determines whether the ASF stream created by the station is to be used for distribution, multicasting, or both.

downloading A method of delivering content to an end user over a network in which media is copied to a client computer and then played locally. The other method is streaming. The methods are differentiated by the location of the source media. With the streaming method, source media is located on a remote server and played by streaming it over a network.

encode For Windows Media Rights Manager, a general term for the process of packaging media files with a key. Once a media file has been encrypted, it cannot be played without the key. For Windows Media Technologies, to produce data in the Windows Media format. One can encode a live stream or save the encoded stream to a file.

end user A person who uses Windows Media Player to play content.

error correction A method of controlling data transmission errors that occur when streaming. If a stream is received via TCP, the risk of error is minimized because data verification occurs between client and server; packets are re-sent if data is corrupt or missing. In streaming media, however, the UDP protocol is preferred because data transmission is far more efficient. The main drawback to UDP is that to gain efficiency, the data verification process has been removed. With UDP, the data is transmitted, but there is no built-in process for verifying that it is received intact. Error correction schemes help correct errors that occur in UDP transmission. UDP resend is employed to partially emulate verification, redundant data is included in the stream, and other measures are taken to fill in missing or corrupt data.

feed A live audio or video signal. A feed is usually in analog form, and can be part of other feeds and sources, which are combined to create a presentation or program for an audience.

File Transfer service (FTS) A feature of Windows Media Services that multicasts files over a network to an ActiveX control (Nsfile.ocx) on a client computer.

firewall A security system intended to protect an organization's network against external threats, such as hackers, coming from another network, such as the Internet.

frame One of many static images that, when displayed sequentially in rapid succession, become a motion picture or video.

frame rate The speed at which individual frames change. The higher the frame rate, the smoother the motion appears.

header Part of the structure of an ASF stream. A header contains information necessary for a client to interpret how the packets of data containing the content should be decompressed and rendered. A header can include information such as codec types and settings, error corrections used, and instructions for how to interpret the data structure of the packets.

home publishing point The root directory for publishing ASF on-demand content on a Windows Media server. Unlike other publishing points, the home publishing point is not given an alias. To open an .asf file that is located in the home publishing point, the URL must contain the name of the server and file (*mms://Server/File.asf*). A server must be assigned a directory to act as the home publishing point. During installation, if a directory is not assigned, a default directory, Asfroot, is created.

I-Frame Another word for key frame. *See also* interframe compression.

illustrated audio An ASF stream consisting of static images that change in synchronization with an audio track, often called a slide show.

Instance Manager For Windows Media Rights Manager, the component that manages the download process. When an end user clicks a file to download from a Web site, Instance Manager retrieves information from the Windows Media Rights Manager database, finds the correct file, and sends it to the end user.

intelligent streaming A set of features in Windows Media Technologies that automatically detects network conditions and adjusts the properties of a video stream to maximize quality.

interframe compression A video compression technique that reduces redundancy in frame-to-frame content. Interframe compression can be used to produce a very low bit rate stream that is suitable for streaming on the Internet. Video frames are compressed into either key frames, which contain a complete image, or delta frames, which follow key frames and contain only the parts of the key frame that have changed. The Microsoft MPEG-4 Video Codec uses interframe compression.

key For Windows Media Rights Manager, a piece of information that is required to play a packaged media file. The end user cannot play a media file without first acquiring a license, which contains this key.

key frame *See* interframe compression.

license For Windows Media Rights Manager, a piece of data issued by the License Service to an end user. The data contains a key to play a particular media file, as well as the following information: a license version number, a signature, the rights of the license, the application security level, and the expiration date of the license. Licenses are unique to each end user, and cannot be copied or shared.

live Audio or video that is transmitted from one site to another as it is being produced, as opposed to being recorded before broadcast time (on-demand). Windows Media Encoder can be used to encode a live stream and store the content as it streams to an .asf file.

marker A name that is associated with a specific location in an .asf file. Markers are added to an .asf file using an authoring tool, such as Windows Media On-Demand Producer. When Windows Media Player opens a file, any markers contained in it appear in a list. An end user can click a marker in the list to move playback of the .asf file to the position defined by the marker. A marker list is often created as a table of contents for people using Windows Media Player.

Media Stream Broadcast Distribution (MSBD) protocol A protocol specific to Windows Media Technologies that is used for internal distribution of ASF streams between components. MSBD is used for the transmission of a live stream from Windows Media Encoder to a Windows Media server. The server connects to the encoder by using a path, such as msbd://EncodingServer:Port. MSBD is also used when saving a live stream to a file on a content-storage server and when distributing streams from server to server.

metadata Information about data. For Windows Media Technologies, metadata, such as content title, author, copyright, description, and rating, can be included in an .asf file and in an .asx file script.

metafile For Windows Media Technologies, a file that provides information about an ASF stream and its presentation. There are four types of metafiles: .asd, .asx, .wax, and .nsc files.

Microsoft Media Server (MMS) protocol A protocol specific to Windows Media Technologies that is used by clients to reference and stream ASF content from a unicast publishing point on a Windows Media server. Windows Media Player opens an .asf file using a URL, such as *mms://Server/File.asf*.

multicast   A one-to-many client/server connection in which multiple clients receive the same stream from a server. To receive a multicast, a client listens to a specific IP address on a multicast-enabled network, like tuning a television to a specific channel. In contrast, a unicast is a one-to-one connection in which each client receives a separate stream from a server.

multicast-enabled network   A network that has routers that can interpret Class D IP addresses.

multimedia   Includes audio, video, and images. A type of content that can be played or displayed on a computer.

multiple bit rate video   A feature of Windows Media Technologies that supports the encoding and streaming of up to six video streams within one ASF stream. A multiple bit rate video live stream or .asf file is created using Windows Media Encoder. While playing a multiple bit rate video stream, Windows Media Player sends feedback continuously to the Windows Media server regarding the quality of the stream. The Windows Media server then switches between streams to optimize the bit rate for the current bandwidth.

NetShow   The name of Windows Media Technologies prior to version 4.0.

on demand   Describes one method of streaming, in which playback of a stream is controlled by the client. The other method is broadcast. The two methods differ in how control of the stream occurs. As a client plays on-demand content, an end user can, for example, pause, fast-forward, and rewind the content. On-demand content can only be stored media. On the other hand, a broadcast stream is controlled at the point where the stream originates, and the source can be live or stored media.

packaged copy   For Windows Media Rights Manager, a media file that has been packaged: encoded, encrypted with a key, optionally signed with a certificate, and contains information such as a license acquisition URL and properties of the file. Packaged copies are the files that end users download from a Web site. Windows Media Rights Manager can periodically regenerate new packaged copies of media files so that new keys are assigned to the copies, reducing the risk of piracy.

packet   A unit of information transmitted as a whole from one device to another on a network. A packet consists of binary digits representing both data and a header. When an ASF stream is created, audio, video, script commands, markers, and control and header information are encoded into a sequence of packets according to the ASF specification.

player   A program that renders multimedia content, typically animated images, video, and audio. ASF content is rendered using Windows Media Player.

playlist   A list of streams that Windows Media Player plays sequentially. Windows Media Technologies supports both server-side and client-side playlists.

port   A number that enables the sending of IP packets to a particular process on a computer connected to a network. Ports are most often identified with a particular service. For example, port 80 on an Internet computer indicates a Web server. Windows Media server components, when in use, bind to particular ports. By default, the Windows Media Unicast service binds to port 1755 and the Windows Media Station service binds to port 7007. If HTTP streaming is enabled for a service, then that service switches to use port 80.

pre-encoded files For Windows Media Rights Manager, files that have already been encoded by using Windows Media Encoder. Encoding files is a CPU-intensive process. Pre-encoding files before adding them in Windows Media Packager reduces the time required to regenerate packaged copies of media files.

privacy statement For Windows Media Rights Manager, explains to an end user how the content owner will use registration data that the end user provides. Windows Media Rights Manager provides a placeholder privacy statement, which the content owner customizes. This file, Regusage.htm, is located in the root directory of the Web site; by default, this location is C:\Inetpub\Wwwroot\WM file.

program One of the components of a complete broadcast station. The other components are a station and one or more streams. A stream is an ASF content source: an .asf file or a live stream. One or more streams are grouped into a program. A program can be thought of as a VCR that plays the streams. If a program contains more than one stream, it plays them one after the other. A station receives its input from a program, and then multicasts or distributes the stream over a network.

protect For Windows Media Rights Manager, a stage in the packaging process to encrypt media files with a key and add information, such as the license acquisition URL.

protocol rollover A procedure that Windows Media Player follows by switching from one protocol to another if it fails to connect to a broadcast multicast stream. Windows Media Player attempts to connect to a UDP stream, and then to a TCP stream. If it fails to connect to on-demand content by means of the UDP and TCP protocols, Windows Media Player then attempts to connect using HTTP if an HTTP URL is designated in the .asx file.

proxy server A firewall component that manages Internet traffic to and from a local area network (LAN).

publishing point A virtual address that points a client requesting a unicast stream to the directory containing the requested media or to a station or server originating a broadcast. A client accesses a publishing point on a Windows Media server by using its alias. The alias, which is mapped to a directory (a unicast publishing point) or a broadcast stream (a broadcast publishing point), then points the client to the stream. For example, a client connects to a unicast broadcast on the MyPubPoint alias of MyServer by using the URL mms://*MyServer/MyPubPoint*.

regenerating copies For Windows Media Rights Manager, the process of creating new packaged copies of media files. Packaged media files discourage piracy because a license is required to play them.

registration For Windows Media Rights Manager, the process of entering information, such as an e-mail address, to acquire a license. After registration information is collected, it is stored in the Windows Media Rights Manager database.

render To produce audio, video, or a graphic image from a data file or stream on an output device such as a sound system, video display, or printer.

scope In multicasting, the reach of a stream. Using Windows Media Administrator, the scope of a multicast can be defined. The scope can be set to reach only an immediate subnetwork, or it can be set to reach the entire Internet. Scope is set by specifying a time-to-live value.

script command Text that is inserted in an ASF stream at a specific time. When the stream is played and the time associated with a script command is reached, Windows Media Player triggers an event and the script command can initiate some action.

security The process of controlling access to resources based on end-user credentials and permissions. In a Windows Media Services environment, security means restricting and controlling access to Windows Media server components, Windows Media Administrator, and Windows Media content, both on-demand and broadcast.

sign For Windows Media Rights Manager, a stage in the packaging process at which to add a certificate to media files. This stage is optional, and only occurs when a certificate has been created and specified in the Packager settings in Windows Media Packager.

source Content that provides the input for some process, such as an encoder or broadcast station. The destination, on the other hand, is where the output of a process goes. A source can be a media file or the output of a device or another process, such as a capture card or remote server.

station *See* program.

stream Data transmitted across a network and any properties associated with the data. A Windows Media ASF stream contains data, which is rendered by Windows Media Player into audio, video, images, and text.

stream format Information about the settings used to create an ASF stream that Windows Media Player uses to render the stream. This information contains such settings as the bit rate, the size of the image, and the codec. Stream formats are contained in the

header of an .asf file and a broadcast unicast stream. An ASF Stream Descriptor (.asd) file contains stream format information that is used for encoding ASF content, and a Windows Media Station (.nsc) file is used to provide the client connecting to a multicast stream with stream format information. Windows Media Encoder and other Microsoft Windows Media Tools provide templates to help users choose stream formats for encoding.

streaming A method of delivering content to an end user, in which media is located on a server and then played by streaming it across a network. The other method is downloading. The methods are differentiated by the location of the source media. With the downloading method, media is first copied to a client computer, and then played locally.

synchronized multimedia The presentation of text, graphics, and other content and effects synchronized with the playback of an ASF stream. *See also* script command.

time-to-live (TTL) In multicasting, a value that defines the number of routers through which a multicast passes before a router stops forwarding the multicast. TTL is equivalent to scope. Using time-to-live, the reach of a multicast can be limited to, for example, the immediate subnetwork, a value of 5; or an intranet, a value of 32; or expanded to the entire Internet, a value of 127.

unicast A type of client/server connection in which each client receives a separate ASF stream through a unique, one-to-one connection with a server. In contrast, multicast is a one-to-many connection in which multiple clients receive the same stream from a server. A unicast connection can be used for streaming on-demand and broadcast content.

unicast rollover A procedure that Windows Media Player follows if it cannot receive a multicast from a station on a Windows Media server. Windows Media Player first listens for multicast data packets at the IP address and port designated by the .nsc file. If no data is present, then it attempts to connect to the server by using the designated unicast rollover URL.

URL flip What occurs when a script command in an ASF stream causes Windows Media Player to change a Web page that is being displayed in a browser. If the script command type string is URL, Windows Media Player automatically opens the default browser if necessary and loads it into the address given by the command string value.

URL rollover A procedure that Windows Media Player follows if it cannot connect to an ASF stream designated in an .asx file. Using the REF scripting element, the URLs of alternative sources of ASF content can be designated in a list. If Windows Media Player fails to connect to the first URL, it tries the second one, then the third one, and so forth until a connection is made. Typically, the URLs point to the same content on different servers, but they can also point to different content. For example, the first URL can be a broadcast stream, and the second URL can be an on-demand file that plays if the client cannot connect to the broadcast.

User Datagram Protocol (UDP) A protocol that is used on the Internet and in certain networks and does not require a direct connection between client and server. Like TCP, UDP converts data messages generated by an application into packets to be sent via IP. The difference is that UDP does not verify that the packets have been delivered correctly to the client. By not requiring verification, UDP can deliver data, such as streaming media, more efficiently.

Because the transmission of data is unreliable, methods such as error correction and UDP resend are used to help ensure quality.

Webcasting The process of broadcasting stored or live digital media content (audio, video, or a combination of both) over the Internet.

Windows Media Audio (.wma) file A special type of advanced streaming format file for use with audio content encoded with the Windows Media Audio codec.

Windows Media Audio Redirector (.wax) file A special type of .asx metafile for use with .wma files. The .wax file includes information about the location of the .wma file on the Windows Media server and the properties of the file.

Windows Media program (.nsp) file A file that contains information about a Windows Media Services program, used primarily in backing up and restoring Windows Media Services program definitions.

Windows Media Station (.nsc) file Contains information that Windows Media Player uses to connect to and play a multicast stream, such as the multicast IP address, port, stream format, and other station settings. Unlike a unicast stream, no header information is contained in a multicast stream. That information comes from an .nsc file. Windows Media Player usually opens an announcement (.asx) file first, which points it to the location of the .nsc file.

Symbols

X–Z